From The Women's Press Ltd
124 Shoreditch High Street, London E1

FEMINIST
LIBRARY

Barbara Deming   *Photo by Joan E. Biren*

Barbara Deming, poet, story writer, essayist and journalist, was born in 1917 in New York City. She spent the last years of her life in the Florida Keys with the writer and painter Jane Gapen, and a community of other women. She died in 1984.

She was active in the non-violent civil rights and anti-war struggles of the 1960s and visited North Vietnam during the war. She put her hopes for change above all in the non-violent struggles of the feminist movement.

She was a lesbian from the age of sixteen. She recognised the struggle to hold to her pride in this sexual self, as her earliest political struggle. *A Humming Under My Feet* tells the story of a year of that struggle, 1950–51. She wrote six other books including *We Cannot Live Without Our Lives* (1974) and *Remembering Who We Are* (1981).

BARBARA DEMING

A Humming Under My Feet

A Book of Travail

The Women's Press

First published by The Women's Press Limited 1985
A member of the Namara Group
124 Shoreditch High Street, London E1 6JE

British Library Cataloguing in Publication Data

Deming, Barbara
    A humming under my feet.
    1. Self-realization
    I. Title
    158′.1   BF637.S4

    ISBN 0-7043-3952-8

Photoset by AKM Associates (UK) Ltd, Southall, Greater London
Printed and bound in Great Britain
by Nene Litho and Woolnough Bookbinding
both of Wellingborough, Northants

Acknowledgments

I thank all the women who read this book in various drafts. I thank especially Minnie Bruce Pratt and Kady, who helped me find my courage to speak some of the story's more difficult truths, and Judith McDaniel, who helped me trim distracting details.

The first chapter of the book was published in *Wash Us and Comb Us*, Grossman Publishers, 1972, under the title 'From a Book of Travail'.

Foreword

I wrote the first chapter of this lesbian story in 1952 – when I was 35; and, working from a journal I had kept, mapped out in rough notes some chapters to follow. Then I put the work down. The few friends to whom I submitted those pages couldn't help showing that they were embarrassed for me. And, hypnotised by their embarrassment, I came to doubt the impulse that had made me begin the book – instead of trusting it stubbornly, as an artist must. One friend advised me: 'If you feel that you have to write this, at least write it in the third person.' And another: 'Try at least to make it a little funny.' Staring into the faces of my friends instead of the face of my muse, I decided that I would be doing a weak thing if I continued – obeying some pathetic compulsion to exhibit myself in infirmity.

In 1971, when I started looking through the short stories I had written, to make the collection published as *Wash Us and Comb Us*, I very nearly didn't bother to reread this chapter, sure that I would find it an uncontrolled confession. But then I did reread it, and received a shock. For I liked it better than any of the other stories. As I was reading it, the same impulse that, almost twenty years before, had moved me to begin, revived in me with force; and I experienced this as a sharp, in fact an almost unbearable pang. For I assumed that it was too late to finish the book.

But I kept experiencing that jolt of feeling. At first I could recognize it only as self reproach – for depending on others and failing to trust my own impulse. That impulse had been strong, not weakling – this was clear to me now. Strong enough to survive in me through all those years. Slowly I came to recognize that my agitation spoke more than a rebuke – told me to be sorry that I had put the work down, but told me also: 'Take it up again! You can't not try now to finish it!' It was to take me a great deal longer to finish it than if I had persisted earlier, for I had to patiently think myself back into that time. But I began soon to stop regretting that I had let those years pass, for they had brought me a much clearer sense of what was really happening in the story I tell.

When I wrote the first chapter of course I had not yet a developed feminist consciousness. I have changed a few words toward the end of that chapter, and added, from my present perspective, the sentence 'Or so I tried to tell myself.' My behavior, as I related it at the time, seemed to me 'very strange'. I understand it now, I think, all too well.

I addressed the book, when I began it, to the woman you will meet in it, Carlotta – with whom I was then deep in love. I address it to her still, for if love is really love, it cannot stop being what it is – though it can stop seeking, as this love did long ago. Then it changes, certainly; but it does not expire. Even when one falls in love again. One's heart then simply breaks open a little wider.

Yes, I address *A Humming Under My Feet* to her still. But I address it too to all my lesbian sisters who are struggling as I struggle in this book – with the difference that we struggle now in less isolation – to believe in our right to offer this kind of love. An odd 'right' to have to struggle to claim – the right to be who we are.

what am I doing here, Angel?

1

Although it is you who have sent me away, Lottie, it's to you that I address this book: a book of travel. Of travail. Spell that either way. You don't wait for me to return. Penelope? No, it's not a name to try to give you. You weave, unweave, in my absence, no image of a future in which our figures are joined. Nevertheless it is you I go seeking. Perhaps this means that I am mad. And yet, as I cast myself upon countries strange to me, God grant me only that I not forget you.

My words come very strangely. I have been talking every language but my own. (And had I ever learned *that* well? At any rate, it never served to persuade you that you loved me.) And now my words are a little mixed with dust and with salt, as I try to speak. I can see you frowning, trying to make them out – your eyes very yellow-black, regarding me boldly. It is not possible to love you lightly. I love you or I love you not.

So I will be bold, too, and whether or not I know how, speak.

Where should I begin? Begin anywhere, you'd say. Let me begin with a tale that may shock you. Not that that's my pleasure. I went seeking you.

I had been gone two weeks. Your first letter had been in Athens to meet me – to speak a welcome and to speak regret. (It would be nice if heart *could* answer heart as face answers face in water.) In the meantime two letters from me would have reached you, and might have cut you from me altogether (I wrote presumptuously); or they might at last, by a miracle, have stirred in you love. That is the letter I waited for: 'I find that I love you.' I went travelling after those words over miles and miles. You will read this in bewilderment. For hadn't I declared to you that I accepted your words – that you did *not* love me? I meant what I said with all my heart. I could read in your every motion the distress my hopes caused you. So how could I do otherwise than disarm myself before you – lay down all hopes? And yet, speaking this, and meaning this, I continued to hope all things. Love is not reasonable. Isn't it, perhaps, necessary that this be so – that, throwing down every weapon it knows, stripped to nothing, it should continue simply to stand before the city it longs to take, the loved walls, waiting for them to fall.

No further letter from you had come, and I left Athens for one of the islands. Take ship, I felt, take ship, and as the world is round, you may reach home again. This is how I had sailed away from you.

The airs above the sea are full of echoes, colliding. I had spoken my love, I had taken my leave. The ship headed out into the wind. That wind circled my head, whirled round my ears, all my own words again. Here was a young man, eyes large, leaning toward me, saying: 'Your life is more real to me than my own life. I feel so confident that I could make you happy. It's unbearable to me that I shouldn't be allowed to try.' Yes, it was Russell. You had given me a letter to him; and he had hardly put the letter down, to smile at me again, before he was in love with me. This won't surprise you. Because he is young, and a poet, and must fall in love as others must eat, or grow faint. So young that he took no heed of where his words might blow. The wind might carry them round and about the boat to where his wife was sitting – whom he wouldn't want to harm. He loved her too, of course. But the world was so immense. I could see his eyes glinting across the waters as the ship moved out over them, his glance nervous. 'It's as though I let life go by me', he was saying. 'Mustn't one catch at it, mustn't one fling oneself after it?' One can't fling oneself in all directions, I was trying to say. But he burned to. I think he would have liked to have flung himself, in sparks, throughout the universe – one spark of him toward the sun, one toward the moon, one toward each star, and on earth too, toward every fire. 'I love Lisa of course', he was explaining. 'I love her very much. But sometimes when we're walking down the street together I have to find some excuse to drop behind, I have to walk at least a few steps behind her, or I can't breathe. I couldn't imagine ever leaving her. And yet I never can let myself think that I'll be married to her all my life.' And he swung his eyes, distractedly, as if to see that far.

There were four of us making that trip together. Lisa you never met. An open-hearted young woman, whose eyes followed Russell as if he were the sun in its course, and that course an amazement to her again each day. She wore that look of one taken again and again by surprise – eyes ashine, mouth half open. And she was ready to go wherever surprise might lead her (as long as it was with Russell). And there was with them a younger woman, an acquaintance of theirs just arrived from Paris – crop-haired, saucer-eyed, a touch of the tomboy to her – making what giro I did not know, but it was somewhere she wanted to get, though I think perhaps she didn't know, either, where that was. She was dressed for the road, in strange, rather charming mixed garb: sneakers, socks, a striped skirt, a plaid shirt, with a worker's bandanna at her throat and on her head a funny little round cotton hat, a canteen over her shoulder, and her guide book swung on a strap – her name was Kit. She talked of someone back in Athens whom she was trying to persuade to go with her to Crete. But this person could never set a date, and she had only so much time before she must return to Paris, to some sort of studies there. She talked a little tough – gay knowing talk. But her very blue eyes were a child's. There was also on board a young Englishwoman, who when she had spotted us among the Greeks had moved in our direction, shy, almost prim, hardly venturing to speak, but placing herself near us. Lisa had soon won her to speech, and as night fell we shared together our assortments of food. We had oranges, cheese and, from Kit's canteen, wine. She contributed chocolate and tea biscuits.

We were travelling as deck passengers. But Russell had come out that morning forgetting the blankets he was to carry. And the Englishwoman had no blanket. I had an old brown quilt and we spread it out to see how many could creep under. Four of us could, the four women. The bit of deck we'd chosen was unsheltered, and the wind kept lifting the edges of the quilt, rippling it over us like a stage-set sea. A Greek rose from a spot mid-ship and beckoned to us to take his place – and simply walked away, so there could be no argument. For that is how these people are with strangers. We moved in among a circle of sleepers. Kit looked cold still, was trying to make the edges of the quilt tuck under us. A Greek woman turned back the striped rug in which she lay wrapped and gestured for Kit to come in with her, and, when she hesitated, spoke to her, in the strange language, peremptorily, humorously; so Kit accepted the hospitality. 'Ah, it's warm as a furnace here', she called to us in a little girl's voice. At the rail, the man who had moved for us joined Russell: 'We don't have to sleep.' Russell grinned, but the look he turned toward us then, through the dusk, was a frail one, forlorn. So some of us dozed. Over us the stars swung as though on cords. And from the rail Russell glanced our way, or out to sea – his gaze wandered beyond the arc of huddled sleepers and huddled creatures, the goats, the chickens, legs tied under them, uttering their quavery cries (the goats, their chins on the deck, eyes flicking, the chickens, heads buried in feathers, but raising them now and then, as on a stick, to complain). Toward midnight, waking, I could see Russell walking up and down flailing his arms. The other man had vanished. At the rail some leaning sailors wailed an ancient, a harsh tune – emptying their throats of it; then flung themselves to the deck and sprawled in attitudes of death. The stars were too close and the sea was too close. I waved my hand at Russell, and he peered across at me like a new-born soul, like a child set adrift on a stream and waiting the hand that will pluck it forth.

Before dawn, islands drew near: a speckle of thin lights, a port, the delicate lights – pink yellow pink blue – making the water smile. We dropped anchor, out from land. And at our side small boats, appearing, tossed like paper, the crews clinging to us with their hands, one rope tossed, and up the flimsy ship's ladder three men clambering, one a crippled man, dragged by the others, thump thump up each step, grimacing but unalarmed; then down the ladder disembarked a disordered (but unalarmed) small crowd, men babies women rugs baskets a green trunk a violin three chickens flapping upside down – and we moved off again, the pale lights vanishing. And we had dreamed it, delicately.

Then at dawn we woke again, rubbing our eyes, and Mykonos shone there. And this time we went in, in one of the crowded small boats, toward the line along the shore of waiting Greeks – the welcoming line shaped there at any hour. The boats moved in quietly (though one old Greek woman in our boat was laughing gigantically at something). Russell looked pale, looked very slight of frame. The young Englishwoman, gripping her small satchel, sat crouched forward, staring toward land, her eyes glazed, her face, in the dawning, full of alarm, full of dreams. The boat rocked and her glance met mine, but her face did not change, she was so tranced. Then suddenly she recognized, in the line along the shore, friends, the couple she was visiting, and woke out of that sleep, and began to wave, giggling, conscious again.

Our shipload scattered, the four of us headed for the house where we had rooms – a house where Russell and Lisa had stayed the summer before (earning their keep on the island by giving English lessons). And here we curled up again, and dozed, until light was full. Then we rose and all day walked that white island. Russell had revived, and as we walked he put questions to me. 'What do you think is the condition of modern poetry?' 'Don't you believe, then, that it's the poet's duty to find a language in which he can communicate with all men of his time?' 'Do you believe in God?' 'Why do you believe in God?' 'Ah, Russell,' Lisa would cry, 'Look, look – how pink the sea is there!' 'Look, look at the flowers on the slope!' 'Look,' she would cry, 'look – do you remember the day we stopped at that house?'

I wanted to say to her: 'You need not fear me. If you knew with what force my thoughts flew elsewhere.' But I didn't know how to say this. Kit meanwhile wanted Lisa to teach her Greek songs, and they walked echoing: 'Su-pa ma-ma – su-pa ma-ma – Mother find me a husband. And I don't want an old man.' Russell didn't know what he did. I was a book he wanted to read. He was a book he wanted *me* to read. He stepped beside me, swinging his hands as if he danced – gesticulating, frowning, sought my eye. And his eye said: 'If I ask for bread, will you give me a stone?'

But I found it hard to reply to his catechism. This island we walked – Rock. A piece of rock set in the sea. But from this rock light strikes sparks, sparks into flowers. Light-struck, here it was that I began to believe: if you would only come (you had spoken of a visit as possible) – if you would only come – surely, this light might strike from your breast love. And so I went dreaming.

At the sea we had our lunch. Retsina from Kit's canteen. Olives. Cheese. The bread had been forgotten. It didn't matter. Joining hands, we attempted a Greek dance, witless, danced into the sea, having to hop out in disorder. We walked a long way home then, a rocky up-and-down-winding shepherd's path, picking the million small blazing flowers as we went, so weary soon that we staggered; and Kit actually stumbled and fell, angry at herself, the canteen flung from her shoulder. At the top of one hill, our tongues out, we agreed to beg some water. A peasant's house was set there high above the sea. The man came out at our calling and fetched us the water in a large tumbler, emptying and refilling it with ceremony, for each of us – his pig, his chickens, and his goat regarding us mildly. Revived, we thanked him profusely; and he stared at us, in the eye, out of his ugly pleasant face, and 'It's not such a very great thing', he said, 'to give you a drink of water.' And we limped off again, down toward the shining whitewashed town.

We ate that night at a tavern on the waterfront, a barnlike room opening on to beach and ships – a crowded mishmash of tables, brown faces gathered. At our entrance there were shouts, arms raised. Russell and Lisa moved eagerly among the tables, renewing friendships. A couple of musicians were flaring away – a violinist, a guitarist. Close as we could to their vibration, we found room at a table. Two men were seated there before us, friends it seemed, but one very different from the other; one was plainly of this island, the other – well, at the other I barely looked, for I was looking at the man across from me. He sat over a great plate of fish, the criss-cross bones scattered to the table, and his glass spilling wine. The table top swam. As we sat, he lifted the decanter and splashed our glasses full. The custom here is to fill a glass only half-way. Not to be uncongenial but the reverse, for this makes it necessary to dip decanter toward glass more frequently. But this man could not possibly stay his hand half-way; the glass must run over. But he could keep the decanter in motion, too, for he would pour again whether or not the necessity had arrived. Russell knew this man and introduced him: Cyclops. Yes, he had one eye – the other lost, not as I began imagining, in some festive act of recklessness, but as the result of a childhood illness. The one eye, very blue, set shining in a long face, set in leather; the other eye out but the blind socket gesticulating still, out of that gone eye tears dropping often, not for grief; the cheek wrinkling, the brow above it lifting, and the tears brimming as the wine brimmed at his hand, out of extravagance of spirit.

'Your health', Kit toasted, suddenly lively.

'We'll arrange for that', he cried – Russell translating. And stared at her with a wise look, which both devoured her and did without; and jerked his head back and laughed; and the tears sprang from his dead eye.

'He is a fisherman', the man at my left announced. 'A bachelor fisherman. And a king.' And he turned to me. 'He is a king.'

The king got up to dance. The musicians had begun a new tune and he pushed back his chair and stepped into the small dancing space somehow managed here among all the tables. He was a long, bony man, dressed in very worn britches, a layer of raggedy shirts, a bulky grey cummerbund wrapping it all together, barefoot. He began to strike the boards with his feet – light, then hard – and move, foot crossing foot, in circles, eyes down, watching the ground he danced, hands hitching up his trousers at the groin, then clapping the air, then, as he bent his knee, clapping the ground.

The other man joined him, laughing. This man was dressed in a double-breasted grey city suit, full in cut. A medium-sized man, and pleasant enough in looks, but a little plump-chested, a little soft. I remember I felt for him at that first meeting a slight spontaneous distaste. He echoed Cyclops' motions now in a dance of his own, the steps the same yet not the same, a subtle difference intruding. He'd been to America, one gathered. He just perceptibly swung the dance. But I still do know how to dance it, his motions also proclaimed, self-consciously.

When he came back to the table, he wanted to talk. Cyclops had tipped back his head and begun to sing, and it was hard to listen to any other. But I did half listen, and he sat there telling about himself with a peculiar urgency. He was telling me that, yes, he had been in America. He'd spent two, three years there at a certain hospital. I muttered words of commiseration, but hadn't heard him right: he hadn't been ill, but was a doctor, and had studied in America, now had returned to his own country to practise.

Most of what he said I lost. Weariness had made me deaf. The evening spun round me and blurred, faces and voices mixed, only one image holding an outline: Cyclops spilling song with wine, his head back, mouth opening as if to yawn, gone eye gesticulating: '*Asemay, Asemay* – Let me live alone, let me forget you!' – a joyous baying. The four of us staggered the ghostly streets home.

The next day again we walked the island, this time taking the opposite direction, the sea on our left (striped violet, electric); walked again to a far beach. Flowers burned the ground and bees the air. The day flung light so wide that the far looked near as the near. We wandered until the day was out; then headed for the doctor's. For the doctor had found us that morning, as we took our coffee on the waterfront, and had sat again to

7

talk, and had ended by asking us for dinner.

His house was set at the edge of town, and half-way up the slope the town climbed from the sea. A raised terrace circled it. One mounted by steps from the street. The doctor was out here, staring down into the town. But the door open behind him rayed light and voices. The other guests were gathered, and the banquet spread.

The other guests were Cyclops and the two musicians. The banquet – was that. The table held lobster, fish, chicken, rice, squash, cheese. The edge of one platter rested upon that of the next. All this had been prepared by the very young woman who kept his house ('She is only a child,' said the doctor – 'a miller's daughter'), and who moved now, as we sat, to set before us still further dishes. A small brother kept her company in the kitchen; stood now in the doorway, lightly on one foot, to watch the plates go round.

The doctor stood to carve the lobster; the violinist to carve the chicken; the guitarist to spear out fish. Each vied to see his neighbour's plate heaped higher than his own. Cyclops stood to splash the glasses full. Their moving arms tangled, a festive vine.

In the passing, Cyclops' plate vanished somewhere – into the kitchen perhaps for some repair. Kit, at Cyclops' side, expressed distress, the doctor translating.

But 'You eat, and I am satisfied', he cried.

Sun had flushed us all, this day, but Kit flushed pinker now, and blinked, her eyes rounding – a bigger, a more startled blue, it seemed, each moment.

The doctor wanted to tell us about Cyclops. 'He's a fisherman, but he is a king', he announced, as he had the evening before. 'He lives with his mother. He goes out and catches as much fish as he needs to keep house for himself and his mother. And no more. When she tells him he's lazy, "Did I bring you home dinner tonight?" he asks her. His bed is right by the door, so that when he comes home full of wine, he doesn't need to look for it; he can fall down and be in bed. He fishes for his living. When he has his living, he stops. Then he's a leisured man. He is royalty. He walks about and he enjoys the world around him. He sits in the sun. He opens his mouth and sings. He pours wine down his throat.' The doctor, talking, rose and wound the gramophone. A tavern melody began to circle. 'This gramophone', the doctor interrupted himself, 'belonged to . . .'

The floor gave a sound like a drum. In one barefoot leap, having, it seemed, not even to push back his chair, Cyclops had left the table. Arms spread like wings, he twirled around the room, a great barefoot bird, stepping, leaping, hands clapping the air, with a hush, the ground. With one final floor-thudding somersault, he rejoined us. The doctor was beaming at us. 'I haven't let him drink all day. That's why he's dancing well.'

The miller's daughter changed the record. In the doorway now her small brother lightly hinted a dance, his feet in one place, scarcely moving, yet dancing; then catching my eye, smiled rapidly in confusion and ducked away. Cyclops splashed all the glasses full. The doctor wanted to talk. He wanted to talk about Cyclops. He wanted to talk about himself.

'I'd thought', he was saying about himself, 'that one couldn't choose a life that would be more rewarding – to make people well again. But it isn't so, it isn't so', he was saying. 'Everywhere there's simply wretchedness.' Russell was straining forward, trying to follow. He was biting his lip, straining toward him. But one couldn't quite follow the doctor. Or perhaps we had drunk too much wine. 'My friend came into my room one day, at the hospital. "What do you believe, George?" he asked me. "Beethoven", I told him. The day I first heard Beethoven, I wanted to kill myself. Who am I?'

Kit was flirting with Cyclops. She wanted the doctor to translate. He translated. Then he got up to look for his album of Beethoven. He came back beaming again as a symphony began to shake the small room. Everybody hushed down. Cyclops cocked his head and listened; then without thinking he opened his throat and began to howl his own ancient tune, more familiar refrain: '*Asemay, Asemay* – Let me forget you, let me live alone!' His blind eye sprang great tears. The doctor laughed and poured Cyclops more wine. 'He'll be in here tomorrow, though,' he told us, 'and ask to hear it again.'

The lobster vanished, the chicken vanished, the fish vanished. The Beethoven concluded. 'Let's dance', said the doctor. The table was pushed back and the plates were carried off into the kitchen. The musicians wiped their hands and brought out their fiddles. Another bottle of wine was found. We had walked this island all one day and the next and we could almost dance, ourselves, Cyclops' dance. He discarded a few shirts now. Arms raised, his foot raised, he again tried the earth. Who is to say, lightly, that it will hold one? He steps out – hush – and again – and kneeling quickly, touches the ground with his hand. Yes, he sets his foot down before him as though it were the day of Creation all over again.

The doctor must dance too. He shed his coat. He shook his leg, put out his arms like chicken wings, then, one hand behind his head – a Greek gesture – flirtatious, kicked off his shoes.

And Russell must dance. He leapt into it, eyes bright. Lisa joined him.

Soon we all danced. The floor thundered. The miller came by for his daughter. And he paused to dance too.

Everybody danced on and on. The doctor danced again until his forehead shone, his shirt clung to him plumply. Cyclops danced, wine in hand, the wine spilling. Danced without thought. His arms, legs danced. The dance danced. The doctor was like a bird trying to fly – but this bird cannot; but cannot stop flapping, running, stretching out all his feathers. He was dancing with his heart in his eyes: Tell me – who am I? Cyclops' great feet struck sparks from the boards. The doctor couldn't help but stare at him. Nor could any of us. He was our delirium, this one-eyed man.

What were we all trying to dance?

It was late when an oldish weary man appeared in the doorway. The doctor, flushed from the dance, turning, still half-danced toward the man, slowing to a grave stop before him. They spoke briefly. Then the doctor crossed to me where I was sitting, drink in hand, catching my breath. And 'Please, would you like to come with me?' he asked. 'I have to go to a patient – a boy with tetanus.' And he got his jacket. We groped our way from the lightstruck room down the stairs outside into the street, following the weary man.

We followed him through the dim maze of the town. The doctor took my hand. And I started to withdraw it. But that seemed an ugly motion. So holding hands, as though we were children, we stumbled the uneven night streets. At the waterfront, by a café, he spoke to the man, who nodded and vanished. We sat down at a table out front. The doctor ordered two coffees, black.

He began to talk again. Beyond us shone the sea. The small boats were tipping in it lightly. We were the only ones sitting there. A dog limped by, turning its head to look at us.

'Why don't you stay', the doctor asked, 'and be my nurse here? Do you have to go?'

'I have to go', I told him. 'I have to go tomorrow.'

'You don't have to go', he said. 'Stay.'

'How old is the child with tetanus?' I asked him.

'He's twelve', he said. 'Stay. The day I came back here,' the doctor said, 'the day I arrived at this island, I stood on the shore, and I looked at the pebbles at my feet, I looked at the boats in the surf, and I started to cry. I had been so homesick – in America. But I'm a stranger after all. And I'm lonely.'

'Were you born on this island?' I asked him.

He had been born on another island.

I asked him about his practice.

'I can't really make any difference at all', he said. He leaned toward me with an exhausted look. He wanted to tell me about a call he'd had one night. A boy in a motor boat had collided with a larger boat. 'His brains were lying on his cheek', he said. 'They came and woke me. It was three in the morning. I said I'd be along. I went back to sleep. They came and woke me again. I got out of bed and started to dress. And I lay down and went back to sleep. they came again –'

We glanced up and Russell was standing there. He wanted to come with us. He sat down and ordered a coffee too. The doctor didn't finish his story. Russell began to inquire about the boy with tetanus. He knew the mother slightly. The man who had come to fetch the doctor reappeared. The doctor drained his cup and stood up. 'Yes, come with us', he said to Russell.

One mounted to this house, too, by steep outside stairs. The room was the first into which we stepped, a whitewashed dim-shining room. There was little in it but the bed in which the sick boy lay, his limbs flung out under the sheet, around him gathered relatives. Russell stood near, joined that half-circle. He knew some of these people. But I felt incongruous there – though they turned to look at me without reproach. I stayed by the door.

Someone went into the back room for a lantern, so that the doctor could see. The doctor whispered urgently, 'Cover the light!' As its blaze whitened the room, the boy's body arched, and he began to moan through his teeth. They shaded the lantern quickly. The doctor turned back the sheet and ran his hands along the boy's anguished limbs.

The boy wanted to speak, but his jaw was locked; and it was as though he had forgotten how to speak, sought again to know what speech was. The doctor covered him again, and sat beside him to prepare the hypodermic needles he must give him. The family, in its gathered arc, watched in silence. One woman covered the boy's eyes with a cloth, and she kept her hand there then, on his head. He had the shaven head of all Greek boys, large domed, and the great widely-spaced dark eyes.

The others bent toward him, their hands by their sides, yet touching him, and touching him with their eyes. And one held the shaded light. The bed in its disarray of limbs was queerly beautiful. His body arched and arched again. The doctor put the needle in his arm and held it there. They had all been standing there, one knew, hour after hour, watching him, trying to read from the hieroglyph of his limbs in spasm: Will he live – will he speak, will he walk – will he be born again?

The doctor gave him several needles. He questioned one of the women. Then he stood up. 'Wish them good night', he told us. We wished them, in whispers, good night. We descended the dim stairs again.

'Will he live?' Russell asked.

'Yes, he's going to live', the doctor said. 'He's lucky.'

And we walked back through the town to the doctor's house. The terrace smelled of carnations. Through the windows, music still spilled. The doctor took my hand. Russell stepped in the door, toward the music, but the doctor, with the pressure of his hand, asked me to stay. I stayed. One could hear Cyclops' bare feet stepping the boards inside. And then Russell join the dance. The air was very clear about us, blue, not black. Below us, along the shore, there were bright small flares – night fishing. 'I am lonely', the doctor said to me again.

Now this is very strange. He kissed my mouth. And then stood close against me – as though he would vanish, if he could, in my arms. And though I had experienced at first sight for this man distaste, I didn't feel now that I could draw away. He led me into the garden to which the terrace circled. I told him, 'I mustn't.' But when he said. 'Please don't say that', I stopped speaking. And felt for this man no desire, but something more difficult to resist than desire. And yes I fell down under him. And though I knew no pleasure, yet for those moments the world seemed to lie there intact, hammered together again. Or so I tried to tell myself.

Then he picked a carnation for me. And we stepped back into the room where Cyclops was somersaulting.

And why have I told you this tale?

2

'And why have I told you this tale?' I asked – before I interrupted the writing of this book for twenty years. I think I told it hoping to become more real to myself. I had failed to resist a thief. Failed to see the needy man *as* a thief. (Failed to see this even when I wrote the story.) Yet my inability to resist him did continue to seem to me 'very strange'. Groping to understand what had happened, I wrote in my notes for a next chapter:

'It's risky to step from one's own country into another. One sets down one's feet. They move no longer to familiar music, stepping to a tune that's not even heard, that runs through one simply as the blood runs through one's veins. In a strange country, this music suddenly is in the air, audible and queer, and it is the beginning of one's life all over again. One looks down at one's feet. They don't yet move. One opens one's mouth. No sound comes out. But the music is urgent, and so one cries out some note and one steps in.'

I can't help remarking my use here of the detached word 'one' instead of 'I'. Yes, longing to dance my life my own – as the fisherman 'king' danced his – I had instead let myself be stolen from myself.

'One travels at risk,' I wrote, 'but it is necessary to leave home.' I'll take up this book again at the moment when I did leave – begin, this time, not 'anywhere' but at the beginning of my travelling.

It *is* necessary to leave home. If I had not, would I ever have met you, Lottie – who had been growing up next to me through all the years of my life until that time? Our families were neighbours and friends. We had been shyly friends. I saw you on to your ship when you sailed for Europe several months before I did. I remember that was the first day on which I believed I, too, would really sail. I'd already made plans for it, but I had to finish a long and difficult piece of writing first; and the trip still seemed only imaginary. My mother's mother suddenly offered me the money for it – just enough to live on for a year over there if I was careful. But for many years Europe had seemed out of my reach. I couldn't ever save enough at any of the jobs I held to make such a trip. My father could have given me the money, but didn't believe in spoiling his children by making them any gifts of money beyond the money for their education. Travel abroad didn't seem to him a necessary part of education. I had thought of leaving as impossible for so long that it still really seemed so. I began to have dreams about it, though – my sleeping self trying to imagine it. I dreamed that I was walking down a street and women passed wrapped in orange and black calico-cat fur coats. European fur! I exclaimed to myself. In one dream, I was lying on a beach and a young man stepped near. I could see only his legs, which were very hairy. The hair was trimmed like the hair of a French poodle. Why, a Frenchman! I recognized within my dream.

Leaving was unreal to me because I was so used to thinking of it as impossible. It was also unreal because at the time I was still in love with somebody else; and she was here on this shore. For eight years my life had been entwined with Nell's. I wrote in a journal: 'She is the knot itself that ties me.' Nell was the kind of woman, full of talent and energy, who, when she loves, concentrates upon her beloved much of her own will to live. She had made much of me, made me her study. And I eagerly sought myself in her eyes. But – a little over a year before, she had married. It was clear enough that I must now carefully loosen the cords by which my soul was bound to hers. But I feared that loosening. During our years together, we sometimes talked as though of course some day we would both marry; and that part of me which listened to the teachings of the world believed this. But that part of me which listened to my own heartbeat had believed that I would always live with Nell.

She married one of my brothers. Ben – the brother to whom I felt the closest, and who had been strong support to me in many life crises. I had often felt toward him as toward a twin spirit. Once, living for a while in a city far from home, I'd looked into a mirror and seen not my own face but his face looking back at me – at which I'd recovered from loneliness. Ben had been in love with Nell for a long time, but because of me hadn't tried to win her. The fact that he loved her too haunted me. One night I dreamed that I was carrying in my arms his slack naked wounded body, as I

15

climbed a green but difficult mountain slope. Even today I can shut my eyes and feel that sad weight against my own body. Soon after dreaming this dream I told him that he mustn't feel he shouldn't woo Nell. He wooed her and he won her. In one part of my soul I felt that this was only right. Back then, the idea of marriage still inspired in me a kind of awe. He could offer her marriage; I could not – could offer it only *through* him, my twin. In another part of my soul of course I felt that everything had gone wrong. And my hope was really still that she would take me back into her life somehow. Even into the life that she and Ben now shared. One part of me knew this was impossible, but another kept hoping that it could be so. We all three did love one another. Ben had even written after a visit I'd paid them, 'We miss you. Home doesn't seem quite home without you.' When I set sail – a few months after you, Lottie – I was carrying with me a weight of memory and of fantasy more real to me than the voyage I was beginning.

I can remember sitting up at the front of the ship after it had left the dock – a small Italian liner, like the one you took. My journal reads: 'A windy spring day. The sun a white blister. The ship now seems empty.' For everybody was below, unpacking, or having tea. I didn't feel like doing either; I wanted to watch our passage out to sea. At quarantine, we swung round and then waited. A small boat came out and the captain yelled across at it over a megaphone. Two stowaways had been found on board and he wanted them taken off. Red tape made this difficult, but after more than an hour the boat returned and did remove them. I experienced a shock of feeling at the sight of them. They were two skinny black youths – one in a navy jacket, one in khaki. Each carried a tiny canvas bag and that was all. They stepped on to the small boat and didn't look back; sprawled themselves out on the deck in jaunty disappointment. And we moved on. Laden. Yes, I remember that shock, remember feeling abruptly: One should travel like *that*; one should travel light; but I am setting forth laden. I had even brought a trunk. A trunk and a couple of suitcases. Everything I could think of that I owned that I might possibly use. And my spirit, too, was overladen.

We moved out the sea lane – past the New Jersey docks, past Liberty holding up her heavy torch – a careful file of us, one ship behind another. Then we were in the open waters and began to separate. Land, home, left behind, we were on our own – we were at sea. I stood at the railings. Papers, boxes, drifted about, clung to the riggings; flower boxes, wrappings, all the refuse of departure, clung for a while, then, one by one, the wind plucked them off.

A new language was shouted over the public address system. 'Attenzione! Attenzione!' We were advised to set our clocks forward an hour. I kept mine at the old time – to mark the difference. Those I was leaving were at this hour still. Those on the shore we sailed toward were of course at quite another. The ship glided eerily between two times.

I climbed whenever I could to the very top of the ship. Touched the riggings and felt the ship's life humming in them. Wished I could feel my own life hum like that. 'Attention! Attention!' Could they catch my attention? As the wind blew in these riggings, so memories of Nell blew through me. The nearer we glided to a new shore, the more I seemed to be standing still tightly bound upon the old. Wordless. My wits caught in the riggings. The ship bore me on and yet there I stood upon the home shore – the memories that bound me there drawn by the ship's motion tighter and tighter.

I did in time begin to take note of some of the other passengers. I remember the woman with the orangey hair and the nervous little dog on a leash, making round after round of the deck, peering into the faces of other walkers – the dog with its squinting eyes peering also. Her husband followed, several paces behind, thin, morose. In the conversations she would sometimes pick up with me, she asked all kinds of questions about where I was planning to go, whether I knew anybody over there. Her questing figure repelled me slightly – yet touched me, too, in spite of myself. For I was adrift and anxious as she.

I remember the stiff young man with whom I found myself at table, who was travelling alone to join his parents overseas. They were in government service. He was troubled several times by seasickness, but it was a point of pride with him never to leave the meal until all at table with him were ready to push back their chairs. He would sit, straight as a stick, his hands in his lap, his cheeks drained of colour, taking not a bite, but managing a few polite words now and then. He probably felt his father's eyes upon him from afar. Sitting across from him, I sometimes felt my own father's grave eyes upon me. For it was because of my father that I was seated at that particular table. Once my grandmother had offered me travel money, he had taken me aside and, to my astonishment, told me to put her money in savings; he would pay for the trip himself. He took me to the bank to sign a year's worth of traveller's cheques. My hand began to tremble as I made the multiple signatures. I'd tried to steady my right hand with my left – hoping that he wouldn't notice my agitation. That agitation was in part gratitude. The extra money would set me free for a much longer time. But I trembled, too, wondering why he was making the gift. A year before, when I was running out of job-earned money I'd saved – that allowed me to write for a while full-time – I'd appealed to him to give me a small subsistence allowance until I could begin to earn a living by my writing. He refused – explaining quietly that he feared to turn me into someone dependent upon him. What would happen to me if he died? I told him that he needn't worry about my ability to find a job if I needed to. What worried me was that I might not find the time to learn my craft as a writer. But I hadn't persuaded him; and that attempt to persuade him had left me feeling an unpleasant shame. Why was he paying for this trip? Because he knew how lost I felt after Nell's marriage? Did he know that I was in love with her? I assumed that my mother knew. I had never talked with her about Nell, but when I was sixteen and had fallen in love for the very first time, I had confided in her. My first love was an older woman and her close friend. She hadn't seemed disturbed by my news, but I was quite sure that she hadn't shared it with my father. Had he guessed anyway? And how much had he guessed about Nell? Had he guessed not only that I was in love with her but that we'd lived as lovers? I felt both uncomfortably visible to him and uncomfortably invisible. And I couldn't help wondering: Did he see the trip abroad as a sort of necessary medical expense – heart's cure? Did he perhaps also hope that I would find a husband during my tour? He had bought me a first-class ticket. This gesture both touched and exasperated me. And I'd been tempted to exchange it for a second-class ticket; but I didn't quite dare risk upsetting him, if he should find out. So there we both sat – the young man and I – two dazed and obedient children.

I made one friend on board, Eva – met her down in second class, where I liked to wander. She was a sculptor, returning to Italy where she had been many times before. She felt freer to work there, she said. A large handsome woman with a head like the head on a Greek coin, a warrior head – the lip notched, as if in battle, the cheek a little wan. A battle-worn figure, and battle-wary. She was accustomed to blows, had made her difficult way on her own. I asked her at one point whether she was in a gallery. She replied tensely that yes, she had shown in such-and-such-a-place for several years. When I said quickly that I managed to miss an awful lot, her face relaxed. The very next moment she said to me, 'You must come and see me when you're in Florence.' I had succeeded in persuading her that I was unarmed. In certain unguarded gestures, she could betray longing that was prodigious. Friends I made later in Italy described arriving with Eva at the tall gate of a palazzo where they were invited to a party. A little path led round the locked gate, but – they recounted in astonishment – on a sudden impulse Eva scaled the gate. This combination of ardour and wariness touched me, and I kept trying to signal: 'Don't fear me; I don't want to put you down.' We would meet and play deck tennis, or meet at the day's end for a Cinzano, sit at the back of the ship and watch sundown stain the wake. We established a certain shy case together.

But a lot of the time I spent by myself. At night I would climb up above the captain's cabin. The stars were as though new to me. It was a long time since I had looked at them hard. Now they seemed to be written across the sky like scattered signal words to be gathered into a sentence if I could. But I couldn't of course. The big dipper hung there each evening like a question mark – turning precarious in the heavens.

One day we sighted the Azores. It was a misty blue late afternoon. I was walking round the deck when the announcement came over the P.A. system that we were approaching and I moved to the railing and stared forward. I could see only blue sea, blue sky. Then I blinked. For I was looking at the islands. Which were blue too. A painter's playful experiment of blue on blue on blue. We moved quietly through them, and then away, and now we were even more at sea than we had been before.

But the continent lay near, and Gibraltar, sighted, seemed at once a fact – a familiar shape, believed long ago. It was beautiful seen from far off, but grew ugly as we drew near – stark official buildings set on the bald rock. And here abruptly actual contact was made with the new, the old country. Little boats were at our side. I hadn't seen them launched, but there they were. Ropes were thrown up over the ship's railings. And up the ropes were sent a multitude of baskets. In the baskets, cigarettes, cheap bracelets, squids, figs in dark leaves. From the boats rose a strong and unfamiliar smell that broke roughly through the dream in which I was wrapped. And sharp unfamiliar accents – 'One dollaire! One dollaire!' – that broke roughly through. The look, too, of the Spaniards standing in their boats to hawk their wares was a look altogether unfamiliar to me, so that I stared and stared. At their bony faces, at their shirts and pants of beautiful colours, lavender, rose, but which were faded rags – these men and the rags on them weathered in a life of which I knew nothing. Here were the first strangers to me who were strangers to every sense. The new, toward which I'd been sailing, had thrown up its ropes over *me* at last. Those baskets of figs in their dark leaves struck me as an image of wonder and promise. Though something moved me to ask in my journal: 'Might they contain the asp?'

A few passengers disembarked and we left Gibraltar at sundown – the Spanish coast blazing for a little while rose and silver. The details of this coast, too, grew small, and as the land receded, belief again receded – belief that we had had that encounter at all. A dragonfly still flew about the deck, above the deck chairs, startling the passengers, who had retired to the chairs, pulling up their blankets. It drifted oddly, lost, above the reclining forms, the only sign that we had touched land.

The next day we arrived at Naples. We came in by night. Picking out the shapes of things by lights, by silhouettes. Which was the mainland, which were islands? Was that Vesuvius? I noticed that the rhythm of my breathing had quickened. Eva was on the ship's bridge with me and she was singing. She was coming home – I didn't know her well enough to know to what, to whom; but her voice contained a wilful wistful note that was an opening out of herself. '*Vecchia Mama*', an Italian would exclaim to me the next morning as we moved into the harbour – 'Ancient mother! She holds out her arms!' And I would feel his words pierce me – to my surprise; feel my own self, too, expand as if in homecoming. *Might* this trip bring me somehow home?

This next morning I climbed out of bed early and hurried to my porthole. There they were. There they were – the stained walls, the history-stained walls of, yes, an ancient mother. Softly glowing. 'Muri melodiosi', I would write – walls that sing. I stared and stared from the porthole, my whole being straining forward – as if to catch at once, across this space of water that remained, the burden of their song. Listening, listening for it as if indeed it had been sung to me in my cradle. Even peering in memory across the space of years, I feel my spirit now concentrate, attentive.

Soon we moved in, to dock. Oranges bobbed round us in the water, and the multicoloured chips of the daily ship's programmes, scattered now, orange yellow green – the voyage over.

Ashore, in customs, I stood next a young American couple I had come to know a little. They, too, wanted a look at Naples before catching the train to Rome, and we walked out into the streets of the city together.

Into the strange air. Filled with the babble of a strange tongue. My journal reads: 'The strange tongue, the strange air. And perhaps above all the smell of this land is strange to me. But look smell sound are one. Antiquity. These walls are streaked with all weathers, with all times, with suns and suns. I smell not this present moment but tumbled yesterdays, and yesterdays. An incense swung out of all time . . . *Muri melodiosi* – how these walls glow! Here as in double exposure, triple, quadruple, countless exposures – as in a vision by which heaven breaks through Time and shows us all time, wavering here – Ancient Mother! Mother! Streaked bosom. Where I want to lay my head . . . When was it that I left home? I cannot remember. And the others here, brothers here. I cannot remember. Their tongue is a strange tongue, strange songue.'

Yes, I can recall still in what a confusion of feeling I walked. I was home at last; all was strange to me; and these two facts were somehow one.

We took a horse carriage for an hour's giro – Tom, the young husband, making the arrangements, for he had been to Italy before. As we walked down the street, cabbies began to offer their services. Tom looked unconcerned. Still another driver called out, and he turned as if vaguely interested. What had the man to offer? A very reasonable sum. But Tom wrinkled up his handsome face. A cabby up the block called out. Tom named to him a much lower sum than the last driver had offered. This cabby shrugged. Impossible. Which it obscenely was. We walked on, round the corner. Trot trot trot. The horse and buggy was drawing up beside us. The driver offered now a price much lower than his first price, but necessarily higher than what Tom had offered. He accepted, and we got in.

And I remember still mounting the steps of one of the old churches to which the cabby drove us. At the foot of the steps a begging child held out his hand – a redhead, a small Harpo, utterly ragged, his face already an aged beggar's face. I expected Tom to make some response to him, but he disdained to, and in embarrassment I started up the long steps. Then half-way up, wishing I had acted on my own, I began almost furtively to slide my hand into my pocketbook, rehearsing the gesture, really, to be ready next time. And there he was, beside me, in an instant, come from all the way down at street level. The mere hint of my hand's motion had brought him – up the long wide steps – as though we were precision-bound by wires. His eyes meeting mine. His fist out. With a start, I felt: Ah, I like your spirit. I half acknowledged to myself the thought: I wish I could ask like this for what I need. Not trembling, not eyes cast sideways. Your fist out, eyes in mine: 'Gimme.' Yes, gladly.

We rode around for an hour, quickly visiting churches, museums, the large arcade – my senses reeling. Then we caught the train for Rome. Just caught it, and it was crowded. I sat for the first part of the trip on my suitcase in the aisle. And stared out the window – at glimpses of the sea, the water blues that seemed new to me; at hills with the trees set on them in ways I had never seen before; farmlands shaped and worked in ways I had never seen land worked; walls terraces balconies spires – even the light that fell on them seemed the light of a day like no other day into which I had awakened.

In Rome, I took a taxi to the pensione where I had reserved a room. And there was a note your aunt Reba had left, asking me to telephone. You were still away in Greece – your first trip there. I was feeling pleased to find that I could handle the Italian language well enough to get about, but the sound of my native language over the wires was a welcome sound. Reba said she and your uncle would let me settle in, but pick me up for dinner. I didn't take time to settle in, but hurried out into the street again to wander about until they came by for me.

I remember that as I walked down one street, a faint sound at my feet made me glance down and a tiny lizard was darting along the sidewalk. It ran ahead of me for several paces, then changed course and ran up a wall, where it froze, pretending to be invisible. Lucertolina, I would come to know the name. They were a common sight almost anywhere in Italy. But how uncommon it seemed to me that day. I think if I had seen a lion or a giraffe moving down the street, it could hardly have seemed to me more portentous.

One day, years before, a woman older than I, a writer who lived in our community, had drawn me out about myself, inviting me to speak more freely than I was used to of my anxieties about my work and about my life. She had listened with a rare attention; told me, then, something of her own life; and we talked together about how fear can hobble one, how one must learn to step free of it. Walking home from that visit, the country mile or two between our houses, my spirit at ease, I glanced up at the wooded hillside, feeling: Something quite new could happen to me now – suddenly thinking: A dinosaur could appear on that ridge and I would not be appalled, but would accept the sight of it. Why should the figure of a dinosaur have occurred to me? I don't know. But it is still real to me, that large odd body looming there on the ridge of a summery hillside. The smaller darting lizard in the street seemed again, mysteriously, a portent of the new.

Reba and Lou took me to dinner in a trattoria in Trasteverie. First they drove a meandering route there, to show me a little of the city. City in which narrow streets keep opening into spacey piazzas, or offering extraordinary vistas: an obelisk, perhaps; or, to a tumble of sound, a fountain in which demigods and creatures rear up and gesture; or wide stairs that lift the eyes to the city poised upon another level. The tawny glowing city. Its colours the colours of grassy fields in late summer – ochre, burnt umber, burnt sienna – the walls of the buildings here changing like the grasses under the changing light.

We sat at a table outside, in a small piazza. Reba made a list for me of useful things to know: how the different buses ran, where to find the American drugstore. And she and Lou together, inter-rupting each other, told me of particular sights I should be sure not to miss. The sabbatical year was altering them both, it seemed to me. Her face especially had relaxed, and he looked much less the knowing scholar of history. Yes, in his face, too, something different shone. A sense of wonder, perhaps. He had not travelled in many years; had sought history in books. Here it was before him in the flesh, in the stone. Overhead, swallows made darting twittering flights. And the streets beyond were filled with the roar of motor scooters, and notes of their horns and their bells, as the youth of Rome, piled often two or three together on their mounts, circled and circled, taking an evening promenade of their city. Dogs and cats, too, were taking their promenades, passing our table.

In this piazza was a small church – dedicated to the Virgin, Lou told us. And there was a fountain. I can't remember its design, but I can remember, it seems to me, the delicate sound of the water – audible now and then when the roar of traffic would subside. And I can remember the dim glow shed by the surrounding buildings, even now that evening had gathered. As though, again, the walls had absorbed the light of years and years, cast back at us not simply the ebbing light of that particular day but day born of day born of day – a magical radiance, I felt, and stared and stared, forgetting to eat. Though the food was magic to me, too. I had prosciutto and melon for the first time that evening. And ripe figs – like the figs that had come on board in baskets at Gibraltar. I stared out into the radiant piazza and up at the clustered buildings that illumined it. A few windows were open, and in the open window at the top floor of one house, a young woman sat in a straight-backed chair, quietly looking out. I kept raising my eyes to that window, I recall. I recall it, in fact, almost as though it were yesterday – not in precise detail but in its dreamlike essence. For I felt a little as though I were experiencing a dream. As though the woman in the window, a stranger to me, was really no stranger but one who knew my fate, and waited there quietly, ready to tell me if I asked it. As in a dream, I had no impulse to ask. It thrilled me, simply, that she knew it. Once I looked up, and she had gone. There was only the silhouette of the straight chair. But a little later still, when I looked, she had returned. She sat on and on, quietly – sometimes leaning her elbows on the still. That evening seemed to stretch and stretch in time – time to stand suspended. In fact, it stands suspended still. I sit there still, glancing up at her.

3

Yes, it is necessary to leave home. If I hadn't left, would I ever have found you? Wandering, I discovered not only the strange but the familiar, saw it as new – the newest of all. But this happened only in travail. I look back in time and can see at once that I had found you – in a moment. But I couldn't see it then.

It was a week or two after my arrival in Rome before you returned from Greece. You were due back almost immediately, but kept changing the date. Meanwhile I was getting myself settled – or rather, I was learning to allow myself to be unsettled. That first week, I woke and woke throughout the nights – to bells, to horns, to the roar of Vespas in the streets – sitting up in bed encircled by the unfamiliar. It was like waking at sea in a tempest, in a chaos. I find in my journal, 'No, you will not be told anything in advance. The sea will look like the sea will look like the sea.'

Mornings I tried to write, but it was hard. Because I was homesick. And the mail was discouraging. My agent wrote me that the book I'd left with her had been rejected by a publisher she'd thought would take it. Another letter let me know that I hadn't been awarded the grant for which I'd applied. I told myself each time that I was not discouraged, but each time I told myself a lie.

In the afternoons I explored the city. Several times your family invited me to drive somewhere with them. Some days an American friend of a friend to whom I had an introduction acted as my guide. But I saw most, in fact, when I wandered by myself. It was always tempting to be in company, but in the state of loneliness I was more easily surprised. Rome, of course, is a city of surprises. Which Mussolini had done his best to annul. The first time I saw St Peter's I saw it on a drive with your family and we approached it along the new avenue the Duce had ordered, its famous dome, just as he had wished, visible for the avenue's straight length. But on another day, roaming on my own at random from one street into another, I rounded a corner, found myself among some enormous pillars, took a few more steps – and then the space around me enlarged as the spirit itself can enlarge; the cathedral faced me above its airy piazza as if created as I stared, by some burst of the imagination. The moment in which I saw you again was a surprise of this kind.

That morning I telephoned to ask for news of you, and learned that you were due back at last on an afternoon train. Did I want to join them for dinner? your uncle asked me. His voice was tentative, and I had taken it for granted that they would like to spend this first evening with you alone. But it was a time in my life when I still too often expected others to throw me my proper cues for action. Instead of saying simply that I'd come to see you the next day, I asked, 'Shouldn't I wait until tomorrow?' Your gentle uncle replied, 'Whatever you wish.' As the conversation ended, he inquired, 'Will we see you tonight?' and I answered stupidly, 'All right.' I decided to say a brief hello but then leave.

Your family lived in a small villa on one of Rome's seven hills. The door was open and I could see, across the room, that everyone was out on the terrace. I knocked and started in, self-conscious, and, hearing the knock, you rose and came inside, yourself. I remember still your voice that day as you walked toward me – 'Look who's here' – bantering, affectionate, a voice familiar to me and yet unfamiliar, some vibration in it that was new. She has changed, she has changed, I heard. I saw that you had. Who is this friend of mine? I wondered, walking toward me with her arms out – bony brown arms sticking out of her sleeveless summer dress, and bony brown legs carrying her, face almost skeletal, and stained a shining nut brown by the Greek sun; short hair caught back in a bandanna, eyes very black and the whites of them very white – your self burned down, worn down, to some essence I had never seen so sharply. Who are you who are you? I was asking myself, and where have you been? You held out your arms and we hugged each other lightly.

Other friends of the family were there, it turned out, so I ended by going out to dinner with you after all. It was to the sidewalk restaurant at the Piazza Navona that we all went – piazza of the three Bernini fountains, in the largest of which a lion comes down to drink, a sea serpent coils, a demigod holds up his hand – in mock alarm, Lou told us; holds it up to prevent the collapse of the building across the way, designed by one of Bernini's rivals.

You and I spoke very few words together. The conversation was general. You had tales to tell of Greece – about the people who gathered round you as you made your landscape drawings; their responses when you turned from the landscape to sketch portraits of them. Your accounts were often funny, and the joke, when there was one, was on you, who were always, it seems, making some preposterously foolish move. But for all your disparagements of yourself, which were familiar to me, you spoke with a boldness I had never seen in you before.

On the day after, your family invited a few people in to see the work that you had done – several of them painters themselves; and I was included. You spread out your notebooks on a table out on the terrace – three or four large books full of work. That afternoon, too, was like seeing you new. As we turned the pages, the air was full of the twitter of swallows, I think I can remember – and the smell of resin, an incense swung from the branches of the pinon pines beyond the terrace wall. The work was in pen and ink or was in watercolour or in crayon. I remember still seeing the strong pink of the Cretan earth in one drawing and wanting to walk on that ground myself. And I remember the electric shock that ran through me, staring at your work – like the shock at seeing you the day before. I wrote in my journal that evening: 'Not a lazy sketch among them!' Your whole being was concentrated there.

You were joking still, of course, as you watched us. The jokes on yourself, discounting yourself. Yet not discounting. As the two other painters – older men – softly exclaimed in spite of themselves at what you had done, I noticed that you accepted their praise with calm – taking it almost for granted. You joked and yet you didn't joke, doubted yourself and yet were sure – the two modes of feeling curiously mixed in you. To this day you clearly know and as clearly do not know how good you are, what authority you have.

Within the week you vanished, to the hill town not far from Rome where you had a studio. And I set forth in another direction – seeking my own concentration of self. I wouldn't see you again for several months. I was headed for Florence first. Your aunt let me store some luggage with them before I left. I was becoming more and more aware that it had been ridiculous to bring so many things. Travel light. The look of you had shocked that through me again.

27

Leaving, I found to my surprise, was like leaving home, like heading out to sea all over again. In Rome I did know your family. Eva lived near Florence and had said to visit her, but I hardly knew Eva, and would visit her briefly. As the wheels of the bus began to turn, I felt again that queer sensation in my soul that was also a physical sensation – of cords tightening upon my body, the many memories of my life with Nell the past eight years.

The bus rocketed along the roads – past summery fields, past olive groves their dusty dusty green, and hills which, as I stared, took their particular shapes – upon them ancient castles sometimes or walled towns. I squinted at all this as at a difficult text. Memory was between my eyes and this land. Yes, seen through the thickness of that pane, the world I wanted so to learn from flickered before me too often as though it were a mirage. I remembered the way in which *you* looked about you, and rebuked myself. The day was very hot, and at one point the driver stopped the bus by a roadside faucet to give the steaming radiator water. All the passengers tumbled out of the bus to take a quick drink. I stuck my feet, one at a time, shoes and all, under the running spout. Not only to cool them. The living touch of the water, I hoped, might shock me out of my dreaming state.

Spoleto we passed through. Assisi, with its glowing stones. Perugia. Arezzo. No town along this route like any other, each its own world. If one had eyes to take it in.

A friend back home had advised me, when I arrived in Florence, to take a horse and carriage up to the Piazalle Michelangelo, built upon a height, and from there take my first long look. And so I followed her good advice. The horse walked at a very quiet pace up the hill, its harness bells tinkling slowly. There was a different rhythm here than in Rome, I noted. And the people glancing at us as we passed seemed more slow-eyed. Even the cats who made their lives in these streets stalked at a different pace. Or was it the dream in which I was caught again that made it seem so? I stared down at last at the domes and towers and spires and roofs of the beautiful city – the River Arno moving under its three bridges, carrying its reflection, carrying its long history – and as I looked there drifted from somewhere behind me the recorded sound of 'Parlez moi d'amour!' sung in a complaining, a lovesick voice. I winced at that music. It was not an adequate anthem of Florence.

And in spite of myself I felt that my presence had somehow introduced the plaint.

That evening I walked and walked the city – hoping to be drawn out of myself. But my own history was still more real to me than this larger history through which I walked. All that I saw kept seeming to me simply a reflection of my own disordered state. Traces of the war were much more visible here than in Rome. Some buildings – especially along the river – were in ruins still, some badly pitted. Two of the bridges that had been blasted were temporary reconstructions still. 'Misera Italia!' an old beggar woman cried out to me, as she asked a coin. Another old crone sat on a stone near the entrance to one of the bridges, humming to herself, humming to herself, out of her mind. There was a quarter moon reflected in the river – as pale, as insubstantial in the sky as in the water, like a wisp of cloud. I can remember looking up at that moon and feeling: Why are we of no more body?

In the days that followed, I did gradually enter Florence – to stare and stare about me. You know its marvels. As I write this, Michelangelo's *Morning and Night* loom before me in their beautiful nakedness. And Massaccio's *Eve and Adam* painted as they fled the Garden in dismay. I stood before that painting for an especially long time, watching the changing light wake in the faces of the disobedient pair – it seemed to me – changing thoughts. The dust of war was still in the air of this city, the smell of rubble mixed with the smell of coffee and of wine. Some of its inhabitants were still crying out their losses to passers-by – stunned. But the deep life of the city ran through it still – persistent as the river that ran through it. Wandering, I just began to sense it – a life that was in the present, a life that was also all the motion of the past.

As I wandered, I thought of you sometimes. Thought of you suddenly in the Convent of San Marco one afternoon as I peered into the spare cells there – bed chair small table; a fresco by Fra Angelico (in each) the one luxury. The paintings light, very concentrated – the subject of each an act of concentration. I thought of your gaunt face, beautifully alert. There was a kind of joyfulness to the Fra Angelicos. The joy was that of concentration of being. Could I learn a concentration that was comparable? You had learned it, it seemed to me.

I looked up Eva. She lived in the rented ruins of a once very elegant villa a few miles outside the city. One very large room, still intact, made a fine studio for her, and she had made a number of other smaller rooms usable. The landlady's sheep grazed on the terraces of what had been an extensive formal garden. Relatives of the landlady inhabited some of the remoter wings of the building. And one of them cooked for Eva. Luxury still – however dilapidated. She invited me to stay for several days. It was a marvellously lonely spot. But she ventured into Florence rather often, where she had friends – and took me with her several times. Two of her friends turned out to be friends of friends of mine. We sat in a series of sidewalk cafés and talked and talked and talked. They were musicians and poets and painters, and all were very knowing. Men, most of them. The talk as often as not went over my head. Everyone was an expert on the ballet, on the opera, on Italian history. Eva held her own. I couldn't begin to.

It seemed to me that Eva was in love with one of these men. He was a composer, younger than she, brilliant, witty, flirtatious in an almost girlish way – with Eva, but also with everyone else. He was a frequent visitor, I gathered from their talk, and they touched each other often. But the attention that he gave her seemed to state (in parenthesis): You understand that at any moment I may have to leave you. Eva kept her poise, maintained an appearance of handsome calm. Just as she never faltered in any of the conversational exchanges, she never let herself seem to be anxious about his intentions. But to display such ease, I sensed, put upon her in fact a very great strain.

One evening which the two of us spent alone at her villa, Eva began to speak a little about herself. We sat in her large studio room – her sculptures in the background, clay hands gesturing (they were thin figures, of rather haughty bearing, but expressing in these gestures a great disquiet). The day paled, but we didn't bother to light a lamp, we let the darkness gather; and, as it gathered, it drew us closer – a shawl round us.

'You are alone, too,' she said suddenly; 'do you suffer from loneliness?'

I told her yes.

'Of course I do my best work when I am alone', she mused. 'But when I am alone too much, it feels wrong; I get scared – that something in me will die, dry up. But then when I am with a lot of people, that feels wrong too; I feel scattered; I get scared that I will lose myself in *this* way, lose whatever is original in me, most my own.'

We sat without speaking for a while.

'Perhaps one needs to be married,' she said at last – posing it as a question.

We both sat and looked at the question, not speaking. The gathering dark kept drawing the room into a smaller size. We could see only each other now, and the low table between us, with wine glasses, with fruit. At a certain point, even, I felt it gather the two of us, strangely, into one person. She put out her hand slowly to lift a wine glass to her lips. It seemed to me that my own hand was lifting the glass, and that my own lips drank. Whether she felt the same, I don't know. But she stared at me rather oddly – as I at her. Then we said our goodnights.

The next morning I left to spend some time in Assisi. On the train I managed a conversation with a group of women sharing the same compartment. They were amazed that I travelled alone. Without either parents or husband. My parents must be dead, then. Alive! And I was here without them! 'Sola!' They whispered it – the word marking me much more a stranger than the fact that I barely spoke their language. When we told each other our respective ages, it was my turn to be shocked by the differences in our lives. One of the women I had taken to be my mother's age was not much older than I. A woman wrinkled as my grandmother was my smooth-faced mother's age. The women were factory workers, worked at a factory that made cheap straw hats – like the one I was wearing, had bought near the Ponte Vecchio that morning. 'There's my hat!' one of them shouted with a laugh, pointing at me as I took my seat. The woman who was not much older than I – but worn already, her lively face deeply lined.

'Sola!' The word kept echoing in me. Word uttered by the women in awe. They had not my privilege to roam. The whispered word named me privileged; it named me also outlaw – one who fit no accepted norm.

In Assisi I haunted the churches – to stare to the Giottos and the Cimabues. I also walked and walked around the outskirts of the city. I remember an ancient grove of olive trees past which I walked. Their silvery grey trunks were gnarled and twisted. Many of them were hollow. And yet the trees were leafy, and they would bear. I remember that I thought of Eva's question to me: 'Do you suffer from loneliness?' And that it occurred to me now with new strength that I might well have to do my chosen work in loneliness, but that one can be lonely and yet bear. I remember, as that thought pierced me, thinking of you again for a moment – as that thought entered my flesh, and my flesh became hollowed wood. While I was standing there in a sort of trance, a skinny beggar woman approached me out of the grove. Before holding out her hand to me she showed me first her faded ragged dress, then her bare ragged feet – holding up the edge of her dress, her left foot, her right foot, in grave pantomime. Thanking me, she gave me a jagged grin, then limped away.

I returned to Rome briefly. You were in your hill town studio and we didn't meet. I set forth for Venice. I had an American acquaintance there, Lee, a former actor who was trying now to become a writer. Lee had become close to Phil, another young American abroad, and I spent a lot of time with the two of them, at their invitation. From the intensity of their concentration upon one another, I guessed that they were lovers. And did they guess that I was 'queer', too, and was that why they spent the time with me that they did? I couldn't be sure. They were a vivid pair. Lee very slight of build, blond and with the kind of pale skin in which every vein shows. A nervous young man. Phil sturdily built and of ruddy complexion; but as nervous a soul as Lee. I had first mistaken him for a calm and centred man, taken a quick liking to him under this illusion. Hoped, for a very brief while, to find in him a kind of brother. As we first sat talking together, he seemed to me to be assuming that we had something to share.

Phil was a painter, a good one, but who sold very little, and he was anxiously engaged in trying to make his way into the social world of those who buy paintings. During the meals we three took together we would begin to talk about our work, or about Italy, or some subject of particular interest. But again and again this talk would be interrupted. So-and-so had called, one of them had to tell the other. Or he had run into Who's-its who had heard from Somebody-else that You-know-who was planning a party – to which an invitation might be had. And wherever we sat, inside or out, their eyes glanced round the restaurant or the piazza to see who might be seated nearby, or might be passing. I'd feel briefly visible to them, but then invisible; visible, but then quite invisible. *Sola*.

My second evening in Venice they had an invitation to dine with a rich American woman who was a patroness of the arts, and they asked permission to bring me with them. She lived in a beautiful palazzo. I felt a little dirty, for I'd been exploring the city most of the day – with three small Venetian children who had befriended me (Luigi, Paulo, Lulu) – exploring, first by foot and then by gondola, the beautiful watery city. So I asked for the bathroom as soon as I'd been introduced, planning to wash my face and hands. At the end of the dusty train ride the day before I'd taken only the basin bath available at my lodgings. The bathroom here was modern, and in its glaring light I discovered that I was dirtier than I had supposed. When I washed my hands a sharp dirt line was visible at my wrists; when I washed my face, a sharp dirt line was visible round my throat. So I kept dabbing a little further and a little further, to make myself presentable – and more and more time kept passing. 'Are you all right, dear?' my hostess asked, when I finally joined the others.

A well-known American actress, in her fifties now, was there that evening. And a Belgian film maker, say my notes. I have no memory of the film maker, but I remember the actress, for she was wonderfully sassy and self-assured and did most of the talking. She didn't pay much attention to my two friends – though, feeling very much on show, they tried to be as interesting as they could. She was more interested in what her hostess had to say. It was the two women who held the stage – laughing a great deal, in competition with each other, for each was very witty; and yet in league, too, I felt. Against a man's world that would like to get all that it could from each one of them. Each of them – refusing to be 'had' – seemed to delight in the other's sister toughness.

I spoke hardly a word, myself. I was dazed still from staring at Venice. Dazzled by its airy main piazza, where the pigeons that rose in curling-up waves of flight added still another intricacy to that wonderfully intricate wide space. Where stone was winged, too – creatures though of stone had flown atop columns and portals. Dazzled throughout the long afternoon roaming in a gondola with the children, under the various bridges, staring at the many-coloured buildings, their continual motion of arabesques. Staring at Venice, staring at the reflection of Venice in its waters. Its reflection in turn throwing back fluttering shadows. I sat now near as I could to a window in the large room, and water-shadows played upon the stones of the building across the way. And the sound of the water entered the room. With the dank slightly rank yet delicious smell of this city – city both delicate and indelicate. On show.

At the end of the evening we were asked to write in a guest book. Weary and self-conscious, I scrawled a misspelling of the Italian for 'thank you' – 'Gracie'. What I had done struck me after we'd left and again I thought of you, for I knew you would laugh – seemed, as I thought of you, to hear the hoot of your laughter. But Phil made a more serious blunder. In the palazzo's entrance there hung a large Calder mobile, and Phil, headed for the door, walked, debonair, straight through it – setting the dangling parts in violent motion. Our hostess ran to untangle the whirling pieces; she cried out, 'How dare you walk through my Calder?'

He flushed deeply; but protested, '*You* walk through it all the time!'

'I know *how* to walk through it!' she raged at him.

I saw the actress flash a look of surprise but delight at this assertion.

Lee, Phil and the actress walked me to the dock where I caught my ferry to the Giudecca and my lodgings – across the large canal. Saying goodnight to me, the actress touched me softly on the back of the neck and said I should come to see her. I was surprised by the gesture, for she'd seemed hardly to notice me throughout the evening. Was it an amorous touch? I wondered – and wonder still; or was it a touch given without any particular thought by a woman of the theatre? Perhaps she suddenly saw herself in me – about to ferry out into the dark.

The building on the Giudecca in which I'd taken a room was a large building, with a huge barnlike double door, and I'd been given a very large iron key with which to open it. But I couldn't make the key work. It would turn – this way and that – but not catch. I knocked – softly, for it was late. No answer. I tried the key again. And again. I knocked a little harder – but not very hard, for I didn't want to wake anybody. And I wasn't heard. So I kept on turning the key. I stood there, jiggling it one way and then another, and then another – beginning to feel very odd, beginning to doubt a little my reality. The key was so very real, so large. It must be I who failed quite to be and to be really turning the key.

Then suddenly it caught. The heavy door swung open for me, and I was inside in the dark. And I couldn't find the light. I felt along the wall to my left, and along the wall to my right. But there was no switch. I tried sliding my hand along a higher, then a lower portion of the wall. Tried grasping the air – for something hanging. Kept on reaching out in first one direction and then another. I really felt like nobody now.

Finally I decided to accept the dark and grope my way up the staircase. Luckily my room was the first room on the first floor. The stairs took various turnings, so I moved from step to step in slow motion, one hand on the railing, one out before me. And found my room at last – and a lamp. In the rosy light, stood for a few moments delighting in the sight of bed, of chair, of open suitcase, table, pitcher, wash-basin, and delighting in my own tangibility. Then clambered into bed.

I wrote next morning in my journal: 'If the land is dark – put out your hand before you and feel your way. If you cannot see to find your way, put out your hand before you and move like a thief toward where you would go.'

4

A friend from my college years was living in Paris and she'd written inviting me to drive with her to the Salzburg music festival. I travelled to Paris now to join her.

Flo was the daughter of an industrialist. What was it that he made? Something that she despised, I remember. But though she disliked her father and the way he lived, he had immense power still to hurt her feelings. She'd returned from one Spring vacation at college with the story of how he had asked her to join him and a friend of his for lunch, then when she appeared at his office in a shortsleeved dress, glanced at her arms and brusquely informed her that he wouldn't ask her to join them after all. 'There's too much hair on your arms', he told her. Her arms had on them a pleasant light fuzz. Flo was an extraordinary poet. I'd heard a friend complain, 'Her poems are cry after cry of pain.' For this was a time still when women were not supposed to cry out. But her cries seemed to me a very wonderful music. She had one book of them published. But nobody took any notice of it. So she stopped submitting her poems anywhere – stopped even showing them to friends, she let me know the evening I arrived and asked had she any I could see. Now she was studying ancient hieroglyphics; wrote articles about them that were published in learned magazines. (And contained, I mused, no traces of emotion that could disturb anybody.) She still did *write* poems, she admitted. But when I tried to say how much it mattered to me that she did, changed the subject quickly. To the subject of our trip.

We were to leave Paris for Salzburg the very next morning. It was a strange experience to enter and leave such a city so abruptly. Flo drove me on a short swift night tour – through the wide Place de la Concorde with its dazzle of lamps, through the Arc de Triomphe, back and forth across the Seine. I can remember still my bewilderment. Nothing was as I had expected it to be. (Nothing in my travelling ever was.) I had dreamed the narrow cobblestoned side streets, but not the wide straight avenues, the formal vistas. (Ordered by Napoleon, said Flo. For military reasons.) And in the morning I would realize that I had dreamed the city in the wrong colours; in reds pink yellows purples, the 'gay Paree' of song – not these muted greys and blues. It was a much more sober city than I had imagined. In the morning I had longer to look at it than we had planned. Before we even left the block on which Flo lived, her car broke down. While Flo went to fetch a mechanic, I stared at the passers-by. How marvellously proper everybody was. Tiny children wore gloves! Even dogs had the proper outfits. The skies promised rain, and there trotted a dog dressed in a light blue raincoat with red piping. Decorum was observed by all, by rich and by poor. For each differing trade and occupation had its distinctive smock, apron, uniform. Even one grizzle-haired old bum who stalked past, a long staff in his hand, a bottle peeping from his ragged side pocket, seemed to assert: 'I look as I should; this is *my* correct costume.' I was always to feel in this city out of step, out of mode, myself – something of a barbarian.

It was a while before Flo returned. I watched the morning light flicker across the sober facades of the houses across the way; and was grateful for this delay. My eyes could now slowly adjust themselves to the city's beauty, so different from the beauty of an Italian city. I remembered, as I gazed, walking in the winter woods around my parents' country house in New York state, after returning from a trip to Florida. The northern countryside had seemed at first grey and dull, after the landscape of the south which was all awash in colour. But as I peered about me, I had begun to see again and to take delight in all the colour that really lived in that seeming grey – in winter buds and twigs and bark; colour that slept or awakened according to the changing light. In a like way this northern city street slowly began to appear to me beautiful.

Flo turned up with a mechanic. He tinkered a bit, declared that all was well with us, and off we set. Before we reached the outskirts of the city, the car broke down again. We had our picnic lunch not out in the countryside but on a bench in the Bois – where I sat marvelling again at the decorum of the passers-by. Many, here in the park, were on bicycles, and often on bicycles made for pedalling tandem – a woman behind a man it almost always was, of course; and almost always the two wore carefully matched sports outfits – the colour, the trim, the same. It was a holiday of some sort, a *jour de fête*, it seemed; which is why there were so many neatly-matched couples out together at midday; and why, too, each time we broke down that day it took so long to find someone willing to work on the car. We broke down for a third time in a small town only a few miles from Paris, and help was so hard to find there that we ended by staying the night – in an inn which had very noisy plumbing. I remember that I washed my hair, and the water pipes were so noisy that the people in the next room began banging on the wall. 'What shall I do?' I asked Flo. 'Bang back in a friendly way', she suggested. This town, too, surprised me – seemed, after the glowing towns of Italy, very stark. The next day we passed through town after town as grey. But again I began to find them hauntingly beautiful.

The car made some odd noises that next day, but kept going. We were able to reach Strasburg before five and by rushing about just manage to get our papers for Germany OK'd before offices closed. We were anxious to push on, because the festival was to start the day after the next, and we were running late. I remember well our crossing into Germany. Not that I recall any exact details of landscape. 'Small farm villages in the darkish', my journal reads. But I remember well the sense of rushing unprepared into unknown, into confusing territory. We were not even prepared in ordinary ways. We'd not had time to change money. And when we decided to rehearse a few key German words and phrases, Flo discovered that she had forgotten the dictionary she thought she'd brought along. We began to sing aloud to one another all the German songs we had ever learned, or half-learned, in school – 'O tannenbaun O tannenbaum!' – trying to find a few useful words to pluck from them; finding very few. 'Hmm hmm hmm nacht, heilige nacht' – 'nacht' would get us a place to sleep perhaps, if we used sign language as well: two hands forming a pillow, cheek laid against them. 'Lerne essen ohne zu klagen', 'Learn to eat without complaining' – my mother had once playfully bought a plate with that scolding saying on it. 'Essen' (question mark) could get us a meal perhaps. 'Gut!' We kept repeating that word, I remember, for reassurance – saying it loudly to one another.

It was more than money and the language that we lacked as we rushed through this night. It was a sense of moral bearings. This was 1950 and the abominations the Nazis had committed were recent past – acts the German people had allowed, claiming now that they had not even been aware of what was happening. This seemed to me a grotesque claim. The United States had not yet waged its abominable war against the people of Indochina – more of us protesting than Germans had, yet even among those who protested most of us allowing ourselves to remain unaware of the full measure of evil that was being acted out. I had still the queer feeling about Germans that they were unlike all other peoples – obtuse of spirit in a way impossible to explain, peculiar to them. I can remember my first sight of one – a stocky blond young man in work clothes walking quietly along in the dusk. There is one of them, I thought – there is a person I can never understand. And this thought made me feel seasick.

We stopped finally at a small village inn and spoke our word: 'Essen?' As though reading in our eyes how separate we felt (and very likely feeling toward us his own antipathy) the innkeeper led us through the room in which others were eating into a room behind it where we sat at table quite alone. After dinner, and a clumsy dialogue in sign language – about our need to sleep and our inability to pay for anything until we could change our money (waving it) into German coin ('morgen?') – we were led down the road to a nearby house. The scrubbed, very courteous but far from friendly woman whose house it was had a spare room for us. On the walls of that room: a pen and ink drawing of a handsome young man in S.S. uniform, and a chromo of Jesus. Flo and I stared at the two pictures – the only ones on the wall. And after the woman had left, we pointed at them, staring at one another. We couldn't find any words in our own language by now. We climbed into our beds, exhausted.

In the morning we found a bank, and we found a store that had a dictionary and a phrase book. We found our way to the big westbound highway, the autobahn, which the Nazis had built – for there wasn't time to take the smaller roads; this was the day on which the festival in Salzburg began. We hurried along the autobahn, past the tidy villages, which had bright flower pots on every window-sill, past the fertile fields. Each field confronted us with the one image: an entire family out working in it, doggedly; or tramping to or from it, hoes, spades over shoulders, a family frieze. 'Field after field the image repeated', my journal notes – 'Industry!'

It reads, 'And the strain in the faces' of these people. But we began to encounter along the road some lordly ones, too: young men astride motorcycles; dressed in greasy lederhosen – the greasier the leather, the more proudly they seemed to wear it. Young men sitting on their noisy mounts as though they could straddle whatever they chose to straddle. I wrote that evening, 'Suddenly there shapes itself the image of war.'

We began to see roadsigns announcing: Dachau. Studying the map before we started out, I had said to Flo that I thought we should stop there, and she had nodded. Then trouble with the car had put us far behind in our schedule. 'Dachau's not far now', I said. She murmured, 'If the car hadn't broken down – '. I didn't feel that I could urge her to stop. For this was her trip, which I had simply been invited to join. But I experienced again – more acutely now – a sense of travelling in confusion, seasick – as we hurried past that obscene place. Just a roadsign: Dachau. Hurried past.

We arrived in Salzburg that evening – though too late, in spite of our hurrying, to hear *Fidelio*. Hunting among the small crowds in the streets, we found some of Flo's friends, and found, with their help, a room in an inn – a room with extra beds in it that one of her friends was willing to share. The next few days we stuffed our ears with rich music; and stuffed our stomachs with rich food. The meals here took almost as long as the operas. This was in part because the waiters were always assuring us 'Ein momente!', then vanishing. To spite us? I was never sure. The food served us was too rich. I remember especially one dessert on the menu: *Kaltkrem mit schlag* – which I still translate as: cream with cream on it. The operas were a true feast. Many of them were Mozart's – true riches. But even the marvellous equilibrium of this music did not restore to me, during these days, a sense of my own equilibrium.

Flo, too, was uneasy. Flo was a person of drastically alternating moods – great quiets sometimes, out of which she would emerge all at once, smiling, talkative, and with gifts to offer. When I had known her at college, days could pass during which she'd keep to herself and not communicate at all; then – she would be at my door, holding out a pot of flowers, or a book she'd like to give me; stepping forward to offer it, with a bouncing step. She had a way of moving that was like a quick pony – a small, plump but delicately-boned woman. Perhaps she made me think of a pony, too, because of the way she cut her hair in long floppy bangs, which she let slide quite over her eyes when she wanted privacy. Flo began now to grow quiet, to grow private, almost at once. Music was very necessary to her. She knew a lot about it, too. And here was a luxury of music. But – there broke in upon the notes of Mozart and Strauss and Handel too many other notes. A man at a nearby table in a restaurant one day was suddenly yelling at a waiter: 'Bastard! Jew!' All the people in the restaurant stared at one another rather as though a marvellous drama that we were attending had been rudely interrupted. Yes, everybody we met was trying hard to pretend that the music of the festival was all the sound that was in the air here. But it wasn't so.

One of Flo's friends – a young singer, the woman whose room we shared – knew some of the USO hostesses who had been stationed here for a long time. We all had drinks together on a couple of occasions. I felt especially depressed, I remember, in the company of these young women – though they were friendly; seemed in fact almost starved for friendship. I wondered in my journal at their 'miserably scarred faces – scars of no disease'. The scars, I imagine, of trying for day after day – as we were now trying – to pretend to themselves that they were not seeing the kinds of things they *were* seeing; hearing the kinds of things they were hearing. All of us kept turning to one another with strained smiles, with friendliness that was forced – seeking to find in one another's company what we were not going to find that easily: a world that gave the lie to Tyranny, a world in which none of *us* could ever count others for naught.

One afternoon we looked up a young friend of mine I'd heard was living nearby. You know her – Lila G. You and I had sometimes wondered together what she would decide to do with her life. Her mother was an artist, a very good weaver, who had managed, stubbornly, surely, to make her own way – divorcing her husband early, bringing up Lila by herself. Lila was clearly going to choose one of the arts, it seemed; but which? She'd wonder aloud about it herself. Would she become a painter or would she become a writer? Probably both – for she had so much to say that one medium couldn't give her room to say it. She was wonderfully sassy about her talents. I'd spent an evening with her in New York City about a year before and marvelled at the frank delight she took in herself. It made her a little drunken. She couldn't walk down the street; she had to dance down it. She couldn't just talk to me; at the little restaurant where we ate, she clearly felt that people at neighbouring tables, too, would want to know what she was thinking. She'd keep glancing round at them. She wanted to share her self. Oh look, oh look at me. How I brim over! It made her burst into laughter sometimes. Here was more life than she knew what to do with.

Lila had married, I'd heard; and I'd heard that she and her husband, who was a mathematician, were living for the summer in a pension a few miles outside of town. So we traced them there. Lila gave us tea, while her husband, Geoff, explained to us – I can't remember what he explained to us, but I remember that he knew that he knew what he was talking about, whatever it was. While he talked – quietly, charmingly – I kept turning to stare at Lila, for her face seemed not the face that I had last seen. I would have said that she'd been ill – if she were not so clearly in good health. Or I would have said that someone had recently slapped her in the face – if she and Geoff were not so clearly on affectionate good terms. 'She is strangely subdued', I wrote in my journal. Yes, all her sassiness had quite evaporated. 'Are you writing or painting?' I asked her when we were alone for a moment. 'I don't do that any more', she said curtly. She spoke as though I had referred – tactlessly – to a former lover. Which I had of course; for once she had loved herself.

'What do you think of marriage?' I asked Flo on the way back to town.

'People do marry', she said. She said no more than that, and I couldn't think of what to say next, myself.

The opera that evening, the last in the festival, was *The Magic Flute*, performed in an outdoor theatre. Tickets had been sold out before Flo had written to ask for ours. We climbed the hill behind the theatre, hoping to hear at least faint strains of Mozart, but policemen had been stationed along every footpath, to make sure that none of us could take this freedom. They waved us sternly back – hands in immaculate white gloves, their gestures of admonition absurdly visible in the dusk. We tried – with the help of our pocket dictionary, and with gestures, with comic grimaces – to tease one of the policemen into relenting. He could only reply that his chief (he found us the word in the dictionary – his 'schiff') was the one to be blamed. We should not blame *him*. We couldn't even make him agree that the orders were 'grausam' (mean). We couldn't even make him smile. We walked off, discouraged, and sat down on a rock just to take the evening air. We heard at last the faraway muffled sound of prolonged clapping. The performance was over. It occurred to us that perhaps we'd be allowed now to catch just a glimpse of what the opera had looked like. So we hurried back up the path upon which we'd been stopped. But when the man heard us coming, he turned in alarm. He jumped quickly astride the path, spread his stiff arms wide.

'The oppressor as ridiculous,' muttered Flo.

The next day we left the town. Flo wanted to return home by way of Italy. We'd head for Venice, we agreed. Estimating the distance between Salzburg and Venice on the map, we figured we'd be there by evening on the day we set forth. We made one slight miscalculation – forgot that the Alps stuck up between. Crossing them required of us a little more time. The car began now to falter again and to steam. After each crawling ascent of still another peak, we'd glance at one another, breathe deeply of the mountain air, and let out our breath again in sighs of laughter. One ascent we almost failed to complete. I wanted to see edelweiss. Was that it? Or was that it? I kept peering out at the slopes to try to know. As the car laboured to the near top of one mountain, we saw a man dressed in leather breeches and with pack and staff, standing by the side of the road. He'd know! I cried – with such imperative eagerness that Flo stopped – and stalled – the car, even as she objected angrily, 'We can't stop here!' The man just happened to have in his hatband a sprig of the very flower I sought. And he'd be happy to sell it, he said – grinning at us, amused, contemptuous. The sprig almost cost us the top of the hill. The car didn't want to start. 'Edelweiss!' The word became that day Flo's private curse word.

We reached by nightfall a town called Heiligenblut, perched on the brink of a final mountain. And should have stopped. But we wanted to leave behind us the great peaks we had been foolish enough to forget about. We hurried on – into the valley and into the dark. And not long after, on road that was level at last, the car spluttered to a full stop, and this time wouldn't start up again. I volunteered to walk back to a farmhouse we had passed; and there found a tired woman with many children who waited patiently for me to find the words in German that I needed, told me that there was a garage not far ahead – and came out to the road with me and helped me thumb a ride from a passing neighbour. I shouted out the window at Flo as we passed her, sitting lonely in the stalled car, and she looked up, startled. The man didn't stop at the garage. He gestured in a lordly way, to quiet me, when I cried out; and half a mile later drew in at a cluster of barnlike buildings, where trucks were parked in the yard, and small groups of men lounged about, joking with one another. He passed from group to group, greeting the others – in words which I could never manage to understand. No one more than glanced at me. I began to wonder whether he had forgotten that I was there with him. But suddenly four of the men turned, nodded at me to follow, and started clambering into one of the huge trucks. One helped me up into the cab, two of them piled into the back, and we roared off. Into the darkness. Fast. The men laughing and shouting. And again ignoring me. I can remember still the feeling of being nobody, a nobody rushed captive through the moonless dark. I can remember pretending to myself that I felt no alarm. At last they pulled up at the stalled car. They leapt out. They yanked up the hood of the car. They all peered in – one of them aiming a little flashlight. For all I knew they would now laughingly disassemble everything. But after a few moments one of them commanded Flo to step on the starter. She stepped on it – and the motor started. 'Austrian mechanics!' the driver shouted – and stared me for the first time in the eye. And then they jumped back into their huge truck and thundered off.

Flo and I sat for a little while, listening to the hum of our car.

'We're damn fools', said Flo.

I agreed. 'Yes.'

The inn we found now had no room for us, but a little boy was sent to lead us through the dark to a nearby house, where an old woman rented us her attic room. The room had a tiny balcony from which we looked up briefly at the stars. Our mattresses were filled with corn stalks, and rustled softly as we turned in bed.

'Listen!' we whispered.

Now I tried to describe to Flo how it had felt to be rushed through the dark in that huge truckful of men.

She muttered, half asleep: 'Yes. A woman. Doesn't exist.'

'We do, though, don't we?' I felt I had to say.

'Oh, we do', she agreed – waking slightly, and shifting her plump body on the cornstalk mattress; 'Listen to the lovely rustling sounds we make.'

5

We reached Venice by sundown the next day; settled in at my old hotel on the Giudecca – and soon decided to stay for at least a week. Flo wanted a long look at that city, and I was beginning to have the feeling of being a little ill that I always suffer from when I haven't been writing for a while. So each morning I stayed in my room, scribbling; and I'd meet Flo over on the mainland later in the day.

We looked up Lee and Phil – and found them in a sulky mood. Phil had just learned that he had *not* sold a large painting he had been expecting to sell. He had wasted a lot of time partying with a rich traveller who'd led him to think that he wanted to add the painting to his collection. The man had just left without buying it. 'A flirt', said Flo. Phil flushed. Lee took us almost at once to see his mother, who had moved to Venice since my last visit. Introduced us – and then vanished, with a quick crooked smile, a wave. His mother was a painter, too. Lee had never mentioned that. She had a studio now in Giudecca, not far from where we stayed. She'd been divorced for some years, was on her own. Alma. A small woman with a face like a worn Botticelli – but unconscious of her beauty, I think. Grey eyes. Hair the colour of honey – pulled back tightly from her face. A sweet smile that contained always the shadow of a frown – frown of anxiety. She was turning out a great deal of work. She let us see it on the second day. Scene after scene of the watery city. Scenes, too, of Capri, where she had lived for a while. Painted with great skill and patience. And strangely mournful. It was as though she saw everything as mouldering – as subtly damaged by the waters that lapped them. I was a little shocked by her vision. And I remember asking myself: are women artists doomed perhaps to express visions of the world that are disturbed? But then I recalled the drawings you had brought back from Greece, and recovered from that thought.

We spent more time with Alma than with her son. She knew a great deal about the city and volunteered to guide us in our wanderings a few times – looking at everything very hard, almost fiercely, herself, as though sketching scenes in air. Lee and sometimes Phil turned up at odd moments – spotting us at an open-air café and sitting down with us, or appearing suddenly at Alma's; but they never stayed long, had always appointments to keep. One of these times Lee left with Flo and me a one-act play he had just finished. It wasn't very good, and when we offered some tentative criticism the next time we saw him, he listened mutely, then stayed away completely for a few days. When he turned up next, at his mother's, he was hunting frantically for Phil – face flushed, clothes all rumpled as though he had slept in them. He'd lost the key to the place they shared and needed to change before attending a dinner that was 'important'. Alma offered to run an iron over the clothes he was wearing, but he said no, he'd better try to find Phil, and darted off again – his mother standing at her door, looking after him intently, smiling and frowning at the same time.

When Lee appeared, Alma always changed. Her son alone had her attention, in spite of herself. An attention that was a queer mix of contradictory feeling – disappointment, I did think I could read, yet at the same time helpless admiration. Though her own talents were clearly very much greater than his, and her own sense of discipline much greater, it was clear, too, that she continued to hope for more from him than from herself; her eyes kept turning to him – shining – as to an unfinished canvas she counted as her only really worthy work.

One afternoon the three of us took a gondola, and she guided us along the city's edges, out past the madhouse built for priests – where a white array of sheets hung on a line in the walled garden, and at an open window one thin inmate stood chanting, chanting as though in an ecstasy. She brought us to visit an elaborate small church nearby, baroque figures atop it, which seemed to lean toward us, gesturing, at our approach. When we left the boat, to see the interior of the church, we had to climb stone steps to the quay, and the steps were slimy from the canal waters. Alma slipped and fell to her hands and knees. I remember still the look on her face as she knelt there for a moment, before getting to her feet again with Flo's help. It was a look suddenly of bitter anger – a look that seemed to complain that everything in the universe conspired against her, ready to bring her down. Her artist self. Her woman self. I kept seeing that look all the rest of the day, and wanting to cry. (For her self. For my self.) Though for the rest of the day Alma faced us again with a gentle smile – marked by just a shadow of a frown.

We headed back for Paris now, at a leisurely pace. Two memories haunted me as we drove: Alma's contorted face; the figure of the Austrian guard astride the path we wanted to take, arms flung out wide. I couldn't throw off the shadows these two memories cast. Flo seemed depressed, too.

We stopped on the second day at Verona's market place, the Piazza delle Erbe – and began to smile at one another again. Under the great array of umbrellas here, you could find – 'Everything, everything!' Flo was murmuring. Here were toys, pets, household objects, clothes or yard goods, food that was ready to cook or – still in fur and feathers. ('Don't think about that', said Flo.) You could buy a pigeon to cook, and the seller would quickly pluck it for you; or you could buy a pigeon in a cage, to coo at you. Mythical, it seemed to us. Each stout umbrella was an upturned horn of plenty, the air seeming to whisper: 'What do you need for your journey? You'll find it here.' Flo and I decided suddenly that what we needed for our journey was the small owl who sat hunched in her cage next to a cage full of rabbits and a cage that held a large stony-grey falcon. 'She keeps following us with her eyes', Flo nodded.

The man with the face of a friendly pirate who sold her to us made us a long leather thong and an anklet – so that we could fly her on a tether. While he was working on the thong he put his pet parakeet into my hand. The little green bird kept escaping from me and running along the ground among the other cages, the men laughing at it. The hawk, behind its bars, watched, not a feather moving. Until the parakeet stepped just precisely close enough. Then it thrust a leg through the bars in one economical lightning-quick move; and its claw grasped the green morsel, which squeaked in terror. The man dropped to his knees, very slowly disengaged his pet from the fierce talons, talking to it all the while as to a foolish child; dunked it into a pail of water that stood there and put it back into its own cage – where it staggered about for a few moments, then seemed to recover itself. I was stammering apologies, for he had put it into my hands. But he shrugged. That was a bird's life. 'And you're a fool', he told the little bird – 'Nara'. The bird blinked at him, nodding.

The owl in her cage rode between us now in the car. At night we set her free in our hotel room, to fly about a bit – watching for droppings, and mopping them up; catching her to return her to her cage only when we turned out the lights. Lunch we took as a picnic always in some field along the way, and there we let her fly as best she could on her tether. We both began to wonder aloud whether we shouldn't simply allow her to fly away, into the countryside. She hadn't been a captive for long, the man had said. But neither of us could bear quite yet to part with her.

Why were we so intrigued by her? She did stare into our eyes – sometimes settled down among her feathers, all puffed out, her gaze steady; sometimes straightened up, a different shape of bird altogether, quite skinny, her head stuck up high upon her neck, her glance in motion and electric. Did we feel that we communed, through her, with some wild, some forbidden part of ourselves that we couldn't reach on our own? And did our recent experience in Austria of the blighting spirit of repression make us especially eager for such communion?

The first night that we had her with us she began to batter about in the cage soon after we'd gone to our beds, and we both got up to see what was the matter. The leather anklet had been drawn too tightly and was chafing her small ankle. I held her so that Flo, more nimble-fingered, could work to loosen it. For a while I couldn't hold her still enough. But then it occurred to me to stroke her eyelids and feathery lashes – gently – and little by little she grew calm and at last lay in my hands as though hypnotised.

'You've hypnotised yourself, too', Flo told me – for I sat there holding her still, though Flo had adjusted the thong. Yes, we did both want something from her.

We spent a night in Milan and a night in Turin. Both cities seemed to me ugly after the cities to the south of them. There were lots of expensive shops. Many of the buildings were new ones, sleek and luxurious but graceless – a different spirit the building spirit here. In the square of the Duomo in Milan a huge electric billboard advertising talcum powder faced the old cathedral, with its carved figures, great brass doors – the ad blinking across at it in neon. 'The cathedral's match, in other terms', I jotted in my notebook. The two masters – Mammon and God the Father – claiming the one space here. On the church door were sculpted the Virgin and Child – the brass in which the Son was figured rubbed smooth and shiny by the worshipping touch of many hands. ('Depressing', Flo muttered.) On the billboard, a contemporary 'mild virgin' smiled a fixed smile.

It was in Turin I decided that before leaving Italy I should buy a motor scooter – the smaller, light kind, a Lambretta. For I wouldn't be travelling with Flo much longer. With a Lambretta, I thought, I'd be free to head in any direction I wanted, and at my own pace – able to see much more than if restricted to trains and buses. In time I would recognize that it was just by travelling in the crowded trains and buses that I saw the most – packed in with other travellers who were after all the people of the country I wanted to learn something about. But at this point it still seemed to me what I most required was the freedom of movement the motor scooter would allow me. I became even a little intoxicated by the thought of this new freedom. It seemed to promise a new measure of control over life itself.

Flo agreed that we could take the time needed for me to make my purchase. The time needed, as it turned out, was more than a little. After some hunting, I found a scooter light enough for me to handle. The padrone at our hotel had warned that because I was an American whoever sold me the scooter would try to cheat me; so a good deal of time was spent discussing the price. A price that seemed fair was at last agreed upon. (The padrone had jotted down some figures for me.) The shop owner then began casually to remove from the Lambretta the lock, the horn – various necessities. Not covered by the price. Extra, if I wanted them. And our haggling began all over again. I ended by putting down the money he asked. Time was in his favour. He knew that we were passing through and wanted to be on our way. And it didn't help me that as I argued I knew I was misusing the Italian language, and felt a little guilty toward him because of this.

We weren't to be on our way yet, however. I had to buy insurance, he pointed out. And before he could give me the machine, I had to take out operator's papers. He told us where to go to get the documents I needed. Both offices he sent us to were closing down – 'siesta time!' – just as we arrived. And when they reopened, we were informed that it was to quite other offices we should really go. Each official I was able at last to apply to had different instructions about just what documents I did need. And so to complete the paperwork, we had finally to stay over until the next morning.

Then the shop owner gave me a quick driving lesson on a side street – offering this himself, very amiable now. 'I'm not going to watch,' Flo said; 'I'll go buy a bottle of wine.' He helped us tie the machine on to the roof of the car. And we set forth. Only to learn after travelling many miles to the French border that I hadn't acquired the correct papers after all, and Customs wouldn't let us pass. And back we turned – driving again through the stony mountain towns near the border (I remember still the lonely stolid figures of women sitting out on tree stumps, each woman watching a few grazing farm animals, and silently knitting knitting as she kept this watch). Back to Turin just too late in the day to do anything more until still another morning.

On this third morning, the same man who had cheerfully cheated me in the sale, as cheerfully left his shop in the care of an assistant, returned with me to the various offices and – patiently interpreting for me now – helped me to replace the wrong papers with the right ones. When I tried to pay him something for all his trouble, he refused with an emphatic gesture. And when I tried to insist, he turned and ran from me down the street. The day before I had been a customer, fair game. But this day I had been a stranger in trouble – to be treated with due hospitality.

And back again we drove. A fine drizzle was falling on the border towns, but the women were sitting out still at their watch, knitting knitting.

6

'Paree, Paree!' As the train which had brought me for the first time to Paris hurried through the city's outskirts, a woman next to me – a Frenchwoman, middle-aged – had risen from her seat to draw on her coat, and she had sung very softly very quickly to herself the city's name. I can still hear the little tune, hear the name sung as a promise. Here – she seemed to hum – I shall be who I am. Who will that be? Here, on the beautiful stage which is this city, my life can become a play that is worth acting.

The tune was repeating itself in my head as we re-entered Paris. City of life, city of life. This time I would stay for a while.

We threw a coat over the owl's cage, so that Flo's concierge wouldn't see her and perhaps object to having her in the house. The owl and I moved in with Flo. Flo's apartment was old-fashioned, with chandeliers and ornate curtain poles, and the bird looked almost at home here – perched on one of these stout branches or another. A woman who was friendly with the concierge came in sometimes to clean. Before her arrival we'd put the stowaway into her cage, and the cage, with a cloth over it, on top of a high armoire. She never uttered a sound, and the woman never cleaned thoroughly enough to discover her – dreaming as she worked of the end of that work. She'd look at me sidewise and chant: 'Boire un petit coup, c'est agréable; boire un petit coup, c'est doux' – to have a little drink, that would be nice. Yes. Her look also seemed to me to ask: 'And who are *you*?' A good question. I had better try to find out.

I wasn't at first going to stay at Flo's for more than a few days. I was going to take a small room somewhere on my own. I did some hunting. But rooms were expensive – or very dreary. Flo had space for me, she was hospitable, and I kept staying. It must have been hard on her to have her privacy taken for what turned out to be almost two months, but she didn't let on. She went out a lot, because of her studies – spending long hours in museums and libraries. She went out, too, with other friends. 'We'll go our own ways', we agreed. I was nevertheless very much in her life for that long time – and all too visibly not finding my separate way very well. It was a more pleasant time for me than it would have been if I'd taken my own place. But it was also easier to move through the days without finding out anything very new about myself. Flo's busy life – though it puzzled me – kept seeming more real to me than my own.

And other lives kept seeming more real. While we'd been on the road we'd received no mail. Back at Flo's a small stack of letters waited for me. Letters from my mother, with family news – one piece of news alarming: my youngest brother, Ned, who had joined the Marine reserves some time back, sooner or later now would be sent off to war in Korea. That war had begun a few days after I'd taken ship for Europe. You and I had some argument about it in Rome. I'd persuaded myself that it must be a necessary war, if the United Nations had decided so. You'd had the wit to be cynical: What did it mean that the UN had decided? Meant that the US had decided. I put up an argument, but really knew that none of it made any sense to me. Whether or not I could understand it, though, the war loomed now as that-which-is-Real. And Ned was about to have to enter that Reality. Had I any right to be travelling about, seeking the shadow which was my own life? I wrote and asked my parents whether I shouldn't perhaps return home. They wrote back promptly: Stay. Ned would only be upset if I cut my trip short.

There was a letter waiting for me from Nell. I had wanted to open this first, but made myself wait and open it last.

Nell wrote that she was with child. Nell wrote that she was with child. (I kept rereading her words.) 'It is a secret', she said. I was the only one, beside Ben, whom she had told. Because she couldn't quite believe it yet – had still to tell *herself* that it was really so. But the baby was due by Christmas. She was beginning to change shape.

I read all my letters the night we got back. The next day I walked out into the city and in the first park I found sat on a bench to read some of them again. The letter from Nell I read again last – in the strange brightly sunlit park; walked on, found another bench, and sat on and on, still receiving this news. It seemed to me that I could feel her child stir within my own body. I also wished that I could be that child and be born to her. She wrote that when she thought of it as a girl, she imagined it to be like me. Reading these words, my heart beat quickly and I imagined myself in her arms again, a tiny girl. That imagining flickered and went out. It was not with my life that she was pregnant. She wrote that her shape was changing. Yes, the child was changing her. And once born, it would change her even more. I sat on, letting this knowledge touch me. Though she had married, I believed she loved me still. Of course I knew that she also loved Ben; but I had clung until now to the dream that our lives could be joined somehow still, I didn't know quite how. Until this letter, her marriage had not been more real to me than the love between us I knew to be still alive. But the child she expected – the child was changing her, and the child would also change the marriage. I sat there, the letter in my hand – in the flower-bright park. Sat waiting for this birth. Not able not to love the child, and not able not to dread it. Sat wishing that I were the awaited new life.

Yes, Ned was real to me, as he prepared himself to encounter the horrid reality of war. And Nell was real to me, as she waited the reality of giving birth. But could *I* presume to be real? I prepared myself neither to make war nor to give birth.

So, for these days, I wandered through the city (on foot or, very gingerly, on my Lambretta) thinking, as I passed along the quays or through the 'places': what a wonderful city this would be to be alive in; moving through it like an actor who looks with approval at the set but – lacks a script.

There were a few lines that Ned had asked me to speak – for him. He had managed to spend a summer in Europe the year before, and on the ship back had met a young Frenchwoman, Diane, on her way to the States to attend one term of a midwestern college. He'd seen her again – and again – when she came east in the late spring, before sailing for home. And found her departure painful. And called her by transatlantic telephone and asked her to marry him. She'd said no. He told me with a grimacing smile: 'A minute after she hung up, the phone rang again, and I thought: Oh! Oh! She's calling back! She's changed her mind! It was the operator, of course.' He imitated the operator's plaintive voice: ' "The charges on your call will be . . ." ' whatever the large sum was. So he had

53

asked me to be his ambassador when I reached Paris, to go to see her and make clear to her that he was serious. Perhaps she couldn't quite believe that. He did think she cared for him. I told him that he'd better simply keep writing to her, but that I would happily go to see her. I'd met her, briefly, in New York and liked her at once.

I called the number he'd given me. Diane's mother answered. (Diane was at work.) Her mother knew no English, and listened with a gentle patience as I struggled with the French language, attempting to leave a message that was intelligible. I'd become just a little bit at ease over the past weeks with simple Italian, and heard myself talking French now as though it *were* Italian. In French, of course, one asks not 'Is Diane there?' but 'Is it that Diane is there?' and so on – adding these little grace notes everywhere along the way. I couldn't seem to add them. 'What's the *matter*?' Flo asked, when I came back from the phone.

Diane returned the call, however. She laughed – 'Ha!' – when I told her I was afraid I might have frightened her mother with my coarse speech; and she suggested that we meet the next day after work hours at the Arc de Triomphe, then find a nearby café.

I hadn't yet dared the traffic circle at the Arc on my Lambretta; I walked to meet her. We both recognized each other quickly. You know Diane of course. How could I not recognize her? Dressed as always very plainly, yet looking not at all plain. Gypsy-beautiful. Her delicately frizzy hair alive about her shoulders. Her dark eyes taking one in – the whites very shining. Brows, boldly marked, arched often, as if to put questions. Her long and very finely modelled nose seeming to take one's scent. She is shy at the same time, scanning one as it were from cover. Just as, walking to meet me now in a strong long lope, she seemed at the same time to hesitate, the stride perceptibly lagging – something in her in contradiction. I think we said nothing at all as we met – just looked at one another, nodded, smiling; and I followed her to the café she had in mind.

We shared a pot of tea at her suggestion. She poured it – her long capable hands making of the simple motions a pleasant grave ceremony. I gave my little speech. My brother, I told her, had asked me to be a kind of ambassador on his behalf. I didn't really know how ambassadors were supposed to behave; and I wasn't sure that I believed in ambassadors. But – here I was. Just to let her know that he had asked me please to be one. She sat very still as I spoke. The moment I stopped, she plucked an oblong of sugar from the bowl. And asked: 'Have you ever tried drinking your tea through a lump of sugar? Like this –.' She placed the sugar in her mouth and sipped some tea through it. 'Try it.' I tried it. The tea was very hot, and I had to sip quite slowly.

That stopped my words of course for a while. And then she questioned me about my trip – offered her help if I should need it in finding anything in the city. But we said little more that day. We sat glancing at each other as we drank out tea, or glancing round the café. Just trying out, I suppose now, how it would feel to be sisters. For some reason – out of reach of words – it felt very natural.

So Diane was real to me. And the life questions she'd have to answer now were real. As I watched her walk off into the city – hurrying to be back in time for dinner with her parents – Paris was real to me as the place which was presently her home. But Paris as a city in which I walked off in my own direction – was not quite real.

I remember that I visited the Eiffel Tower soon after this. My notes speak of 'the wonderful crazy erector set view from below. Gay ascenders. The silly tooting of a whistle. We go up to that little sound.' And then below – was the beautiful sober wide perspective of roofs, 'places', monuments, parks, the meandering Seine. And I remember thinking: Yes, here is a city where I should be able to shake myself out of my stupor. It seemed – in its northern sobriety? – more a world which I could truly enter than the world of Italy. And yet it kept remaining for me a world seen from apart. Yes, as from a tower. In which I was locked.

I told myself that I could perhaps escape from this locked state if I would learn to get about on my Lambretta. So I set about to master its ways. I practised first in the courtyard of Flo's apartment building, then in the sidestreets of that neigbourhood – keeping the scooter at first in low gear; and ventured gradually forth into the mainstreams of traffic. The machine stalled easily. As you know, to start it, one jumps vigorously on a little pedal. I was wearing flat oxfords that were actually men's shoes – the only comfortable shoes I had been able to find when preparing for this trip; and because they were made for men they were a little loose about the heel for me. When I'd jump on the starter, a shoe would sometimes fly off – into the thick of traffic. So I had to learn, too, the technique of recovering this flying object, without being run over, or letting the scooter fall – as I held to a handlebar with one hand, reached out, out, with another hand, or a foot. I did become at last adept at this, and at ease in the scooter's saddle. The day came when I dared to enter even the traffic swirl at the Place de la Concorde – and to ride on and enter the agitated circle at the Arc de Triomphe, into which the vehicles of one avenue after another charge. Flo volunteered bravely to accompany me on this ride – which was my initiation. I was grateful for this. Her trusting presence gave me the added courage that I needed. 'Hurrah!' she cried from behind me as we entered the thickest of it. 'Hurrah! You've done it! Keep going! Hurrah!'

Now I could take Flo on here-and-there trips around the city. A young man who kept dropping in and sitting moodily to stare at her – a fellow Egyptologist – I took soon all the way to Versailles at her suggestion. I can find in my notes about Versailles only that the young scholar lingered in the Hall of Mirrors (for he was a handsome fellow – had blue blue eyes, and a neat little scholar's goatee he liked to keep touching). I note in more detail that on the way home, traffic was stalled for a long time, but we rode blithely along the green at the side of the road, undelayed. At such times now, astride my Lambretta, I could experience a strong emotion of relief. I seemed to be tasting independence. Here I was – wasn't I? – getting about sassily on my own. But this mood was always short-lived. Once I had dismounted from my at-last-obedient steed and simply walked about as my single self – who did I think I was? And what did I think I was doing here?

There was a small church cemetery on a corner near Flo's apartment. On one of the tombstones stood a delicate stone angel. I can remember turning my eyes to that angel as I'd pass, seeking her stone wide-open eyes. What am I doing here, Angel?

I wrote in my notebook (trying to write about myself as though I were somebody else): 'She had the feeling that anything might trap her; at any moment she might say it, might spill it – might give the one thread. As though she were a person caught in a great lie, and she might by the slightest motion, unconsidered word, uncover it all – start all unravelling. The lie? That she was a person, an integer, someone with work to do, which she knew how to do – a worthy.'

Actually, I soon had a real enough task to perform. Another letter came from my agent, telling me that the book she was trying to place for me had been turned down by still another publisher. I decided to cut it boldly, and I spent a succession of long mornings doing this; and then had the still-quite-lengthy manuscript to retype. But so many editors by now had seen my book, and failed to give it the response I'd hoped for, that to be working on it again didn't help me much to feel that I was flesh and blood.

While I was sitting writing, I knew well enough what I was doing. But as soon as anyone asked me about the work – all my assurance would evaporate. I'd fear, then, that what I'd done was naught – fear to be looked right through. If I had been living still with Nell, I would have turned to her, and she would have begun at once to talk me back to life: 'They don't know it – even though you're right there in front of their eyes; but you're good. *Very* good. Too good for them to be able to see yet.' She would have wrapped round me, spun round me, clothed me quickly in her silken words. But Nell would soon now have another child to keep alive, to clothe in confidence.

I myself thought continually of that child about to be. I consulted with Diane about where to find a tiny bracelet for it. At the fleamarket I found some mosaics shaped as little flowers, and hastily bought these, too. Charms. I was trying to transmute my care for my own life into care for the child's life. Trying even, I suppose, to pretend to myself that we were the same person. For then Nell would be my life-keeper still.

Through all these days, it was strange to be sharing a life with Flo yet sharing so few of the deepest feelings that were agitating me. I could let her see my distress about Ned's having to go off to war. But when Nell was mentioned – Flo knew her a little and when a letter came would ask about her – I had to veil my feelings. It occurred to me that Flo might have guessed – long ago – that I was in love with Nell and be veiling from *me* the fact that she *had* guessed; but it seemed more likely that she hadn't. And I couldn't help wondering whether if she came to know, she'd be disturbed to think of how she and I had travelled together. During our trip we had almost always shared a hotel room, and one night when that was all to be had, we'd shared the same bed. My feelings towards her had never been more than simply sisterly. But would she doubt this? The cliché about lesbians was that they were tormented by lust. Might she feel that her privacy had been invaded? I tried to put such thoughts from me. So I was too often veiled to myself as well as to Flo. One evening when we had dined out and were driving round the town, the need to touch my own more naked reality made me suggest to Flo that we visit a lesbian bar in the notorious Place Pigalle. I had never visited one back in the States – had found it easier to hold to my pride by not making any such visits. Easier to repress thoughts of society's view of us. But now I felt the need. I tried to sound casual, and merely curious – remarked that we should perhaps see a little of the 'naughty' side of Paris. Flo assented cheerfully enough.

It was a small place, down some steep steps from the street. We sat up at the bar. I remember the bartender was a handsome young woman, her shiny black hair cut in a short boyish bob. She wore a tuxedo jacket and black bow tie. I liked her direct glance. Women were sitting at small tables or dancing in the cramped floor space directly in front of us. At a certain moment the dancers on some impulse joined hands in a haphazard circle dance. A few of them were rather tipsy. One woman wore a flimsy blouse through which her breasts were quite visible and one of the tipsier dancers darted forward to touch her nipples in a gesture of admiration. I flinched at this, afraid that Flo might find the gesture gross. But Flo gave no indication of being shocked. Suddenly a man came rushing down the stairs and up to one of the dancing women. He grabbed her by the arm. The woman tried to pull away. Some of the other women were shouting. The woman he was yanking at burst into tears and he let go of her and she ran up the stairs and out of the bar. He glared about him in a dazed way and rushed out after her.

I asked the bartender: 'What just happened?'

She looked at me for a moment and then she replied quietly, 'I don't think your French is good enough for me to be able to explain.'

I like to remember her words – for their grave wit. But I had taken it for granted that she would recognise me as another lesbian, and realized now with a shock that she took me to be a tourist. The very tourist I was pretending to Flo to be. I left the bar with Flo feeling very oddly – feeling now more distanced from myself than when I had entered.

Flo and I never exchanged a word about our impressions of the place.

It was at about this time that our small owl flew. The young man who kept turning up at the apartment, Alex – who was, I began to see, wooing Flo – had never much to say; or possibly he had never much to say except when alone with Flo. But one evening, just before taking his leave, he decided to speak at length to our owl. He'd learned somewhere to imitate a mating call. He stood there staring into her cage (we had just removed her from the chandelier and placed her in the cage for the night) – he stood there, staring at her, and uttering plaintive and repeated hoots. At which she straightened up, startled, her feathers all standing, and her head moving nervously between her shoulders. 'I think you're really disturbing her,' Flo said at last; 'Alex, stop it.' And he really had disturbed her, as it turned out. That night she managed to squeeze out of the rickety wooden cage – which we found in the morning latched still, but empty. She must have flattened herself like a feather pancake to escape – through the space just above the tray one pulled out to clean the cage, we guessed. And she'd flown through the window Flo always opened at night, leaving one white dropping on the sill. How would she fare? we wondered. Had she been captive too long and would she be helpless? Or would she find a park or belltower in which to nest and fend for herself perfectly well?

I missed her wild presence. And I missed, too, sharing *that* with Flo. There was a sense, I felt, in which we let ourselves be known to one another through our caring for her.

Flo was angry at Alex for causing us her loss. But Alex was plainly proud of himself. To appease Flo, he visited the bird market and brought her back the gift of two pretty little South American birds with delicate markings. Flo always had flowers in the apartment – dried flowers if there were no fresh flowers to be had; and these birds, when not in their cage, would usually settle among the flowers. People are not observant, and her visitors didn't usually notice them. It amused Flo, if she was having a small party, to wait until drinks had been downed, then to pass by the flowers, giving them an inconspicuous jostle, so that the little birds would fly about the room all of a sudden – causing the drinkers to wonder what had been put into their glasses.

Diane was one of the few visitors who noticed the birds at once – walking over to them quietly: 'Hallo, my pretties.' She had begun to drop in now and then after work – staying briefly, never accepting an invitation to dinner; but chatting for a while, asking how my work went, asking where I'd been wandering.

One afternoon late I returned from some exploration of the city, and as I was parking my scooter in the courtyard, Diane's thin figure darted out from the shadow where she had obviously been waiting for some time (she darted out from the shadow of all these days through which she had been waiting) and standing close to me, peered into my face. 'I have to talk with you.' She spoke very low. She had a letter in her hand – in its envelope; and she showed me the envelope, with a quick gesture. 'He has asked me again to marry him.' My eyes asked her what she meant to reply. She put the letter away, she took my hands in hers, with a strong grasp, but didn't answer.

Was it that day or was it the next day that we took tea together again – at the café where we had first talked? I think it was the next day. I think she was late for dinner already that evening, and hurried away. Yes, daylight was still casting changing patterns on the café tablecloth. I remember that in her distraction she put the steaming teapot down on the cloth instead of on the little mat provided for it – and it left a singe mark, at which we both stared and smiled, as though it were a sign of some sort.

What she had to tell me was that she wasn't sure that she *should* marry Ned. She said, 'I'm afraid I'd make him unhappy. I don't think I'm really quite alive, you see. My body is really dead, and my mind is really dead.' I sat amazed at her words. 'My body is really dead', she told me – eyes alight, the hairs of her head softly alight, her hands alert, as she spoke, to make additions, hand-notes, to her ready words. 'My mind is really dead', she told me – who, moments before, had described a couple passing in the street with the most accurate wit.

I sat staring at her. 'All I can say to you,' I told her, 'is that you are very alive to me.' She ducked her head for a moment, as though to hide her face; but then looked me in the eyes – how? I try to remember her look across the years. It spoke a long question, I would say: 'If you see me as alive, am I perhaps alive?'

Perhaps, she went on to tell me, it was living the years of her adolescence under the Nazi occupation that had taken her life – trying to come to her sense of herself in a Paris that had just been lost to itself, made subject. (I can't remember her exact words. They are not in my notebook. But this is how I remember her speaking.) The conditions of life then simply on the physical level depleted one – if one belonged to an average family as she did, her father a minor official in the post office department. They had too little to eat, too little heat. She told of how the four of them – she, her father, mother, older sister – had sat evening after evening huddled together round the dining table, a blanket draped over it, low, and a small heater under it, so that their legs at least could be warm. She had developed chilblains. She showed me the swollen knuckles of her long fingers. (One couldn't always be sitting round that table.) But it wasn't the going hungry, going cold, that had taken her spirit. It was the sight of those stranger soldiers walking round the city. Walking as if they owned it, yes; but their eyes knowing that it wasn't theirs to own – their eyes cold and lost. 'That look in their eyes haunted me', she told me. 'In secret, I'd make a little sign after them, a sort of attempt at blessing – at taking that terrible look away. Knowing I'd be named a traitor, probably, if anybody knew what I was doing. My sister would have been outraged. Of course the bullies were damned, she would have said. Good at least that they were damned. But I couldn't put them from me that clearly. I was possessed by them.'

I don't know what words I found. Her story moved me very much. I know I told her that I thought her one of the most deeply alive people I had ever met. At which she shrugged her beautiful shoulders, smiled a wry little smile.

We left the café to walk through the city together for a while. Before we turned off to take our different ways, she told me shyly, 'If I do say yes to him – let me say that I would like having you as a sister.' I told her as shyly, 'And I would like it, too.' And walked home musing and musing about her. For some reason it didn't strike me at the time as inconsistent to wonder how she could think of herself as not quite alive, when that was just the way I thought of myself.

A few days later she came to the apartment to tell me that she had written Ned, accepting him. But, she'd written, the trouble was that she hadn't the heart to tell her mother that she would be leaving home, leaving France. Her mother had so very little; her small family was all she had. She didn't know how she was going to make herself tell her.

Before she could leave for the States, Diane had of course to acquire an immigration visa. Long careful letters began to arrive from my father, dictated at his law office – letters about how best to get the visa swiftly. Or as swiftly as possible. 'According to my information here, it will take a month, at the minimum, after you are registered in the quota immigration waiting list book . . .' (My father sent me carbons of each of his letters to Diane.) Ned – who was now at a Marine training camp – was expecting a ten-day's leave at Christmas, and was hoping that the marriage could take place then. 'Please, therefore, apply to register at your very earliest possible convenience.' (My father had these words typed in caps.) Ned told him of course about Diane's reluctance to speak to her mother; and I received the cable: 'Hope you stay Paris until everything clear as to parents.' I'd written that I'd be heading back to Rome soon.

So I now saw Diane almost daily. The American Embassy became familiar. And Paris became for me above all the city Diane would soon be saying goodbye to – a difficult goodbye. Leaving those who had always been close to her, to live now with a young man who was really a stranger – though a stranger she wanted to learn to know. 'Your smile is like his smile', she told me; and I could tell a little about her feelings for him from the way she said it. This stranger whom she would begin to know a little would abruptly vanish – possibly within a very short time. Leaving for the hideous war. From which he might never return. And if he did return, he might return maimed. He would certainly return altered: a different stranger now, smiling that smile she liked. She was stepping off the edge of the world, really.

So of course was he. The letters he wrote me were painful to read, for though he kept up a good 'face', they were clearly enough (and quite naturally) written in a state of shock. It seemed to me that I could read in them some panic about his approaching marriage, as well as about his approaching initiation as a soldier. 'Anyway, Dad's very proud of me', he wrote in one letter. Was he being solemn, when he wrote this, or sardonic? He didn't know, himself, I guessed – was being both at the same time.

Our father's presence did, I think, loom over these days for both of us – a weighty presence which could make the waging of a war seem an act of reason; make this risky marriage seem only sensible too; occasional doubts about either striking like mists against the rock of his assurance – to thin and dissolve. 'This is the way it is', he seemed to assert. 'Young men do go off to war. And though we fear for their lives, the fire of war proves them. Young men do ask of women that they leave all that has been familiar and cleave only to *them*. And this is the testing of women. Don't doubt. This is the way it is.'

Meanwhile Flo had begun to see a great deal of a man much older than herself who had turned up in the city – an American professor she'd known for many years, married, but here without his wife. They were out together night after night. And Alex began to pay *his* visits looking pale and anguished.

'Alex is painfully in love with you, isn't he?' I ventured to ask.

'Oh, I don't think so', she answered curtly.

I asked in surprise why didn't she think so.

She was silent for a while. She seemed to be standing listening, still, to my first question. When she answered, her voice was tense: Her friend Celia thought that Alex was really homosexual.

I was silent for a while myself, seeking my balance. Then I asked: Didn't she believe that it was possible for each of us to fall in love with either sex? Wasn't it just a matter, really, of finding the particular person with whom we were happy? For some people that was much more likely to be a person of the other sex, and for some a person of their own sex. 'But there's not some stamp on each of us: You're this or you're that.' I knew very little about Alex, I said, but it did seem clear to me that he was altogether in love with her.

'Then why doesn't he say so?' she asked. And the flare of her anger took me by surprise.

'Perhaps he's a bit in awe of you', I ventured.

And for the first time now it occurred to me that Flo might be more interested in Alex then I had suspected.

The professor moved on to some other city.

Alex began to wear a look less anguished.

One weekend, Diane and I took the train to Chartres together. She was a fine companion on such trips because, like Flo, she knew how to be quiet and let one look for oneself – though she could have delivered non-stop commentaries if she'd liked. Her country's history was very real to her. In the States, I had met few people of whom this was so. To some, the history which their own lifetimes spanned might be real, but beyond that – well, there is little enough that remains to speak to us of anything beyond that; those who build what is new here are happy enough to demolish what has come before. Staring at the so very beautiful time-blunted faces of the figures in stone at the cathedral's doorway, sitting then for a long time in the great airy interior, choosing a place where one of the high rose windows cast its glowing stain – the light through that marvellous window cast for me, too, the thought: how very much she is leaving. She gives up not only family and friends. I glanced at her sideways. She was standing a bit apart, with a smile on her lips, and yet, despite the smile, a look – it suddenly seemed to me – worn as the look on the faces of the ancient figures who were stone of this building's stone. Just for an instant I let myself wonder: Can she really endure this displacement? Can she really become an American?

But I didn't let myself hold this doubt in my mind. The choices being made were not mine, of course. I was also greedy, by then, to have her in the family.

Yes, during all these days, events in the lives of others seemed grave events to me. The people I cared for seemed caught up in what was real, what had to be taken seriously. The word I received from or about them marked, for me, the passage of time. My own actions seemed traced in air, insubstantial.

At one time of day – or rather, at day's end – I did sometimes seem to myself less ghostly, seem a flesh and blood inhabitant of this city. And the city, because of this, became for me, at that evening hour, especially beautiful. Flo's apartment was on the Left Bank, not far from the Place de la Concorde. Often after dark I would walk out to mail some letters at a huge domed air terminal down the river, beyond that wide Place. The night stretched between me now and any further messages I could receive about those other lives for which I was anxious. Something in me dared to recall that I sought my own life. And dared to accept that I would have to seek it; it would not be given to me.

I wrote in my notebook after one such evening walk: 'At this hour, schedules are broken, the night stretches beyond the eye, the hands of the clock refuse to mark the time. This is how it must always be.'

I wrote: 'I must travel alone. Or I can live for weeks in a city and yet not really walk it.'

I wrote one evening: 'I must set off where mail cannot reach me. Then return. But always set off again. Or I am not really here. I pass the time until the next mail.'

I would walk along the shadowy quay. Across the Seine shone the great lamps of the Place, and the fountain spilling under the lamp's light. The lovely darkness filled all the spaces between the lamps, and ran on the river's back, under the bridges, and out beyond the city, out toward the world's edges.

I wrote: 'A possible life – this is how one travels toward it: believing, unbelieving, believing. But go. Unbelieving. And yet not ceasing to believe even when afraid that it is impossible.'

By day it was harder for me to remember that I had written these words. Daylight washed the words from the page. It made visible a city strange to me, in which I walked about with nothing real to do. Lost in admiration, but with nothing real to do. And veiled even to myself.

And then one extraordinary day – but then one day unlike any other – *you* turned up in Paris. You telegraphed that you would be arriving, and suggested that I meet you at a certain café if I were free. I think it was at the Deux Magots – a place where writers and artists liked to gather in those days.

And so I met you at the Deux Magots.

As you read this, you will be thinking back across the years, and you may remember the encounter or you may just as easily have forgotten it entirely. It was a very simple event.

You were accompanied by a young architect, American, with whom you'd made the trip from Rome, I think. But I can't remember this surely. I can't even remember the purpose of your trip. Had the young man – who had a grant at the American Academy in Rome, I think – had he proposed a few days off from work? He had a car, as I remember. Or had you followed your own impulse and come to see the work of some painter you admired, on exhibit just then in Paris? No, I can't remember. I can't remember a thing we talked about, either. You were probably full of questions about *my* travels. This is your way, always: to ask for life statistics as you chat – whether with friend or stranger. You can keep them in your head, too. You ask more questions than you'll answer. This, too, has sometimes filled me with awe. I've never known how to turn questions aside. You gave the attention he required to the young architect, of course. I can remember that.

But what I remember clearly – remember as clearly as though it were yesterday – is simply your living presence on that day, seated at the café table; simply your being there – present for the young man, present for me, and – this is what took me by surprise again – present to your own self, too. You didn't seem to doubt that you were where you were. I remember still your alert head, the quiet forward thrust of your shoulders as you'd speak; I remember the direct energy of your glance. Very simple things. A very simple event.

And yet because of these simplicities everything began to change for me that day. After being with you for that hour or so, I found that Paris had become a different Paris. It was no longer a wonderful picture at which I stared as I had stared at the wonderful pictures hanging in the galleries of the Louvre. I was in the picture now. The marvellous stage set I'd been wandering through had a play afoot, and now I saw that I had a part in the play – as you had. Not that I had any clear idea of how to act out my part. But I believe that I did have one – if you had. For this gift of belief, I thank you again, dear friend, across all the time that has passed.

7

But I've jumped ahead in time, remembering this gift you brought me. I've left out a trip to London, taken before that vivid meeting with you. A trip I must have talked about, for it was the first long-distance trip I'd taken on my motor scooter. (It was to be the last, as it turned out.) I would have talked about it only lightly – wouldn't have spoken of another kind of distance I ventured to cross, making that trip. Though perhaps you made your own guesses, when I told you that I carried a passenger on the back seat – Ned's classmate, Pete Bannigan. We were to talk of him a lot when you and I met again, but I never did recount for you the story of that crossing. That is the right word – 'crossing'. With all its collision of meanings.

Pete. One late afternoon he had suddenly appeared at the door of Flo's apartment – on his head an enormous French beret, set at a jaunty angle. I'd thought at first the beret was a take-off, and laughed merrily. But my laughter confused him, I could see at once. The beret wasn't a joke at all. So I tried to translate one kind of laughter into another: the merriment of reunion. Pete, as you know, was to enter public life a few years later – that life in which (as Virginia Woolf has remarked before me) the wearing of costume is taken very seriously indeed. Down through the years I was to see him, in one news photograph after another, wearing a succession of funny, not-funny, more and more important hats. The beret had its place, I guess, among these others – the proper happy decoration for a Young Student Especially Chosen To Study Abroad. Pete had just received a Fulbright scholarship to the London School of Economics, and was spending some days in Paris before work got under way.

He had gone to college with Ned, and had often turned up with him at our family gatherings – shy in our midst, and more especially courteous than most young men, but quick, too, to get in a humorous word. My family loved his wit – and loved this tall skinny youth with the round pink-cheeked face, very active eyebrows; who moved rather like a recently-born colt not yet entirely accustomed to being on its feet. Yes, for all his height, he was built really like a little boy still – small, flat buttocks, very bendy knees – and had a look about him tentative, unarmed. This made me feel: 'I think I could know you, Pete.' On the other hand, he had sometimes a look in his eye that announced: 'Nobody knows me. And if you think me frail, I'll surprise you.'

A number of days before I sailed for Europe, he had begun to ask me out – to my surprise. We'd eat at Moal's over on Ninth Avenue, then walk and walk through the city, talking as we walked. Pete doing much of the talking. Telling me of his life – which, to date, had been a hard one. His father had abandoned the family years before. His mother had somehow coped, ran a bar now – where Pete often helped out. He had lots of tales to tell about the bar. And tales about some of the rough jobs he'd held as he worked his way through college. And one tale which he told with angry pride. He'd saved up enough money – somehow – to throw a real wedding party for his sister this past year. He'd meant to use the money for something else, but was damned if his sister was going to have to invite people to a wedding where there wasn't enough champagne. Enough champagne had flowed to 'float a duchess'. His eyes glowed as he spoke of this.

At the end of the evening he would walk me to my door, remove his hat and make a low bow: 'Good night, Miss Barbara.' The gesture would jolt me each time. Was he mocking me? Was he mocking himself? Did he really believe in that distance between us?

We'd had dinner together the night before I took my ship. We'd eaten at Moal's again – and sat on and on at table. Pete putting down a lot of wine. And I enough to begin to feel soon that everything was happening in slow motion.

Half-way through the evening, he told me, 'You have the unhappiest eyes.' I didn't know what to reply to that. Turned the conversation, I think, on to the subject of the quest for joy. I'd heard, I said, that in the Catholic church one couldn't be canonized, however worthy, unless one had the special quality of communicating joy. This made deep sense to me, I said. And no, I'd never be canonized, I tried to joke.

Pete said of himself, then, that he expected always to be unhappy. 'And yet,' he said – emphatically – 'I have a joyous nature.' And he ordered another bottle of wine.

He began to talk about the church. He'd been raised a Catholic. Hadn't been to church in many a year. Though he often felt a sharp nostalgia for it. Yes, classically. Actually, he confessed, he was afraid he'd come to feel a certain contempt for those who were not Puritans. Did he really belive in that northern tradition, he wondered, or was he merely its victim? Abruptly he confided that the lines Milton gave to Satan were very real to him – 'I would rather reign in Hell than serve in Heaven.' '*My* fight is with God, too', he said rather loudly. Then lowered his voice: 'And don't tell me that I'm a homosexual, because my father had too many children and so I don't want to.' It hadn't occured to me to tell him any such thing. In fact, I couldn't see the connection. I rather often couldn't quite see the connection between his thoughts.

Nevertheless a little later he accused me – though gently – of having a 'know-it-all' look. 'There is no truth', he instructed me. 'One can know nothing.' He said this with a tight small mouth. A moment later his lips went soft again (he had a small rather pretty rather childish mouth) and he let his head drop forward on his long neck – in a motion I had seen him make before, the head dropping forward suddenly as if to allow itself to be cut off. And he stared into his wine glass.

Toward the end of the evening, he said very slowly: 'I don't know whether or not I know how to love. But if I ever did love, it would be you I'd love.' We sat in silence, then. I felt quite numb from the wine. His surprising words kept repeating themselves slowly in the silence.

Now here he was in Paris. I'd had a joyful note from him about receiving the Fulbright grant. Or rather, a half-joyful note. 'All of this is spoiled by Korea', he wrote. His letter suggested that of course he'd be finding his way to the mainland at some point. One day, without further notice, there he was at the door.

He was delighted that I'd acquired the Lambretta. 'That was an inspiration! A wonderful thing to do – wonderful!' he kept exclaiming. I took him on a number of tours round the city – his long legs tucked up on the stirrups somehow, his voice eager behind me: 'Let's stop and look at this! Ahhh! And now, where next?' These first days, his voice kept breaking oddly. He was so very keyed up, so thrilled to be in Paris – but trying not to show it too much.

One day he asked, 'How would you like to drive me back to England on your wonderful scooter, when I have to go?' It seemed a fine idea. I wanted very much to try a long trip. What better first venture?

In preparation, I went shopping for a coverall – a sort of Winston Churchill zipped-up-the-front mechanic's suit which I'd be able to wear over skirt and jacket. The trip might be dusty, and it might be cold. It was October by now. Pete appreciated the Churchill suit – though I've forgotten his witty comments. Diane, when I showed it to her, was especially intrigued by it, and tried it on.

Some days Pete would turn up, and some days he wouldn't. He had other friends in the city. And he didn't speak of love again. He just – happened rather often to wander by. He was very debonair. If we'd set an appointment, which we occasionally did, he wasn't at all apt to be on time. I learned not to expect him to be. If he was very late, I'd just go on about my way.

Often we'd join Flo and Alex. One night we all went together to a small restaurant Pete had heard about where the woman who ran the place was known for throwing plates when annoyed. She threw only one plate that evening, to Pete's disappointment. A small and wiry woman. I remember the abrupt flare of her anger – made a show of but real enough, too, my guess was. Pete and Alex were laughing as we left. But I glanced at Flo and she looked uneasy. The woman's anger wasn't funny to her, either. But we didn't talk about it.

Pete wanted to taste the café life, and we sat at the favourite cafés of the time till late at night on a number of nights. He was interested in each new person who turned up, and clearly loved the perpetual motion of evenings like this. The more he drank, the livelier he became. The more I drank, the sleepier I became. I hadn't yet learned simply to pretend I was drinking.

The happiest hours we spent together were those of the afternoon he took me to *The Magic Flute*. I remember at the opera's end lingering with him at the top of the steps of the Opera House, a little bewildered by one of the transformations I had watched – transformation of the Queen of the Night from Good Mother to Mischievous Mother – but entirely enchanted by Mozart's music; each of us just standing there, smiling at one another. And what were the words he spoke in those moments that surprised me? They were words to the effect that nothing, nothing matters more than music like this. And if music like this can be made, perhaps much more than we assume is possible is possible. I remember taking his arm at that – surprised and touched to hear him say this. And we went pacing down the steps, and wandered along then, arm in arm, through the streets – not caring which way; Pete for once saying little, both of us moving to the music still, our steps light and at one.

We'd agreed on a day to start off for London, to get Pete there in good time to begin his studies. I figured that before that day I'd have finished copying and editing my manuscript. But long before the time – in fact, the day after we'd heard *The Magic Flute* – Pete turned up at Flo's earlier than he'd said he might, first asked could he take me out to lunch, and then announced that all his plans had changed. My journal reads: 'Funny look in his eyes when he came in.' His eyes were dilated queerly – as though he were hurting, and bewildered to be hurting. He didn't tell me his news at once, just stood there, looking at me. I was reminded again, as he stood there, forlorn, of a young slack-limbed boy. Then he told me that he'd had a wire from the friend with whom he would room at the school. There was some complication about payments and registration. His friend advised him to turn up at once to straighten things out. He knew I wasn't ready to leave yet, he said. He'd catch a train the next day.

He didn't speak any tender words. He didn't say anything about it being hard to leave me. He just stood there looking like a large motherless boy.

I said, 'Let's go have something to eat.' We ate – around the corner somewhere – without saying much. His eyes still had that glazed look.

Some time toward the end of the long slow-motion meal, I decided, 'I *could* just put the manuscript aside, and get myself together and leave today.'

He sat up, suddenly tall in his chair, his eyes lightening, his eyebrows quirked up high. He asked, 'Could you?'

I'd have to get to a bank; I'd have to find Flo and let her know what I was up to; I'd have to pack. But I could – yes – meet him by five o'clock at the Deux Magots, I decided. Could *he* be ready? He started nodding his head: yes, yes.

So I hurried to the bank. I traced Flo without much trouble and told her my plans. 'Off you go, then', she said quietly. I called Diane to let her know I'd be away for about a week. And I quickly packed. I'd wear the dark plaid skirt and jacket I wore most the time. They didn't show the dirt. So I needed only some shirts and under-things, which fit easily into a small sack I could sling at the back of the scooter. And Pete had said he'd bring even less; he'd send everything of his ahead by train. Diane turned up just as I was climbing into my coverall, and she rode with me to the Deux Magots. 'He'll be late', I told her. We sat down to have a tissane and wait for him. I guessed that he'd come strolling in almost an hour late, looking as though he were a little early. And so he did – carrying in both hands the small leather toilet kit he would leave by mistake at the very first stop we made for gas. We started off before sundown.

My journal is terse: 'Gas near the Trocadero – and Pete left his only luggage. Pontoisse about 8. Search for rooms. Finally the Reynard. Pete stayed up late at bar with two French communists.'

I think back across the years, past the meagre words. And though the countryside through which we travelled is now vague in my memory – except for the verge of trees along the highway, the blowing October leaves – I can remember still many of my feelings on that long-ago voyage.

I remember the sense of venturing forth. The sense that it was *necessary* to venture forth – as I had admonished myself: yes, out of reach of the mail, out of reach for a while of news of those *other* lives that sometimes seemed to me more real than my own. Purring along this highroad on my scooter, through the brisk autumn air, I had for a change the feeling of reaching out toward my own life. I was quite at ease by now with the Lambretta, and pleased with myself for being so at ease. The machine did falter near the tops of high hills. We had even sometimes to dismount and walk it up the final way. A friend would advise me later that I should have been cleaning the sparkplugs regularly. But there weren't many very steep hills. And having to dismount now and then didn't spoil my feeling of being on the way somewhere – on the way perhaps to a life that was not just living in the lives of others, that was in my own grasp, as the sturdy handlebars of the scooter were now pleasantly in my grasp. None of this was in words to myself. It was all in feelings. I try now to put the feelings into words.

As I rode along – Pete in the seat behind me, now and then humming a little tune to himself – the question began to touch me lightly, as the very light wind through which we rode kept touching me: Might this young man on the back seat somehow, fatefully, belong in the life I could be on my way to finding? I can see now that the fact that I and not he guided the scooter, the fact that he merrily accepted the very unlordly passenger seat, made it easier than it might have been for me to bear such a feeling. I would phrase it, as I heard it: Could it be that this young man – who seems either to love me or to want to learn to love me – could it be that, if *I* could learn to love *him*, he would prove to be a beloved brother-journeyer my life needs? His hands, which clasped my waist as he kept his balance there behind me, clasped me like a brother's hands; that light whistle in my ears seemed a cheery brotherly sound.

I can't remember Pontoisse or our supper there. I remember that there was no room at the inn, and so we rode on, into the dark. And at the next inn we came to along the highroad, there was only one room vacant. Pete went in to inquire and came back out and told me, 'They have just one room', and climbed back on to the back seat and we rode on again. And I remember that the question now began to knock against my ribs more loudly: Is it possible that if I allowed myself to draw close to this man, my life might simplify? Some part of myself of course still dreamed that my life was with Nell. But another part of myself knew this to be dreaming and strained to wake from the dream. And the question knocked: If I allowed myself to lie next to this man, might I wake?

I remember that I began to drive more slowly and drove in this way for about a mile. I remember that I pulled the scooter off the road – under a large tree. I remember the leaves of the great tree fluttering above us there in the dark, fluttering questions, tentative desire.

I said, 'It's late, and I'm tired, and you must be, too.' I ventured, 'We could, of course, take the one room.'

His eyes widened.

Embarrassment made me add quickly, 'With me in my Churchill suit, we'd be proper enough.'

73

He nodded. I was the one to decide, he said.

I turned the scooter round.

We looked at the room they had to offer. It was a nice clean room with a large double bed. You'll laugh at what followed. Pete said he'd go downstairs while I settled in. Our washing had to be done in the corner of the room, where there was a wash-stand with basin and pitcher. He'd have a nightcap, he said. So I undressed and washed and then did get shyly back into my coverall before climbing into bed. And I lay there and waited for Pete. But Pete had taken my words about propriety literally and he stayed and stayed at the bar.

The bar was just down the stairs from our room and I could hear his voice rising and falling in excited conversation. He was talking French, so the rhythm of his speech was not as rapid as usual, but his laughter burst freely. And another voice went on and on, too, and broke into laughter sometimes. And a third voice sometimes interrupted. I lay there and waited. And more and more time passed. Should I go to the top of the stairs and call? I asked myself after a while – and answered: No. Should I go downstairs and join them? I wondered a little later still. I didn't feel at ease about doing that, either. So I lay and waited – half-laughing at the situation, half-exasperated. Could he really not read my feelings any better than this?

Was it an hour or was it two hours later that he climbed the stairs? He came tiptoeing into the room – and found that I was still awake. And he stared at me. And then he blushed.

I turned my face to the wall while he bathed. He bathed quickly and climbed in under the sheets next to me. 'You were waiting for me', he said. And I told him, 'Yes.' 'Perhaps you should take off that suit', he said – with logic. And I took off the suit. His kiss tasted of whisky and toothpaste. It was a boyish kiss that asked my mouth few questions. He almost immediately took my hand and placed it upon his swollen penis. 'Can you feel how much I want you?' he asked.

I think it was now that he said he had imagined I must either care nothing at all about sex or a great deal. I cared a great deal, I told him – and decided I should add that in the past it had most often been women for whom I felt desire. He was quiet for a moment. But now I wanted him? he asked. I told him yes. And again – his hand on my hand on his penis – he asked me could I feel how much he wanted me.

74

I can remember quite clearly – across all the years – what it was I felt as he asked that question. I felt it very strange to sense that this penis of his was supposed now to *be* he – supposed, so it seemed, to stand in his place and speak *for* him of all his feelings, and to act them all out. Whenever I had made love with a woman, we had spoken together with eyes with hands with lips with tongues with breasts and thighs and genitals and with every inch of ourselves – even when shyly; desire living and desire speaking itself in any and in every inch of us. Lying there, with his penis in my hand, where he had solemnly placed it, this penis seemed for a moment monstrous to me – seemed to loom between us now, not a simple member of a friend's body, but some swollen idol, of which we were both supposed to be in awe. What had this to do with the possibility of our loving one another? For a long moment (that didn't in fact ever end – I remember it still) my own desire drew back – alarmed, and affronted. I didn't speak of it to Pete. I lay there trying to wait the feeling out.

After he had entered me, and our bodies were clasped together, I recovered from the affront. For there was the length of him in my arms, and all seemed comradely again. It seemed a comradely motion to rock together in this way – rocking him in and out of me. We moved together in a sweet tidal rhythm that was like breathing in and out. A sweet way in which to meet.

But I told him soon: 'I don't want to get pregnant.' He had no condoms with him. That anxiety came between us now. Soon he slipped out of me. And we should get some sleep, we agreed; tomorrow would be a long day. We curled up together and did sleep. I liked the feel of his long back, as I lay against it. And I fell asleep full of vague hopes of our drawing very much closer to one another.

When I woke the next morning, Pete was already up and dressed, and his manner was carefully casual. There were to be no morning caresses. I hadn't expected that we'd make love again – for we had to be on the road soon – but it seemed queer not to touch at all; not even to hug; not even to touch softly for a few moments with our eyes.

At breakfast, he had the map out. And we talked about the route we'd take. I remember my bewilderment. The good country eggs had no savour for me. I remember sensing in Pete a dim hostility. I remember that I felt, confusedly, in the wrong. We ate quickly and were on our way again.

My notes say: 'Figured we'd better not go by Rouen. Too little time. Lunch at place where a crooked-handed man was eating moules and a cat and a dog were visiting. (The town was Gronaye.) After this took wrong turn. Through the smell of apples, and leaves falling on to our heads. Dieppe by dinner.'

I don't remember the crooked-handed man or the visiting dog and cat. I think back and can remember the smell of apples in the air, and leaves falling, blowing. And I can remember on my tongue the taste of melancholy.

At Dieppe we found there would be no more boats for England that day. (We could as well have seen Rouen.) We took a room at a hotel called the Normandie. But went out at once. Ate at a brightly-lit café on the waterfront – and then decided to see a movie. The movie, aptly enough, was one called *We Were Strangers*.

Our room had twin beds. Pete made no gesture toward me. I climbed into one bed and he into the other. The night air was damp and chill. I couldn't get warm. I got out of bed to fetch an extra pillow from across the room, to use as a comforter.

'What are you doing?' Pete asked.

I needed the pillow as an extra blanket, I told him.

'You're cold? That's crazy', he said. 'Come over here.'

So I climbed into bed with him. He wrapped his arms around me in a simple companionable hug. And was perhaps ready to drop off to sleep. It was I who began to caress him – to touch his back, his chest. Pete seemed to be unfamiliar with the language of caresses. He scarcely touched me with *his* hands – and seemed only to be able to read mine to be saying: 'Enter me.' So he entered me again, and we rocked together as we had the night before. 'We're good', he said. But again I was afraid of his making me pregnant, and again we drew apart after a while. He was perhaps greatly frustrated, though he didn't say so. I felt awkward, and yet filled with tenderness.

I woke to find Pete up and dressed while it was scarcely light. 'I want to explore the Nazi caves along the shore', he told me. So I turned over then and dozed till late. The boat wasn't to leave till midday. I lay confused. Whenever I had made love with another woman, our lying naked together had seemed an act of asking to be known. And always upon waking I had felt, with awe: Now I am more known to you, and now I know you so much better. Yet Pete and I knew each other no better. And the reason for it eluded me. I lay bewildered, lay half-awake half-asleep, wondering why Pete found it so urgent to get to know about the caves along this coast – why we could not be lying in one another's arms, becoming a little more known to one another.

Once up, I did a bit of wandering myself. And I noted in a shop a beautiful horn and bought it for the Lambretta. I had been wanting an alarm both louder and lovelier than the bell it had. Pete reappeared – and agreed that it was a beautiful horn. We had a meal at the same waterfront café. And no doubt he told me all about the fortifications he had just explored. We made our way to the dock; were given rope to lash the scooter to the ferry's railings. My notes read then: 'Green and pink foamy wake – carnation green.' And I can vaguely remember those churning waters and their very bright tint. This voyage I was making had begun to feel not quite real. The pink, the green, seemed painted colours.

The too-brightly-painted waves ruffled on and on behind us, the coast of England very slowly drawing near. Pete studied the other passengers – especially those who were clearly British. Here were the people he'd soon be living among. We didn't say much to one another. It was dusk by the time we were on the road again. Driving now required an especial concentration. For I had to keep to the left, in English style, and at turnings remember to remember not to turn into the right lane. Resisting habit, my body soon ached. 'Ugly row on row of dwellings', my notes say. 'Glimpses of sea as darkening.' My first sense of England was one of great homeliness. But a homeliness that made no apologies for being what it was – was just what it set out to be. The scooter began to give trouble again on the hills. Night fell. We stopped for a bite and a cup of tea at a pub – where an energetic dart game was in progress. And pushed on. Some time after eleven, we arrived at London's Marble Arch. We both stared at this impressive gateway – then smiled at one another an exhausted smile.

'You did it', Pete said.

End of our voyage.

Terminus – that was the name of the small hotel where, with Pete's help, I finally found a room. Pete himself had decided he should move in at once to his rooms at the School. He suggested a final cup of tea before we said good night. But the hotel-keeper said she couldn't let me go out. She had no key to give me, and it was closing time. When I told her of the long ride I'd just had, she looked at me as though I had forgotten my good manners. Pete gave me a quick tired kiss and went on his way.

I stayed in London four days. I found another hotel – where I was allowed a key and could come and go at what hours I chose. Pete had school responsibilities to attend to, so most of the time I explored London on my own. But we did some sight-seeing together. He showed me first the London School of Economics, and his rooms, and his room-mate. I remember that his room-mate admired my plaid suit (as we sat at tea, in front of their small gas fire) and Pete chided me later for responding that I'd been lucky to find the skirt at one sale and the jacket that just matched it at a sale in quite another shop. There had been no need to tell him this, said Pete. I felt again not up to the British in the matter of manners.

One of the first places I decided to visit on my own was Westminster Abbey. I was running eagerly forward when I saw guards in front of me. They lowered their bayonets. 'I can't go into Westminster Abbey?' I asked, bewildered. 'Madam, these are the Houses of Parliament', one of them informed me with weary hauteur. I did find the Abbey. And lingered in it. And lingered by the dark Thames. And drove slowly round and round this city, looking at towers and monuments and cathedrals and parks and stately homes – looking, too, for a long time, at the great areas still level after the air raids. And scanned faces. Drove round and round. I had expected to feel on more familiar ground than I had in France or Italy. But I found myself looking as from a very respectful distance. Found that I was not at ease even speaking our common language – had to listen with strained attention to understand what was being said, and even to ask rather often: 'Excuse me?' 'What did you say?' With patient courtesy the English would repeat themselves.

On the second night of my stay Pete and I were invited to a party thrown by one of his room-mate's English friends. Pete and his room-mate decided at the party's end that the Britishers had been quietly mocking them all evening. I didn't think so. I thought they were simply being their own very different selves. The next night, Pete decided that *he* should throw a party. Most of the guests were people living in his building. It was a party to introduce himself. It went on and on. Pete looked flushed and happy.

My last day I wandered on my own in the morning, but sat with Pete in front of his gas fire through the afternoon. And we talked a little, each of us, about our lives. It was a relief to be conversing again. He made no amorous gestures. It was I who, before we left the room, stood close up against him for a moment – needing to acknowledge that we had, after all, spent some time in one another's arms. At one point he did tell me, with a smile, 'I was really crazy about you in New York, you know.' The next time that I visited, he was to tell me, 'You know, I was really crazy about you in Paris.' He never did find it possible to say to me that he loved me in the present moment.

His room-mate turned up again by dinner time, with friends, and we all went out together – went, for a treat, to a rather expensive restaurant, where the food tasted exactly like the food in the cheap restaurants to which we'd been going. Then Pete and I wandered off alone together again. And we walked the streets until late. Turning into one old square after another. Admiring the handsome city. But feeling very out in the cold. Here were no cafés at which to stop for a while. One just kept walking. At a certain point we started hunting and hunting for some refreshment. A man at one street corner had pickled eels to offer. I was tempted to try them, but Pete hurried me past. At midnight we were able to buy two drinks of milk at the railway station – and stood, then, and watched a youthful railway worker play snap the whip with a hook-up of small baggage carts. And Pete walked me to my hotel. And we kissed gravely goodbye. Early the next morning I found my way again to the railway station, and put myself and my Lambretta on a train.

I had been back in Paris a week or more when the wire came, saying that you'd be arriving in the city, and suggesting that we meet.

By then I had finished editing my book, and had sent it off to my agent once again (to go the rounds again and be refused in this new form).

I was still lingering in Paris because Diane, although she had her visa, had yet to tell her mother that she was leaving. She couldn't bear to. When we'd meet, I'd look at her with a question in my eyes, and she'd shake her head and stare at me, stricken. 'I can't.'

My days stood strangely still.

I waited for Diane to find the nerve to give her news.

I waited for letters from Nell.

I thought about Pete. Remembering him in my arms. And remembering, felt a kind of eerie longing. It wasn't like the longing I felt still for Nell – a longing for a person real to me, well known. It was like longing for a wraith – longing for the wraith not to be a wraith.

My life stood still.

And then one day, in the very simplest way, time began to move again.

I walked into the Deux Magots and found you sitting there. You rose to hug me. We sat talking. As we talked, you glanced about you, noting the life around us – frowning slightly, as you do, with your look of staring into the light. You sat with shoulders slightly hunched forward – hunched forward into that moment in which we lived. Your knobby-knuckled hands, in quick motions – finding speech even before your lips did – sketched in the air between us pictures, comments, precise details. And I felt something quietly unlock in me. For all was in the present tense. You are. I am. This is. It was as though I had stepped into cold bright water. I felt my blood begin to circle in my veins.

I realise suddenly that I've omitted the young architect in this second recounting of our meeting. He was present, too – though more present for you than for me.

I now remember sharply one particular moment between you. We had left the café. We were stepping out into the street. You were just a bit ahead of him. He leaned forward, as we walked, and gave you the lightest little slap on the buttocks.

You straightened up, flinging up your head, and taking a slight half-skip foward, not looking back at him. And the motion of your body seemed to me to say to him two things at the one time. To say: 'I'm glad that you're taking notice of me. But to say also: I belong not to you but to myself. The little slap had expressed both flattery and condescension. You accepted the flattery, refused the condescension. I felt a kind of awe that you knew how to do this. I felt also a flick of anger toward him.

We met again the next day, and the day after, alone. 'Good talks', my notes say. You asked me where I planned to head next, after Paris, and when I said Rome again, you seemed pleased. You weren't living in Rome itself; you still had your studio in the hill town outside of Rome. But we would be sure to meet. I'd talked with Pete about making another trip to London over the Christmas holidays – or perhaps taking a trip somewhere together. But after this sight of you I knew even more surely that I wanted to return in the meantime to Rome.

A letter came from you a few days after you'd left. A sweet letter, my notes say. But I can remember reading it with an odd sense of disappointment. I wondered why I felt this disappointment, and I couldn't at the time admit why it was. The reason is obvious to me now. I was looking in the letter for words 'I love you'. Yes, I was looking for those words without letting myself know that I was looking. It would be several months before I'd say aloud to myself that I loved *you*.

8

As it turned out, I wasn't to see you again as soon as I'd hoped. Diane did at last find the courage to speak to her mother. (She brought me to meet her. A woman of deep sweetness. I could see why Diane found this parting very painful.) And then I took a train for Rome. But when I got there, you were at first in your hill town studio, then left for what was to be a brief trip to Brussels and – as you'll recall too well – you managed to leave your pocketbook in a taxi, with passport and traveller's cheques, and spent then day after day after day waiting for cheques and passport to be duplicated by the proper authorities – who take their proper time about being of help. It was almost Christmas before you turned up again.

I, meanwhile, settled in at a cheap hotel I had found after some searching, the Albergo del Sole across from the domed Pantheon – that sombre ancient monument whose circular moat was however a very lively place, for many cats of all sizes and colours made their home in it. Several old women came regularly to bring the cats left-over-spaghetti, which they spread out carefully on newspapers, lingering to carry on conversations with the cats who were their favourites. The small sidewalk café on the piazza was an active spot, too. Just by looking out the window here one could feel a part of ongoing life. I kept changing rooms until I found the one I was happiest in. The rooms were large and sunny, though unheated. For heat I relied on my hot-water bottle – which I was able to fill at the caffé espresso machine down the street. One night the bottle sprang a slow leak and I woke to find the mattress soaked through. I had to ask the management to have it carried out into the courtyard to dry. But except for that one disaster – which was the cause of some hilarity – the system worked well enough. I could see my breath in the air as I sat at my typewriter in the mornings, but the hot-bottle tucked against the small of my back kept me from freezing. And if I began to shiver in spite of it, I could on most days step out into the piazza and stand for a while in the direct sun. In which the cats would be basking. This was before the days of smog. Do you remember them? One could still stand out on a city street and have the sun's rays find one – still look up and see the great clouds moving over white as any white. At day's end the clouds would be a glowing pink. And – unless I am dreaming – they would often remain pink even into the nights. At night the cats, who had been lying about most of the day, would be on the stroll. Yes, with all the other citizens. Romans do love to stroll about their city of an evening.

I loved at all hours to stroll about – and found myself as surprised now as if I had not spent time here before. I had half-forgotten the radiance of these walls – stucco walls the many tawny colours of the city's many cats. Half-forgotten the daily music of these bells – the air again and again alive with their notes. And – I wrote in my journal – 'The smell of this city! I had forgotten this, too, really! Wine, coffee, urine – and antiquity.' I added: 'Smell of the jungle, it sometimes seems – or the animal cage.' (Scent of the human male, it was, of course. Men peed against the walls here whenever they liked. We women held our water till we got home.) And I had half-forgotten the very particular sense of space here – always altering as one wandered; or even as one sat in one place: the eye drawn on a continual voyage, space opening, closing in, opening out again and again, in lovely bursts like the bursts of water from the city's many fountains. I liked to walk close to the fountains – walk into their spray. After feeling so oddly aloof in Paris and London, it was a release to feel here sharply touched by the city's life, the bells, and the voices of the fountains, sounding in my innermost ear, the bold scents taken deeply into my lungs, the fountains' water smarting upon my face. It wasn't exactly that I felt at home here. But I did feel in more vital contact.

Of course perhaps it had something to do with the knowledge of your proximity.

I wrote in my notebook, after revisiting the fountain I loved most especially – the many-figured fountain in the Piazza Navona: 'Anything is possible. Yes, yes. Fountain of surprises! A lion has come down to drink. There is a sea monster in the stream. A palm tree is growing here. A snake stares at me. All things are possible.'

I revisited the small church of Santa Maria Cosmedin – which displays in its portico the Bocca della Verita, the Mouth of Truth. A flat wheel of stone, on a small pedestal – eyes, nose, a gash of mouth, carved in it, the mouth ajar; one eye a round hole, one a hole the shape of a tear; and a break in the stone running like a scar from this eye to the stone's rim. Legend has it that if you stick your hand into the mouth, and if you speak a lie, the stone will close upon your hand. I remember thrusting my hand into the mouth. I remember asking the stone: Help me to speak the truth. Asking: Help me to dare not to look away from it. As I asked this, your image came into my mind – as I had seen you on your return from Greece, brown and thin and shining-eyed. I remember, still, the feel of the stone cold against my hand. And as I stared at the rent in the stone, the long scar, I can remember, too, flinching in spite of myself – remember feeling, in apprehension, my own face struck and cracked.

Most of my wandering I did on my own. But at dinner time I very often joined your aunt and uncle at one sidewalk restaurant or another; and they were usually joined, as well, by young artists from the American Academy. Lively dinners these very often were. Reba has the gift of bringing about spirited exchange. Before she resigned her own career to be wife and mother, she must have been an extraordinary teacher. She remains that teacher – but given small scope. Within which, yes, she burns and burns. Her special gift that of attention. Even when she is doing much of the talking herself, she can make another person feel seen and valued – found out. Several of the young men from the Academy seemed half in love with her. Among themselves, as working artists, there was a good deal of rivalry and tension. (I began to understand well why you had chosen to work outside this atmosphere, away in your hill town studio.) Each sought in Reba's eyes the judgment that he was unique.

Do you remember Dwight – the young man who made metal sculptures; who loved to carry a cane and wear expensive hats and elaborate vests? I made the same mistake with him that I had made with Pete – burst out laughing one day at his costume, thinking he was play-acting. But he was playing at being himself. Dwight bewildered me by expressing a yearning for several million dollars, with which, he said, he would love to build a great realm which would be his very own kingdom. My own dreaming wish had more and more become that of the young woman in the fairytale who is given by a fairy a light nutshell out of which she can draw, at will, whatever she finds she really needs for survival. But Reba was fascinated by Dwight's fantasy and drew him out about it. Curiously, a dinnertime soon after ended with his giving a letter-perfect recital of *Little Boy Blue*, the poem by Eugene Field about the boy who dies but whose faithful toys – the little tin soldier, the little toy dog – stay, down through the years, just where he has kissed them and put them at bedtime, put them and told them to stay till he'd wake to play with them again. Dwight was pretending, as he recited, to be making fun of himself, but tears shone in his eyes. Your uncle looked down the table at me with a smile that was like a wink, but Reba watched Dwight closely and at the end raised her glass to him, then dashed the glass to the ground – 'Because I love you.' This was soon before she and Lou were to leave for the States. Dwight sought out her company again and again before that parting time.

Reba gave her attention to me, too, of course. This was, for me, both comfort and discomfort. When she and Lou took me along on a brief trip to Capri, 'Have I brought you to a beautiful place?' she asked. We had just arrived and stood sniffing the spicy air of that island. The question has stayed with me, and often when I think of her I hear her asking it – her resonant voice suddenly light, almost whispered. She wanted to be the one who does bring others to beautiful places, bring others to life. And I loved her for this. It was nevertheless too clear to me – it was painfully clear – that she felt I very much needed to be brought out. She had a way of glancing at me at table as though to say, 'Speak up. Don't keep such silences.' She even one day suggested to me in private that I should think of padding my bosom. 'Just a little bit. It would give you a different sense of yourself.' I didn't take her advice. And for a few evenings was more silent than usual at table.

Now and then one of the young men who gathered round Reba and Lou would invite me to some outing apart from these group dinners. Brian, the young composer, after taking me out only once, suggested that he and I become lovers. I can remember where we were sitting when he proposed this – at a small outdoor café near the city's edge, at cloudy sundown, bats twittering along the trolley wires that ran above the nearby street. 'Pipistrella', he gave me their Italian name. He made it very clear that he was suggesting a liaison that neither of us would take seriously. A little light music. I wasn't tempted. The proposal, in fact, made me feel as estranged from my own body as Reba's suggestion that I pad my bosom.

There was one young man with whom I felt at ease. Aaron wasn't one of the artists at the Academy, but had a friend or two there. A self-labelled 'perpetual student', he was taking time off between academic degrees to make his own study of Europe. Very quietly. That was what put me at ease with him. He felt no need to let me see just how much he knew – or to test me on how much I knew. I see him, standing in some old church we have entered together, standing against a pillar, in the shadow, staring for minutes on end at some detail which intrigues him – falling into a reverie. And he doesn't follow the reverie with a lecture, but simply with a nod at me and a smile. A tall thin fellow with long face long hands long feet, a bush of soft frizzy hair.

One kind of knowledge he *was* quick to communicate: knowledge about how to get along on the very least amount of money. It was he who told me about the cheapest restaurants to be found in Rome – the ristorante economico, where you could stand and eat a hearty meal for pennies. And it was he who told me about the ship from the tip of Italy to Greece which let passengers sleep on deck and pay a fare very much lower than on any ship the travel agencies would tell you about.

Aaron was not without vanity. We lost touch with one another after we returned to the States, and then years later he found himself in the town where I lived and telephoned. His first words after my 'Hello?' were 'It's me!' I was supposed to know at once who 'me' was. But his vanity was blurred by genuine tenderness. He liked to take care of those in trouble. When I met him he was travelling with a young Irish woman whom he had rescued from dangerous trouble. She had taken a young Frenchman as a lover; tired of the affair and tried to leave. The young man, determined to keep her, became threatening. Aaron helped her to escape from him – though she lived in dread of his finding her. Now she and Aaron were lovers. Peggy was small, quick, wiry. Had a very agitated manner. I found her manner irritating, until I learned the cause of it. They didn't confide to me at once that she was in fear for her life. She was a language student. Sometimes, Aaron told me, he would wake at night beside her and hear her urgently chattering, chattering in a language that was an incomprehensible blend of all the many languages she knew.

Aaron and Peggy stopped by rather often to suggest some new exploration of the city. And a friend of a friend from back home, travelling through Italy on her own, looked me up and *we* spent time together. Ellen. I remember she was fighting a cold from the very first day, and was wrapped in a great belted leather coat that almost touched the ground. Wide dark eyes stared from a plump face – an air about her at the same time helpless and wise, as though she saw more than she knew how to handle. The second time we met I learned that she was 'trying' to be a writer. When I asked could I read something she had written, she showed me an extraordinary short story – every word of it alive. 'But you are an amazing writer right now!' I said. She looked at me with an expression I didn't know how to read – as though she were thinking of something else, preoccupied by other words she had heard spoken to her. And over the years since I have never seen anything of hers in print. Though I've heard of her marrying, divorcing, marrying again.

One day we visited together the ruins of Hadrian's Villa, an hour's ride from the city; left in the morning on my Lambretta, took with us a picnic lunch – and walked and walked and walked and walked, amazed, through the many miles of this extraordinary dwelling; walked slow-footed, more and more slow-footed, I can remember, as our amazement grew, and grew too large for us, became oppressive. I name it oppressive now. At the time, I felt our own senses to be inadequate. But they were telling us a truth: Too much was being asked of us. Here was Dwight's fantasy – acted out. But Hadrian had more than a mere million or so to spend. And numberless subjects to do the work of building. He apparently went on adding to this 'setting' for his imperial Self year after year after year; bringing back loot from his many travels; improvising one new structure after another to display this loot. We stumbled through not just one extraordinary palace-in-ruins, but I forget how many; not just one great courtyard with stumps of colonnades, but many; and many temples, many theatres, many baths – interlinked by underground passageways, some surrounded by curious moats. Each very beautiful – even its brickwork or tufa grey-brown shattered skeleton beautiful. The work of genius. And of the skilful servants of that genius. I remember especially the many many small stones, carefully placed. But there was too much here. 'I can't really take it in', Ellen began to murmur. 'Can we just sit for a while?' We sat for a while. The small sounds of birds flitting among the tumbled stones were a comfort.

If this had been a small city, we could have covered the very same ground, I think, without experiencing vertigo – if this had been a community of dwellings. But one man had made this his space. Off the great rooms, of course, were clusters of small rooms; he provided his servants and followers with sleeping-space. But all the spaces that were beautiful were spaces which belonged especially to him – spaces through which he strode, surveying all, casting about him his imperial eye, like God on the Seventh Day naming his creation good. Except that *this* God kept beginning all over again, never calling the work ended, feeling a need to create this World all by himself again and again and again. The structure I remember most clearly is a high high long long long straight wall – enclosing nothing, but allowing an amazing look down its length and into the distance, into time, space, into endlessness. He wanted, I suppose, to be able to feel that he could cast a Fatherly eye upon infinity itself.

I don't remember trying to name my feelings on that day. My journal's entry at the day's end makes no attempt to do so. And Ellen and I made no real attempt to speak. We were too exhausted by our feelings. I remember that we would look at one another and shake our heads, or look at one another and shrug our shoulders. The gestures of children who feel themselves constricted – feel themselves to be under observation, under Daddy's eye. (I recognise the gestures now.)

No, I haven't heard from Ellen in many years. And I haven't seen anything of hers in print. Though I suppose her work might have appeared somewhere and I have missed it. I hope this is so. I find it unbearable to think that she let that gift go unused. I remember the wonderful wild rush of her words in the story she showed me. Then I remember her stumbling, silent, through the grounds that we visited that day. Overawed. Her words all gone.

Our sense of privacy had been wrenched from us that afternoon. I do think that is why I couldn't find my tongue to write in my journal about the place. And Ellen – when she entered marriage not long after; divorced that man but married again – did she *keep* finding herself in imperial territory (however small her lover's realm)? Is that why she lost her tongue? For lack of her own space? Married now or single, may she have made that space for herself again, somehow!

As I write these words, I think suddenly of my father's house. The house in the country. My father's house, not my mother's, for she wasn't sure that she wanted to live outside the city, and so she left all the planning of this house to him. Of course she regretted this later. How he loved the place. And how mixed her feelings were about it – even when she came to prefer the country to the city. 'Some day,' she would muse, 'I'm going to live in a *cosy* little house . . .' For yes, again, here was too little privacy. For others, not for him. This is what he most loved, I think: the sense that all was under his eye – for safekeeping. The door from the living-room-dining-room into the high music room is a glass door. A window from a room in the second storey peeks down into this room, too. Small eye-level arches – which my mother nicknamed 'eyebrows' – enable one to peer from the music room into the long room in which my two older brothers used to sleep. (My mother did insist that these be plastered up.) And except for a back door to the kitchen and one to the cook's rooms, the house has only one entrance/exit. Hard – as in a castle with drawbridge – to slip in and out unobserved.

I am in the garden, talking with a friend. (The garden is enclosed by a curving masonry wall – my father's protective arm thrown around it.) We are talking. My father wanders near. He stands, just a little way off, listening to us. He is not eavesdropping, not spying. He is quite openly listening to what we say. Making sure that all is well. We are under his keeping.

My father loved to stand at a certain spot in the garden from which he could look about him at all he had built and all he had planted. And all the changes he had made in the landscape. For he had done a lot of banking up of low places and smoothing down of hilly places. My mother loved to quote the scripture about him: 'Every valley shall be exalted, and every mountain and hill shall be made low.' He could stand on one spot just looking about him for minutes on end. One day he stood brooding for so long, and so quietly, that a rabbit came along and hopped right on to one of his big L. L. Bean boots and sat there for a while.

When I think of my father's loving but too God-like eye upon me, my spirit flees from home – flees The Garden. But I love this story about him and the rabbit. And I like to think that there were long moments during which he'd let himself relax out of his anxious sense of himself as Father-of-All – to feel simply like one creature among others in the natural world around him. As you probably know, he had once thought of becoming a naturalist, before his lawyer father persuaded him (as *his* father had persuaded *him*) to become a lawyer – and so be in a better position to raise a family responsibly. I remember the day he came upon two lines quoted from Andrew Marvell and was enchanted by them – repeated them to me softly:

Annihilating all that's made
To a green thought in a green shade.

Did my father, even as he delighted in these lines, begin to imagine the green thought taking it upon itself to think up Everything all over again all by itself? I hope not. I hope he felt able to leave this to exuberant Nature.

When Ellen and I decided that we'd stared long enough at the ruins and should head back for Rome, we had trouble finding our bearings, figuring out just where we had started from. We went hurrying along the verges of the place, among the tall cypresses. Peasant women were working in the olive groves nearby – picking. The day was ending, and they were soon ending their work, loading the olives on to donkeys. Singing, they began to climb out of the men's pants they'd been wearing under their dresses, for greater working freedom. We followed the path they took, for a while (they grinned at us), but then they took a turn which was obviously not ours.

'Buona sera!' – they sang out the words. 'Good night.'

'Buona sera!' we called back.

Ellen's voice sounded full of sudden yearning.

As we stumbled along, she began to confide in me that she was wrestling with a difficult decision. She wanted to go on to Greece, before returning to the States. But she'd received a letter from her parents saying they thought she'd been abroad long enough and should now come home. And she didn't know what to do. Had she enough money to go to Greece? I asked. She had just enough. And no, her parents gave no particular reason why she should return – except that she'd been roaming 'long enough'. She shrugged her shoulders, and suddenly stared into my face, her eyes wide with a hunger for further roaming. Couldn't she just explain to them that here she was – so close – and she might never again be able to make such a trip?

'I don't know, I don't know', she said. And gave a little shudder. And pulled her great coat close around her.

Now we came upon a lone peasant couple, and a few cattle. The woman carried an immense sack upon her back. The man carried a tiny switch – with which to keep the cattle moving. We walked along with them until we came to their small house. At which we asked them for directions to the parking lot. The man told us graciously that his wife would lead us there, if we liked. We both answered quickly that we'd find it all right. And hurried on.

'I suppose he'd have sent her off with the bundle still on her back', Ellen said under her breath.

Ellen did go on to Greece. But before setting forth she quite succumbed to her cold and had to take to her bed. And it was on a trip to her hotel to see that she was all right – or rather, on the trip home after seeing her – that I took my fall with the Lambretta. It was a drizzly evening and the cobblestones over which I rode were slick. A car darted out from a sidestreet as I was coming down a hill. I put on the brake, felt the machine slither under me, and found myself sitting on the street, the Lambretta writhing beside me. I got to my feet and went and leaned against the nearest building, just staring at the fallen scooter still in the middle of the street. Some passers-by ran to pick it up for me. I seemed not to have broken any bones, so I climbed back on to it – feeling a little ghostly – and rode back to my hotel.

If it hadn't been for my fall, you and I might not have spent Christmas together. I'd promised to visit Pete over the holidays. But my lower back kept on hurting. I visited one doctor who told me I was just bruised. But went on hurting. Visited a second doctor who told me I had dislocated my coccyx – my tail bone. This doctor was a young Englishwoman, and why she was practising in Rome I forget; but I remember well the touch of her gentle hands. And the touch of her sympathy. I was in low spirits by now, and feeling very much alone. You were still in Brussels; Reba and Lou had sailed. Her kindliness made a deep difference to me. In fact, I came very close to falling in love with *her*. She recommended an operation. I could put it off if I wanted, but she recommended that I get it over with. The price she set was ridiculously low – just what the operating room would cost her. Dr Alberta Jeans. Are you alive still? I hope all is well with you.

For a while I kept changing my mind about what to do. I wrote to my brother Ben for advice, and he wrote back urging that I wait till my return to the States to have any surgery done. Unless, he said, it hurt too much to wait that long. Some days I felt I could wait, but others days I hurt quite miserably. I exchanged letter after letter with Pete. He wrote that I should have the operation in London. 'You can get it for free', he reminded me, and 'I should be around to bring you goodies.' And I wrote back, agreeing. Then the doctor pointed out that there was a flu epidemic in London and I was in poor shape to risk catching it. So I wrote Pete that I couldn't go, and suggested that he visit me in Rome. But he wrote back that this was impossible for *him*. 'I am absolutely dead 100% broke. The reason I am broke is that I have spent all my money on gin.' I offered next to pay his fare – pointing out that I would have paid the same sum to get to London. He wrote, 'That was a cruel letter. I can't go and now I want to go . . . You're wonderful and you were damned good to offer to let me go on your terms which, incidentally, are the only terms on which a self-respecting young man could agree to go to Italy in 1950 – as the paid companion of a beautiful rich young woman.' But – he couldn't go. There were appointments he shouldn't cancel. And – the reason that mattered: he was awaiting orders from the Navy. He was in the Reserve and most men in his class had been called up by now. If he wasn't called up soon it would mean they'd decided not to bother with him till he finished his year of study. But even in that case, he wrote, 'I shall have to decide for myself. I mean to get in pretty soon – like I say, the chow's so good.'

I wrote in dismay: 'Why the HELL are you going to throw

yourself at them? Why the Hell, why the Hell? It just sounds stupid and compulsive and heartbreaking. It makes so much sense to be where you are – a place you didn't come by lightly and shouldn't toss away lightly.' He replied, 'Young lady, anyone alive in the second half of the 20th Century who allows himself to get further than taxi distance from a battleship simply deserves the fate in store for him. Not this fellow.'

He wrote, 'Once and for all, Bobbie. I don't mean to talk to you in terms of the knights of Christendom once more marching forth to meet the asiatic hordes. I merely wish to put it in quiet terms as follows: I'm a young man in whom has been deposited a particularly strong consciousness of the western tradition and a peculiarly large dose of what might be termed civic curiosity. What happens to our civilization matters to me, and for that reason the prospect of going into the Navy is for me a pleasant and proper one.'

I shouldn't have been surprised. In the letter he'd written from the States back in July he had declared: 'We are at war now, Bobbie, and we shall be at war the rest of our lives. In time it will touch if not devour us all. We must expect it, prepare for it.' But I had chosen to forget those words. For my spirit refused to identify – as his seemed ready to – with that warring 'we'. I had not yet discovered myself to be a pacifist. I had even decided, naïvely, that that particular war in Korea must be necessary. But the vision of a continued state of war, that was inevitable, that had to be accepted – this seemed to me both repellant and nonsensical. My spirit refused it, refused it. And I can see now that I was trying, too, to refuse to recognise the fact that Pete *was* able and willing to accept this definition of reality.

His letters began to show a little impatience. At the time I supposed this was because I had changed my mind so often about whether or not to have the operation, whether or not I could make the trip to London. Looking back, my guess is that he became impatient because of my failure to appreciate his warrior spirit.

A few days before I went to the hospital, he set off for three weeks of military training in Germany – without sending me any word of his plans. (He hadn't been called up, never was called up. This was some kind of training cruise for the Reserve.) And 'in a fit of derring-do', as he named it later, he tossed his address book back on to his desk – so that he'd not be able to write to anyone while away. It wasn't for almost a month after the ordeal of the operation that I had any word from him at all. If you'd not been back from Brussels and met me at the hospital; if Aaron and Peggy hadn't asked me to stay with them while I healed – I would have felt very forgotten. 'I shouldn't have done that,' Pete wrote, once back in London; 'I realized immediately I got a moment to write you and couldn't do so. But wot the hell I'm a young thing and will make damn sight bigger mistakes than that before I'm through.' And no doubt he has.

At the time I felt no anger toward him. Or I acknowledged to myself no anger. In fact I persuaded myself that if anyone was at fault it was I. After receiving his laggard letter I wrote him: 'I know you got damn sick and tired of my run of letters and wires, each contradicting the one before. And at this late date I apologize. But one day getting on a train would seem possible, and the next day it simply wouldn't. Walking across the room would seem like quite enough. I'm ashamed that it was so but it was so.' At *this* late date, I am ashamed that I was ashamed.

But I am getting ahead of my story again. There are more people in this story than Pete.

In mid-December word came that Diane had reached the States safely.

Word came, too, that Flo and Alex were engaged.

And a few days before you arrived back from Brussels, a letter came from Nell. She had given birth to her child. A daughter. They had named her Nan. 'I think she looks like you', Nell wrote. My heart turned over in my side at her words. I went limping, at random, through the streets that day – forgetting that I limped. Receiving the news. Receiving this child into my life. Rejoicing and at the same time forlorn. I sat for a long time at the fountain of Trevi – in which sculptured horses of the sea rear up, and the fishtailed sons of Poseidon, the Tritons, try to tame them. Sat listening to the water spilling from one level of the fountain to the next. Bewildered. Listening to the water.

Just before Christmas, I heard from someone at the Academy that you'd recovered your passport at last and were due back. You called my hotel and we met for lunch. My notes say simply, 'Lunch with Carlotta.' But I can still remember the spirit of our meeting. We laughed like children – who like to laugh till they are silly – about the disasters that had befallen us since we last met. You imitated the fit you threw when you discovered that you had left your handbag in the taxi. And imitated every grotesquely unhelpful official you had visited – and the various states of despair into which they had thrown you. You dabbed the tears of laughter from your eyes. I found myself laughing and crying, too – shaking with a wild sense of relief; for it was all right to *laugh* one's tears – as I listened to your tale, then told my own; told of falling with the Lambretta, told of turning from one doctor to another, one plan of action to another.

'Two helpless nitwits abroad', you declared.

And we smiled at one another the shining smiles of those who have found a way to dare to shed long-pent-up tears. We had shaken them all loose with our cackling laughter.

At that meal you invited me to your hill town for the holidays. We could take a bus together on Christmas Eve.

'You're up to a bus trip, aren't you?' you asked.

And – nodding that yes, I was – I wiped away a few final tears which welled up. For I was surprised by the very gentle tune of your voice as you asked that question.

9

I bought a Christmas tree at the Piazza Navona – a tree just not too big to carry on the bus. I dragged it to my hotel room, through a slight drizzling rain. The wet pine needles smelled sharp and fresh, and breathing their air, I remembered that the tree now called a Christmas tree was once the object of pagan worship – a Tree of Life. I felt suddenly light of heart.

I made more than one trip to the Piazza, found there more than our tree – the place, at that season, crowded with improvised booths of holiday wares. Wonderful wares. I suppose that by now everything for sale is made of plastic. But at that time – do you remember? – everything was cunningly made by hand, of wood or tin or ceramic. I still have a child's toy I bought for pennies: a tin circle set on a thin tin staff; a tiny tin fish, painted red, attached to the circle, which is painted blue. Twirl the tip of the staff and the circle spins, giving the illusion of a globe. Turn the base of the staff, and the fish glides slowly through the imagined bowl of water.

I found for our tree some ceramic angels, playing horns, flutes, drums, cymbals. I bought, too – at your suggestion – many bags of candies wrapped in bright papers. To hang on the tree for the children of Anticoli you had befriended – who would strip every last candy from the branches. What did I find to give you? A leather box? A painted scarf?

I spotted in the crowd the wife of one of the painters at the Academy, Penny. She was without her skinny little son this day, which was rare. On a sudden Christmas impulse I bought a small jack-in-the-box and ran across to her and put it into her hands – 'for your child'. And she turned to me with a look of such surprise, and such hungry gratitude, that I felt the shock of it deep in my being. I mean the shock of her loneliness. I had assumed that with husband and child she could not feel so alone. Jugglers were entertaining the crowd which milled there, and we watched them together for a while. Then she hurried off. 'Ken is watching Danny for me.' I began hearing a shrill skirl of music that rose and fell – like the jugglers' balls – above the heads of the crowd; and I followed the music to its source. Several shepherds in their rough country clothes stood together by one of the fountains, playing on goatskin bagpipes. They had come down from the hills outside the city. One of them had pale pale blue eyes, I can still remember, which held a far faraway look. The shepherds seemed from a different world altogether. When I told you about them, 'Ah, you'll hear that music again', you said.

We took the afternoon bus to Anticoli on the day before Christmas. The bus did jounce, and my body did ache. But your company was distracting. You had, as always, wonderful tales to tell. And tales to imagine – as you looked about at our fellow passengers and speculated about their lives. You did this sometimes in whispers, but sometimes in full voice – forgetting that one or another of them just might understand English. I would try to shush you; you'd look at me in surprise, and lower your voice – but after a while forget again: 'Look at that man with the red face. I think . . .' (whatever you thought was so of his life). As we drew near Anticoli, you grew silent, and began to peer out the window at the countryside from which you had been exiled for all these weeks. To peer intently – as though you stood again at your easel, brush in hand. I love that almost-fierce look – of seeing, seeing.

We reached your hill town near dusk. I heard you let out your breath in a kind of singing sigh, and looked ahead. I saw it first as simply the hill itself. Then saw it was the town – town and hill of one substance, the houses like outcroppings of the hill's pale stone of which they are built. As the bus laboured up the winding road, the place became a town indeed, and I could hear the lively boiling of its voices above the noise of engine and wheels. We were let out in the central piazza, with its spurting fountain in which four green carved creatures – out of one's dreams – grin water. A woman filling a jug at the fountain greeted you with raised arm. A young boy ran forward to help with our luggage. You called out to the woman. You began to jabber affectionately with the boy. He was one of the children who often posed for you. Dragging our tree, I followed the two of you up muddy cobbled streets to the building, once a small castle, one beautiful corner of which was now your studio. Was there a note there from Pepinella, the spinster – yes, peppery as her name – who worked for you? Or did she come to fetch us? We were invited to share supper that evening with her family. 'Strong spaghetti' my notes say of the supper. It had a hearty country taste that was new to me.

Before eating, we sat by their fire, drying our shoes. The mud on these streets got so nicely churned up, you'd explained to me, because sheep and cattle and pigs and chickens walked here too. I'd noticed the drinking troughs in the piazza, and noticed a couple of wandering pigs on our way to the Muzzis. The air had a good animal tang to it – pierced by the sweet smell of burning charcoal.

When I'm tired, the words of any foreign language I've learned – indeed the words of my own language – fly out of my head. I sat tongue-tied through this meal – trying to make up for it with responsive gestures and grimaces. No one minded. And words didn't fail *you*. Your Italian was far from perfect – even I could tell – but wonderfully fluent. You just kept going, any old way, inventing words if necessary. Pepinella stared at you, with her black black eyes, as if hypnotised – as you told of your captivity in Brussels, questioned the three of them about what had been happening here in Anticoli in your absence. It was clear that you hadn't hidden yourself away here at your easel. You had let the life of the town touch you and touch you.

'You'll come to the midnight mass, won't you?' the family asked.

We said that yes, we'd be there.

'You'll want to see the baby born, won't you?' Pepinella whispered.

'The baby?' you asked. 'Whose baby?'

Mother and daughter looked at one another and giggled merrily.

'Whose baby?' you repeated. And they giggled.

You looked at me and shrugged. 'They like to tease me.'

'Devil', you said to Pepinella – who looked pleased to be called that.

You said, 'They'll tell me what it's all about when they choose to.'

After supper, we returned home to decorate our tree – with the angels I had found, and with candy after candy, hanging each piece carefully by a bit of string. The tree soon glittered prettily.

'That was an inspiration,' I told you, 'to trim it with candy.'

'Do you think so?' you asked in a little girl's voice.

You decided. 'It does look nice.' Then added, as if in anger, 'It won't last long!' But your anger, if real, dissolved the next moment. You asked, 'Why should it last?'

The church was just across the street from the Castello. We got there early, and so did almost everybody else. The whole town, I think, packed itself into the church that night. With all its children. Innumerable little boys sat scrunched together under the altar rail – squirming, dozing, winking, grinning or staring solemnly, say my notes. In my memory, they squirm alive again. I hear, amazed, the shepherds' bagpipes. You had said I'd hear this sound again, but it wasn't within church walls that I'd expected to. And I hear the villagers' voices lifted in almost screeching song, that shakes the air like agitated water, shakes the walls. I think I grabbed your hand. I think you smiled at me and pressed my hand hard – you, too, amazed at the wild and wonderful sound. Yes, I felt, how much more likely that a new hope would be born to an outbursting like this than to the sedate chords sounded in any of the churches I had yet attended back home.

At midnight the priest strode down the steps from the altar and was joined by several candle-bearing acolytes. The skirted men went into a huddle in the side aisle – just across from where you and I sat. And then suddenly the solemn huddle parted and the high priest stepped forth holding in his arms a life-size brightly painted wooden image of a baby. You glanced at me, eyes wide. And I glanced at you. Ah! We had seen the baby born! The Christ. The giggles of Pepinella and her mother were explained. You were shaking your head. I think back across the years. Could it be that the two women giggled as merrily as they did because they knew that soon these solemn men would go through motions that let them feel *they* – the men had given birth? I hope they were giggling at least in part at this – even if not admitting to themselves why the giggles shook them.

If the priest held forth the child as though its birth were *his* doing, the people of the town swiftly claimed the child as theirs. This I remember best. The little boys swarmed upon it first – like a cloud of bees – kiss-kissing it, with loud reverberating kisses, then running out of the church, home to bed, with bright eyes. Everyone else rose and pressed forward, filed past, a blind man one among them, carefully led. The bagpipes skirled again, the voices skirled in a final tempest of sound – as some kissed the child quickly, shyly, but many covered it with kisses, loud kisses – kisses that made 'The Word', that night, flesh indeed.

Did you and I kiss the child, too? I suppose we must have. I don't remember this. But I remember that back in your cold rooms we stood for a moment in a hug before going to our beds. 'Good night, Good night!'

We slept late, woke to country sounds. Chickens nearby. Pigeons coo-cooing on the windowsills. The rather melodious grunting of some pigs rooting along the street. I walked out on to your long back terrace, to look at the town by daylight. Down the hillside, in close irregular succession, tile roofs shimmering in the sun – a wonderful changeable red, dimming or brightening in the altering light, as though with the life of the town, as though that life gave their colour. And sweet smoke rising. Far below, a river winding – through fields and through vineyards and olive groves. We were high enough on the hill to look down on the backs of birds as they skimmed the roofs, as they skimmed out across the valley and toward another town on a hill. 'Roviano', you named it for me. You were smiling. 'Yes, I'm lucky.' Your painter's eye skimmed the roofs, skimmed the valley. 'I'd better try to deserve it.' Now you were scowling.

Our breakfast eggs were country fresh. We built a fire in your studio fireplace and, sitting in front of it, opened our gifts to one another. And talked. You told me you'd decided that it was especially the children of Anticoli you wanted to paint. Or perhaps they had decided it, you said. They'd simply kept turning up at your door: Here I am. You showed me some sketches you'd made just before you'd left for Brussels – the children there in all their pride.

'Enough', you told me suddenly; we should go for a walk. And you should introduce me to the family of your landlord. So we took a walk – wandering up and down the narrow lively streets. And then we climbed the stairs to the apartment of the padrone – and invited the family to come and have a drink toward the end of the day and see our Christmas tree. You had invited the Muzzis already. We'd been downstairs again for only a few minutes when the padrone's daughter knocked at the door – to suggest that we enlarge the party. It would be sad for us just to sit and drink a little wine. Why not have music and dancing? They could bring a bagpiper. They had relatives who would love to come to a dance. It might be fun to dress in costumes. She had a cousin who would love to dress up. You looked startled at her suggestions, but quickly assented. 'Dancing – yes – of course.' 'Ha!' you exclaimed after she'd gone. 'It's because I mentioned that Brian might be turning up. All the girls want to meet the young American gentleman. He probably *won't* turn up, of course.'

And you were right: he didn't turn up. But the entire family of the landlord did. Sisters and cousins and aunts and great-grandfathers and sisters-in-law thrice removed. Yes, several of the young women had dressed in festal costume. And if they were disappointed at the absence of Brian, they danced their dis-appointment away. The daughter had brought a shepherd – with a shining leathery face – who blew and blew upon his pipe. And when he tired, someone fetched a man who played the accordion. You and I did most of our dancing with the children, as I recall. I remember especially one little boy I had noticed serving as an altar boy the night before – an apparently meek little soul. When the music started, he came quickly to life – asked me to dance and began hopping as though his feet were on fire.

Pepinella, though, was the most determined dancer of us all. She danced with the men and she danced with the women, too. Even when it was a man with whom she danced, she seemed to be doing the leading. And when she clasped one of the young women round the waist with her strong lean arm, she led indeed – striding through the dance as though it were some joyful contest of wills, her face in great concentration, her sharp chin thrust forward. One partner she twirled and twirled round the floor – one of the young women in a lacy costume – the young woman laughing, Pepinella unlaughing, her face fierce, but shining. Does she know herself? I wondered. Does she know what she is feeling? And what do these others make of her? I wondered. I couldn't decide. I kept following her with my eyes in spite of myself.

And did she ever dare to ask *you* to dance with her? I can't remember. Probably not. I remember well enough, though, that she did dare to tell you what refreshments to serve. We had set out nuts, fruits, candies. And all the wine that you had. We watered the wine, to help it go round. 'There should be more', she'd say – as the nuts, fruits, candies began to vanish. '*What* more?' you'd demand. You'd brought some long hard bars of taffy-like candy for the children – as well as the candies we'd hung on the tree. 'We'll chop those up', Pepinella would say, darting into the kitchen. So the three of us would take up knives and break the bars of candy into smaller sections. They were very hard; it took a lot of whacking. Then these goodies, too, would vanish. 'There should be more', she'd order again. Until you'd brought out every bit of food you'd bought for the coming days, and she had improvised some way to serve up most of it. There was the candy on the tree itself, of course. 'Take it from the tree', she began to instruct the children. And the bright candies were stripped from the branches – only the terracotta angels left.

The company began to sing now as well as dance – songs of a kind I hadn't heard in Rome: the voices, as in Flamenco, high-pitched, very tense, often breaking – as if denied feelings were demanding vent. These voices churned my own feelings. I remember catching your eye and thinking that you, too, looked haunted. You turned quickly away. I'd stopped dancing early in the evening, for my back had given warning twinges. Now suddenly I got the hiccups. And couldn't stop them. The padrone's daughter noticed and brought me a drink of water and showed me *her* trick for curing them. But her cure didn't work. Pepinella's mother showed me *her* way, and that didn't work either. I went and lay down for a while on my bed, and they stopped, but when I came back, they started again. 'My poor friend', you said in distress. But I decided just to disregard them. I wanted to take some photographs of the party, and with the help of one of the young men climbed up on a wardrobe and took some shots from there. Noticing that the camera jerked in my hands, he volunteered to take my place. None of the pictures ever turned out, of course – for all was by candlelight and all was wild motion. At about ten-thirty the guests began to shoo each other home – Pepinella, in a clanging voice, telling the last of them that they should go. You warmed our beds with the ancient bedwarmer that hung in the kitchen, and we hugged again, and I sank into dreams in which all was still wild motion.

I remember of the next day a walk we took together up toward the hill's top, along a path the shepherds used. The shepherds we met carried large umbrellas made of stout patched cloth – against sun as well as rain. Umbrellas rather like the one Robinson Crusoe had carried. We both could remember the same illustration of it in a book read in childhood. We didn't talk much on this walk. But now and then you glanced at me as if to ask: 'You see why I choose to live here, don't you?' And I did see. Now and then, too, it seemed to me, your glance said, 'I'm glad you are here.' I was glad, too. And from now on whenever I'd think of you I could see you in my mind's eye so very much more clearly. See you in this remembered place, among these people. A lonely figure among them, for all your mutual interest in one another. But able to work. In equilibrium, I mused in awe. Able to be your artist self.

Back in Rome, I thought of you often. My back now began to hurt more and more, and I accomplished little work of my own. I liked to think about the work you were doing.

The letter arrived from Ben which advised me to put off any operation until I was in the States again – unless it was too hard to wait. I began to think it might be too hard. An impatient letter came from Pete. And a letter came from my mother describing Ned and Diane's wedding. It had been celebrated in my parents' house. Ned had worn his Marine dress uniform; Diane a gown she and Ned had chosen in a quick shopping trip the day before. 'Everyone seemed pleased with the way it went', my mother wrote. 'Everything went – the food, the drink, finally the bride and groom, at last the guests, and then I started to unwind like that thing that goes down the stairs (you know?)' She meant a tight wire coil we had seen once, in a comic film, flip on its own – unwinding – down a long flight of stairs. Diane was to give me added details when we met again. My father knelt in silent prayer for his son throughout most of the ceremony. First he'd acted as father of the bride, since Diane's father could not be present. As soon as he'd 'given' her to Ned, he knelt. (He was not a church-going man, but at solemn moments was used to inventing his own prayers – spoken or silent. I loved this about him.) The family dog – shut up in a nearby room – howled without let-up. 'Oh we were a merry lot', Diane would recall.

Early in January you came into the city and we celebrated your birthday together. I was pleased that I was the person you chose to be with. We went to a performance of *Peer Gynt*, I remember, and you kept up a wonderful running commentary about the performance in loud whispers.

You made other trips to Rome. You'd reclaimed from friends the little car your aunt and uncle had bought for their stay. So now you could drive in for events at the Academy – concerts, lectures, parties. Sometimes you asked me to go with you. At one party to which you took me Brian and another young musician, long-faced Kurt, began to dream aloud about a brief trip to Sicily – to find a little sun, to thaw their frozen fingers. Playfully they invited us to join them, and in the spirit of play we 'planned' the trip. I think it was this bit of fancy that gave us the idea later of heading for Sicily by ourselves.

After the party you told me, '*You* really *should* head into the sun, after your back is fixed.'

I ventured, 'You wouldn't come too, would you?'

But you just smiled.

It was a solo trip to Greece you were recommending at the time. You brought me a copy of Henry Miller's *Colossus of Maroussi*, to tempt me. You also brought me a little electric heater – to make a difference in the meantime. 'You can't live like this!' you'd complained about my room; 'I can see my breath in here! And don't tell me again about your wonderful hot-water bottle.' You also told me that you'd be meeting me at the hospital when the day came.

Meanwhile, I moved in with Aaron and Peggy. I'd first made special arrangements at my hotel. The bellboy had agreed that, if I felt too rotten to go out for meals, he'd fetch me trays from a nearby restaurant. 'Of course, of course! Food, flowers, medicines – any errand that you wish!' The man at the desk was enthusiastic, too. 'Have no worries. You'll be safe with us. We'll rename ourselves: l'Ospedale Del Sole.' But then Aaron and Peggy dropped by and told me it was nonsense. I should move in with them till I was OK again. He put his hand very lightly on my shoulder: 'We want to take care of you.' I can remember that brotherly touch still.

And I wanted to be taken care of, of course. But I wasn't sure that I should want this. I had, in fact, assured myself so firmly that it was good for me to be handling this alone that I said no. 'Anyway, come and see where we live now', Aaron said.

They lived in a small house on the outskirts of the city – a house in the landlady's backyard, in her garden: studio, bedroom, kitchen. There was room for me, they insisted, because 'Look' – they had a large bed in the studio and already preferred sleeping there. It was a pleasant little house. The garden had a lovely scent, for the landlady grew lots of herbs. Sun poured in at the window of the tiny bedroom they said should be mine. And if I could help a little with the rent – it would actually be a help to *them*, they argued. Before the day was out, I said yes – packed up my few belongings and moved in.

And I soon wished I hadn't – as soon as we'd said 'Good night'. Mocking word. My mattress was an ancient one, and its twisted springs jabbed my body all that good night long – whichever way I'd turn. At breakfast I told my friends that I had better return to my hotel. Aaron hurried across the way to ask the landlady if she hadn't a newer mattress. But she hadn't. Then one of us had the idea that perhaps – just perhaps – the management at my hotel would have an extra mattress they'd be willing to loan. And we headed for town. And they had and they would! (I thank them again.) 'This way you won't have left us', said the manager. We fitted the mattress into the back of a carozza and brought it home. 'Wonderful sleep' my next day's notes rejoice.

Dr Jeans had a hectic schedule, and postponed the day of the operation several times. I spent my days of waiting lazily. Often just sitting in the garden – watching the cats climbing among the padrone's vines; watching the midges bouncing in the air; watching the life of the street. My notes tell me, 'Write of that little girl in her jonquil dress of crepe paper.' But I can't any longer remember the little girl. My notes tell me, 'Write of the strange barricaded room of the padrone.' I can dimly remember the padrone's room. She had collected so much old furniture in there that she could hardly move around. She collected facts about her neighbours, too. I remember one day when Aaron and Peggy were out, seeing her head suddenly sticking in the window, peering about. She had assumed that I was out, too. 'I thought I smelled smoke', she lied calmly.

Peggy was upset when I reported this, turned to Aaron with a glance of alarm. 'It doesn't mean anything', he said quickly. 'She's just a bored old woman.' They hadn't yet told me Peggy's story, and I thought her agitation peculiar. But a day or two later they told me. I walked into the kitchen to see her drop a letter from her hand and fling herself against Aaron's chest, uttering trembling cries. I left the room, but they called me back in to explain. The letter, from a friend reported that the young Frenchman's car had just blown up. He had been hoarding dynamite in it, which had been accidentally set off. Luckily, no one was hurt. 'It was meant for me! It was meant for me!' she kept repeating, in a whispery voice. Aaron soothed her: 'He's not going to find you!'

When Peggy left the house on some errand, Aaron told me gravely: 'The young man was a virgin. She awakened his sexuality, you see.' I can remember listening very gravely to his very grave words. It was clear that he would do his uttermost to protect Peggy from this young man. It was also clear that he felt for the young man a deep sympathy. At the time, this didn't shock me. Instead, his words produced in me a kind of awe. And mingled with my alarm for Peggy, I felt a vague shame for her.

It was like the shame I felt for myself a few days later – when the mail brought a message for *me*. I'd had my operation and was resting back at the little house, when Aaron brought in a package my mother had sent – forwarded by the Sole. She had written me to expect it: some warm woollen underpants. For Reba had reported to her that my room at the hotel was cold. As I unwrapped the package, a slip of paper fell out: 'Hi, Barb – I'd like to yank these off you!' Some postal worker had added his holiday greetings. Today I would feel rage. But then I felt bewilderment and dread and shame. My body, after lying on the operating table, felt like not quite my own body. Now it felt more alien still, and more sore. I think I showed the slip to Aaron but not to Peggy. He shook his head and patted my shoulder: 'They can't help themselves.' But when you visited and I showed it to you, you crumpled the paper in your hand, your face twisted in outrage, and I felt suddenly all right.

The morning of the operation you had been waiting at the door of the hospital with a large bunch of roses in your hands. When I looked at your face, *you* looked rather pale and haggard to me, though carefully smiling. 'Are *you* OK?' I asked. 'Of course', you said.

That morning had its comical moments. I was kept waiting for a very long time. You sat with me, keeping up a conversation – or rather, a wonderfully inventive monologue. And I kept burying my face in the roses, to breathe their reassuring fragrance. Then a nun came to take me to a little room where I was to change into hospital clothes. But no one brought me these clothes. Another nun – a very young one – arrived and told me just to follow her as I was. She brought me to the operating room – where the doctor looked at me in astonishment and asked the nun why I was still in street clothes. The flustered sister went running off, saying that she'd try to find the right things for me – 'Oh Dio!' I ran down the stairs to the little room again. And, dressed at last correctly, in large white pyjamas, ran back up the stairs as fast as I could, and climbed on to the operating table.

The doctor laid a gentle hand on me. She told me to lie on my side with one knee pulled up high. The little nun tied my hands and arranged a kind of tent over my head – so that I could do no evil and see no evil. I was given a local anaesthetic. A strange faraway pluck-plucking at me began. It was a blessing not to feel pain as the doctor began to cut. But to feel that far away from my body was disturbing. And the position in which I lay was putting its strain on me. After a while she told me that she wasn't going to have to remove my tail bone; she'd be able to manipulate it back into place. That was good news. But now I began to feel what she was doing in spite of the anaesthetic and to utter some grunts and groans which I couldn't help. (Each time she would ask sadly, 'Am I hurting you?') I began to feel that this would just go on and on. 'Something that happens to time', my notes comment. Yes, time seemed to stop being time and to become eternity. I began to say Nell's name, and Ben's, over and over to myself for comfort. But at last I felt stitches being taken. And then the final stitch. And I was bandaged. The little nun removed the covering from my head – and, to my surprise, gave me a friendly little slap on the behind. The doctor helped me off the table. I apologised to her for doing so much groaning, but she told me, 'You were fine; it's a very painful operation.' At which I felt a rush of relief. She looked at me intently. 'Are you all right?' The little nun ran off to search for my shoes, which she'd put she couldn't quite remember where. And I was allowed to walk away – back to the dressing room, and then to the room where you, blessedly, waited. 'Look at you!' you hailed me. 'You can walk!'

I reclaimed my roses from you. You found a cab, and rode back home with me. After you'd left, I lay on my bed feeling surprised at how composed I seemed to be. It wasn't till the middle of the afternoon that I felt suddenly demoralised. I began to relive in imagination all I had tried not to experience as it was happening that morning. I lay again on the table with my head covered and my hands tied and my body plucked at. And time again refused to move. I turned my head to the wall, whispering Nell's name and Ben's again, and cried hard.

I had an appointment with the doctor to have my dressing changed. Again you insisted on going with me. And again when I looked at you, you seemed to me strangely haggard yourself. Then you admitted that you had been feeling poorly for days, and I persuaded you to have the doctor see you. So you took your turn. And you came out with a luminous grin on your face. 'I've been pretty sick!' you announced – as though you'd been telling me that you'd been granted an award. 'I've had virus pneumonia!' you said. And then you admitted to me: 'I'd been afraid I was losing my nerve – that it was some sort of psychic depression.' Again you grinned at me.

'Perhaps we should *both* go some place in the sun', I said.

'Perhaps', you nodded.

The next day when you came for a vist – bringing Kurt – I made the suggestion again. I think I now suggested the south of Spain. But 'I can't go', you said that day, quite firmly. When Kurt left the room for a moment, you said to me quickly, 'I've had a strange letter.' I looked at you, waiting for you to say more, but that was all you would say. I was to learn later of course. You had had a proposal of marriage.

You called the next morning to say you were taking a very quick trip alone to Capri. You said, 'I just need a few days of sun. But I'll be back before you're ready to start out somewhere. Don't go before I get back. I'll see you off.' Your voice vibrated with a false cheeriness. I wished that I knew what was really happening with you.

I spent the next days just lying about, low in spirits. I'd written Nell and Ben about the operation and a cable from them arrived – signed 'Nan'. I wondered why Pete didn't write. A letter came from my agent, telling me of another rejection for my book. I was getting used to these letters. And then a letter came from my mother, telling me that Ned, who'd left with Diane for a Marine camp, and had expected to spend he didn't know how many weeks in further training, had suddenly been ordered to Korea. Into battle. The tears I wept now felt to me like the tears of a mad woman. I had persuaded myself that this war must be necessary. That is, I thought I had persuaded myself. I could speak of this persuasion glibly enough. But some part of me had never been persuaded. This part of me received the letter now and shrieked: 'Why have they taken him? What is it all about?' And now my body did really feel under assault. It felt snatched apart. Ned is nine years my junior, as you know, and when he was little, I had taken delight in mothering him – cuddled him often in my bed or on my lap while we whispered together an endless and delicious nonsense. Even today I can remember the sweet smell of the nape of his neck – like the smell of newly baked bread. Now I felt that child body snatched from my body. And without reason. There was no longer reason in which I could believe. And I thought of Diane, of course.

Aaron heard me weeping and came in, and I showed him the letter and he sat with his arms around me. He didn't have to say anything. He had argued steadily against the war – any and all wars. He was going to refuse to be drafted.

When I told *you*, upon your return, your eyes blazed with anger. 'Hateful! It's hateful! And there's that poor girl. What is she going to do now?' Diane had returned to my parents' house.

You didn't look rested. Your face was lined and taut. I stared at you. I had met you in town – for tea. Our tea time stretched to nightfall. You told me finally about the proposal of marriage you had received. Your suitor was a young American you had met here in Rome – who had taken you out a number of times; had driven out to Anticoli to visit then had flown off home; but suddenly had written this bold letter.

'Do you love him?' I asked.

'I don't really know him', you told me.

I stared at you.

'But perhaps the time has come', you muttered. You said, 'He's very determined.'

I had met him once, myself, at the Academy. In fact he had taken me to the opera one night. He was a bright young man with very good manners, black-eyed, intense. I can't remember his profession. But I remember he was well-to-do. I didn't know what to say.

You mumbled suddenly, 'I guess I'm having a nervous breakdown.' And then laughed loudly – in scorn. In scorn for that condition.

'One thing I do know', I told you. 'You're still not recovered from your bout of pneumonia. So how can you think straight?

Why don't we both go to Sicily?'

You sat there for a few minutes silently and then you nodded. Your face seemed to smoothe in relief. 'Yes, you're right,' you said, 'I'm exhausted. All right. I'll look after you and you'll look after me.' You reached out and took my hand, and we sat holding hands as the day faded.

10

The train we took south left early in the morning. We both dozed groggily as far as Naples, then began to revive and stare out at what we passed. The train was following the line of the sea. 'Gardens against the sea', my notes recall; 'Large olive trees. Oranges! A wonderful light.' A light reflected from the water – the sometimes blue, sometimes rosy water. We nodded at one another. The south, the south.

A little later, 'So beautiful,' you said, 'but most of the people down here are miserably poor.' The small fishing boats we saw offshore, putting down nets, had sails made of patch upon patch.

Once you said 'Look! Quickly!' I looked. And in the distance on the flat strand stood the ruins of a Greek temple – a jumble of later buildings nearby, and the sea shining beyond. Then the vision was gone. This was Paestum. You studied my face. 'So you liked that?' you asked; 'Yes, you'll find your way to Greece', you told me.

To cross to Sicily we had to dismount from the train and climb on to another, which was loaded in sections on to the boat, taken across, unloaded, hitched together again – a lengthy, complicated, noisy process which had you shaking your head. 'What boy genius figured all this out?' It was dark by the time the little bus that met the train climbed the steeply winding hill to Taormina. By then we were very tired. But the air blowing in the windows was a fragrant air. 'Balmy – balm', you sighed. I can remember that we began to grin at one another, going up the hill. The hotel we had chosen, The Bristol, stood near the top – and at the sight of it we grinned more widely. It looked like a skinny cardboard castle that a child might have built. With turrets along the top. 'Safe at last', we agreed.

They gave us a large simple airy room with twin beds. We climbed into those beds early. And you must have fallen asleep almost at once. I lay remembering some of the route we had travelled and then began to hear the sounds of what is too lightly called love-making in the room next to ours. The walls were thin. The loud-breathing man sounded enthusiastic, but from the woman came the muffled singsong repeated pleading cry: 'Mimi, mimi!' And again: 'Mimi, mimi!' (Which means 'no! no!' an Italian friend would explain to me one day.)

I asked you in the morning whether you'd heard any of this. You hadn't. You had been sound asleep. But the next night when the pleading cries began again, you were awake and – to my astonishment – leapt out of your bed and ran to pound on the wall between the rooms. There was abrupt silence. And then, after a little while, the low murmur of voices. The next night, not even murmuring could be heard. The couple had left the hotel or changed rooms. You and I never spoke again about it. Back in those days, one didn't speak as easily of such things. At any rate, I think you granted the poor woman one good night's rest.

In the mornings, our room was aglow with sunlight. French doors opened on to a balcony from which we could look down at the sea. When we opened these doors wide, we let in the sun in a flood. The beach was a steep climb which we didn't yet feel like making; but our room was our beach. We spread out towels on the floor and bathed in the sun right there. Talking very little. Just taking our ease now, together. Down the hall was a fine bathroom with a large tub and plentiful hot running water. Back in Rome I washed at the handbasin in my room. In Anticoli you had to pour water into a tin tub. Now we both soaked at length – then stretched out, slack-limbed, on our sunny floor. 'Like a couple of cats', you murmured. Luxuriating.

Midday we'd wander slow-motion the short distance to the centre of the town, and have lunch outside at one of its several cafés, lazily staring about us – staring, say my notes, 'into the bright white sun'. That first day, there appeared out of the glare a wiry figure with waggling dark eyebrows who pointed a finger at me: 'I know you!' Sasha it was – an actor who had been part of the theatre group I helped direct the first two summers I was out of college. And what was I doing here? And what was *he* doing here? In reply, he stood and, gesturing, treated us to a monologue about his life in the theatre over the past ten years. He had said goodbye to the States – a hopeless country – and now considered himself a

European. I glanced at you as he talked on and on, so sure we wanted to hear it all, and it seemed to me you were lightly sketching his portrait in your mind. A good way to sit out a non-stop talker. But he did stop at last, for someone waited for him somewhere. Off he sped, first quickly combing his hair.

Slow-motion we explored the little town; then 'Let's go back and nap', you suggested. And we napped away the afternoon. Rose for early dinner in the hotel's almost empty dining-room. Went early back to bed. And woke to lie all morning in the sun again. Side by side. Shy of being quite naked, but almost naked. Half awake, half asleep. The sea murmuring in the near distance.

Our second day, a light frisky wind was blowing. In the piazza where we had lunch at a table under a tree, children were throwing palm fronds up into the air to see how far they would blow. But under our large tree it was calm. We ate, as we had walked, slow-motion. 'One is supposed to chew each bite fifty times', you said. 'Down here, I feel I have the time.' And then, 'Another nap?' you asked, 'after all this exercise?' 'Another nap', I agreed.

As we woke mid-afternoon, you asked, 'Should we or should we not go to see Dewey Otls?' You'd learned that Dewey, whom you had met a number of times back in the States – and I had met him once – was living in a rented villa on the outskirts of town, working on a new novel. 'I'll drop him a note and leave it up to him', you decided. But as we walked toward the post office, Dewey himself, just emerging from that building, greeted you with joy – in his high child's voice, or would you say old crone's voice? A small figure, in shorts and sandals and a pretty shirt, with a long light-coloured scarf wrapped round his shoulders as if by some michievous hand, wound in an odd tangle.

'Lottie! Lottie! Is it really you?'

'Well, it's almost really me', you told him.

At which he laughed in delight – an owl's hoot. And then recognised me, too, to my surprise. And lowering his chin, looked out at us from under his blond brows, scanning us carefully; then asked us to tea the next day; told us how to find his house, and darted off – raising one hand as he went, as if to bless us as well as wave bye bye.

That evening, two Sicilians dining at our hotel asked us whether we wouldn't go dancing with them. We told them we were too weary, thank you. 'But a nice weariness it begins to be', you said to

113

me as we climbed the stairs to our room.

We stood then for a little while on our balcony, looking down at the shadowy quietly-moving sea.

The next afternoon, we made our way to Dewey's house – down through a grove at the edge of town, following a twisting sloping path that goats used, too. We encountered a number of the small animals, and you stopped each time and stared at them hard, as if to memorise their delicate knees, their mobile ears. We also met on the path an old woman in black, with hair in disarray and muttering to herself. 'My landlady', Dewey told us. 'A terror and a dear.'

He came out at our knock and first showed us the garden – where many plants were in flower, though it was February still. The sea was very close. And yes, it was the colour of wine, we agreed. As Homer said. But not 'wine-*dark*' this day, but wine-ruddy; it was streaked with the colour of rosé. There were almond trees about the house, blooming. You stared at them, too, with your wonderful fierce squint.

Dewey had bought a fruit cake for our tea. He served us at a table in the garden. And was full of questions. But all I remember with any certainty about our conversation is one remark he suddenly made to me. He leaned forward and said 'I miss seeing your essays about the movies in *Partisan Review*. Are you writing for some other journal now?' I remember because my feelings took me so by surprise. I had been receiving news from my agent of repeated rejections of the book into which I had expanded those essays. And each time another 'No' had come, I'd stood back from myself to study how I took the blow. Each time I decided: 'Ah, I take it well; in fact, I think it is making me stronger.' But now as he spoke his words of affirmation, I felt confidence begin to circulate again in my veins, and at its revival, I recognised for the first time that it had been taken from me.

As we climbed slowly back up the path to town. I described to you the effect his words had had on me. I'd felt it in my body, I told you. And it was like feeling my blood begin to circle, after being cold and still. You nodded gravely. 'Yes, I could see you brighten up.' You added after a moment, 'But they can't ever kill us off completely, can they?'

Then we stopped to let some goats go by – their large eyes looking into ours, their ears swivelling to one point of the compass and then to another.

You wanted to buy some postcards in town, so we stopped to make that purchase, and in the shop fell into casual conversation with a lean-cheeked young man who was looking through postcards too. He suggested tea together at the nearby bar. 'Why not?' you said. We'd had one tea, but another wouldn't hurt us.

So we joined Mario – his name was – for a pot of tea. He was from Chile, it turned out. A young businessman. With impeccable English. He was living in Rome, he told us – had a little house on the Appian Way; but had come here for a rest. He'd had his car driven down by a mechanic, and a good part of our tea hour he spent complaining about that young man, who had taken his time, and left a lady's dress in the car – then had the nerve to charge him for the further time it would take him to rest up in Rome from the tiring train trip back. Oh, the masters in this world had a much harder time of it than anyone allowed, you said with a smile. As a matter of fact, yes they did, he told you wearily. If he had a car, how would he like to take us on a little trip the next day, you were bold enough to ask. He looked surprised, but 'Good idea', he said. He'd like to look around, himself. Not too early in the day, you told him. For we were still lazily sunning in our room each morning.

So the next day he turned up in his comfortable Mercury and drove us off to some nearby towns. At one of these towns, one could climb to the ruins of a castle. We let Mario make the climb and stayed below; shopped for bread and wine and cheese and fish for a picnic; and gazed about us in the bright bright day. The light, this day, was so intense that nearby Mount Etna seemed a mirage, paper thin. And the sea, too, was sometimes so light-struck that it could seem to disintegrate before our eyes – turn to mere space. I remember one moment, as we stood gazing, in which the pink of the town's roofs, the pink of the sea, and the pink of the almond blossoms became one wavery blur. 'Oh pink, oh pink!' you sang.

Back in our own town again (dusk, and both sea and hills now a ruddy purple) Mario suggested we visit Taormina's castle, built by Saracens. You wanted your nap, but suggested that I go with him. So I did and was soon sorry. Once we were sitting up there on the ramparts, he first asked me why I wore such ugly stockings (I can't remember those stockings, but I must have liked them, myself); then he tried to kiss me. 'I don't kiss strangers', I told him. 'Then let's not be strangers any longer', he replied of course. And now I was tired, I said. And I asked could he drive me back to the hotel. He agreed promptly enough, but half way there, decided he wanted to read his newspaper; pulled over to the side of the road under a street light that had just been lit, and proceeded to do just that – reading even the comics. I was too weary to get out of his car and walk, so I sat waiting, astonished at him. 'I'm sorry, sweetie – is this boring for you?' he asked once, lightly; and turned another page. Until the paper bored *him* and he took me on home. 'A punishment of course, for your not giving him a kiss', you said, when I told my story. I'm not sure that this had dawned on me, clear as it is to me now. 'We had a beautiful ride, though, didn't we?' you said.

After dinner we both felt, for the first time, lively enough to take a stroll. We took slow steps, staring up at where the delicate colours of the stars shone. You said, 'I think there are more stars here than anywhere.' We walked among almond trees, and staring up into their branches, you said – I can remember – 'The blossoms are stars, too.' We stood where we were, then. 'And smell the night, and smell it!' we said. Though this was many years ago, I can remember still how your face looked – in that starlight, blossom-light. Your eyes were very wide and you looked as though you were listening, puzzled and yet contented, to some faraway unfamiliar sound.

Then you said suddenly, 'We should go see a movie.' So we walked up into town where a movie called *Blue Skies* was showing; and watched a little bit of it. Half way through, you said, 'This is silly, isn't it? Let's go back home and get another good night's sleep.' So we walked back home together through the soft night.

The next day was to be your last day in Taormina. You'd decided that you were better enough to get back to work. Of course I tried to persuade you to stay on, but you knew your mind.

Mario had said he would call in the morning: perhaps we should take another drive. But he didn't call, and we were both glad. We decided to go to the beach at the foot of our hill. After lunch we took a cab there. And sitting on the sand – after a little wading, and a little watching of some fishermen who were mending lobster pots – we finally talked – do you remember? Why had we waited this many days to have that talk? Well – we'd been resting; we'd been taking time out. But now that luxury was ending. You talked about Leonard. And I talked about Pete. You had a way and still

116

have, during such exchanges, of managing to ask more questions than you answer, and in the end I'd told you considerably more about myself than you told me about you. But our stories were comparable. Here we were both past our thirty-third birthdays, and still unmarried. Here were two men who had turned in our direction – though Leonard was taking a good deal more initiative than Pete. And the question we were both very obviously asking *ourselves* was: Hasn't the time come to accept what we are all taught is women's natural fate?

I assumed as we talked that you knew that Nell and I had been lovers. But we didn't speak of this. And we didn't speak of the close bond you obviously felt with your stepfather, Seth – which had, I guessed, kept you living, working, still at home, in the studio he'd long ago helped you set up next his own – though you had moved into your own place once or twice and went off rather often on trips like the present one. I'd returned to my parents' home at intervals, myself. Neither of us had found making our own living easy. But we didn't speak of our lives before the present. As I've said, we each knew well enough what almost anybody would say was the reasonable step for us to be taking now. And what we were doing was to look at this prospect together – to hold it up before us and ask: What do you think? What do I think? Would this be possible? I don't remember much of what you told me about Leonard. I remember only your musing, anxious face, your hushed voice – your staring at the question we had raised. After you had drawn me out a bit about Pete, you said suddenly very tenderly and with a lilt of hopefulness in your voice: 'I think you're in love with him.' The statement surprised me. But something about the sweetness with which you said it made me suddenly wonder: Could you be right? Could it be so? We sat without saying anything for a while.

We had told Dewey we'd meet him for drinks, and asked the cab driver who'd brought us here to pick us up at a certain time. But he didn't turn up, and after waiting a while we decided we could climb the very steep steps that led up the cliff. A young fisherman sold us, first, some sea urchins – ricci – freshly caught, and showed us how to suck the sweet meat from the spiny shell. It was my first experience of that salty-sweet exotic taste, and I think yours, too. I taste it again, as I remember. As we climbed the stairs, pausing often to rest, another young Sicilian joined us – full of questions and of talk. Cosimo. Learning that I was a writer, 'I scribe a bit, too', he announced. And he sang us some songs he had invented – mocking songs, which mocked especially some of the typical characters who'd turn up in Taormina. Dewey was suddenly named among these. We were on our way to see Dewey, you informed him. 'He won't mind if you don't turn up', he said – and rolled his eyes. We didn't reply. He sang us to the top of the long flight of steps.

We were both tired after that climb. Back in our room again, you stretched out on your bed to rest a little. I started to do the same, then sat on the edge of your bed for a moment, next to you. For I had to say: 'What I really feel about Pete I'm not sure that I know. But one thing I do know: I love *you*.' You stretched out your arms to me, smiling. I leaned into your arms and kissed you on the mouth. And you returned the kiss warmly. A sisterly kiss, of course, we understood it to be.

We were both sweating still from mounting all those stairs (I can remember still how your hair lay damply against your cheeks) and I was surprised as I bent toward you to breathe the sweet warm scent of your skin. We had hugged before this, and I had caught your scent. But I had never before smelled this deep smell of you. It was like breathing your very essence, and it threw me into a reverie, the kind of reverie that has no words – the kind of reverie one falls into when lying, eyes shut, in a summer garden, drowned in sun, when the humming of bees and the humming of one's own blood become sounds one can't distinguish and one is filled with wonder.

I went to my own bed and stretched out. And we both lay resting for a while – neither of us speaking. I didn't know what to say to my own self. You may find it strange, but I still didn't tell myself that I had fallen in love with you.

After a time we washed and dressed and made our way into town. Dewey was late, but Mario came strolling along and sat down with us at our café table. When you told him that we were waiting for Dewey, he was eager to meet him – though what he really wanted, he said, was to see what the place he lived in looked like. You bantered with him as only you can banter, and finally got rid of him by suggesting that he might like to take us somewhere nice for dinner. Mario had wealth, we assumed, but was clearly stingy with it. He decided that he had telephone calls to make. But he did stay long enough to meet Dewey.

Dewey was late, he explained, because troubling letters had arrived in the mail that he'd had to think about. Someone was feuding with him, he said, and then laughed merrily. He was distressed to hear that you planned to leave the next day, and did his best to dissuade you. Then – at your questioning – he told us a little about the feud.

You and I had a quiet dinner alone at our hotel. We had a last quiet stroll among the almond trees. Early the next morning I took a cab with you to the station. You suggested a farewell glass of wine. No matter the hour. We toasted each other. And – you were gone.

I decided to walk back up the hill to the hotel. And as I walked I began to work again on an old poem I had once started. 'Love shakes me', the poem began. 'Love has its hand upon me', the second line formed in my brain. Did I know at last that I was in love with you? No, I didn't know it yet. I was simply writing a poem about love.

As I was walking along in the very bright day, a big car slowed to a stop beside me. And there was Mario in his Mercury – with two passengers, a couple from Minnesota he'd befriended – and they were heading up Etna. Would I like to see the volcano?

I would, even in the middle of a struggle with a poem. So I hopped into the back seat and, happy to be alone back there, stared out – as we climbed past the sooty towns that lay on the mountain's flank. And past level after level of terraced vineyards, the terracing carefully built of volcanic stone. A queer sulphurous smell hung in the air. What was the taste of wine from these grapes, I wondered. And what was the taste of life here on this mountain side? The people were very poor indeed. I marvelled at how one family managed to travel on a single bicycle: father pedalling, a child on the handlebars, another child tucked between the father and the mother who sat behind him, a third – the baby – balanced on the mother's hip!

A snow line began – a small sooty snowman marking the place. And across the snow, we began to see the cold grey nubbly vomit of lava flow. And I began to shiver. I had dressed that morning in shorts and shirt and hopped into the car without thinking that the drive would mean a climb into different weather. Mario had left an extra jacket in the back seat and I huddled into that. I was to shiver for a long time. When we arrived at the parking lot for tourists near the top, Mario slipped out of the car, saying he wanted to look about – and disappeared. The man and wife from Minnesota took a few photographs of one another, with the faintly smoking mountain top behind, but soon grumbled 'Enough!' and began to hop up and down – as I was doing – and slap their hands together to try to keep warm. Mario came strolling back at last. 'Let's get out of here!' we all chattered. And he drove us back down Etna.

Home again, I sat down at once to write you, giving you a comic report of our trip – and declaring I'd not hop into Mario's car again. And I continued to struggle with my poem. I wrote:

Love shakes me.
Love has its hand upon me and with
Obstinate motions
Unmakes what I am.

The next day, too, I struggled with this poem – on a long walk during which I was distracted by the sight of warblers darting among the almond trees. I wrote:

Love shakes me.
Love has its hand upon me and with
Obstinate motions
Unmakes what I am.
It circles its seven times round me:
I am down.
Who says that love has gentle ways?

Dewey had asked me to come to dinner. And he mourned again that you hadn't stayed on. It was the first time I had met the man he lived with, Joel Kelly. I don't think you met him before you left: a shy intense man, a writer too. 'But we don't read each others' books', Dewey confided. 'This makes it much more possible to live together.' Joel went upstairs early, but Dewey and I talked on till midnight. I found myself very much at ease with him. A moment had occurred soon after dinner that gave birth to this ease. Dewey prepared the meal. Joel then made and served the coffee. The three of us were sitting round their fireplace (I made the small fire), and as Joel leaned forward to fill Dewey's cup, a loving look passed between them. I saw the look and it made me happy to see. Dewey, glancing up, saw that it did, and gleamed at me a very tender smile – a smile of welcome, of kinship. Yes, from that moment on I felt that we *were* somehow kin – no matter how very different we also are from one another.

For the almost three weeks more that I stayed on in Taormina, we saw each other at least briefly almost every day. He always headed for town in the late afternoon, to go to the post office. Then he would stop at one or another of the town's several cafés to have a drink. I would wander into town at about the same time, and either he'd find me and join me or I'd find him. Others would often find him, too, of course. Sometimes I'd walk him part way home – along the path the goats wandered; and sometimes he'd ask me to come the full distance and stay for dinner (a few times, perhaps, asked me when he hadn't really intended to). One evening, after Joel had climbed the stairs at his usual early hour, he suddenly asked me: 'Have you ever been desperately in love?' I told him I'd been *utterly* in love. And I spoke a little about Nell. 'And how did it end?' he asked. I told him about her marriage to my brother. He sat shaking his head. He told me, then, about a lost lover in his life; and told me of finding Joel. He had a recurrent nightmare now, he confided. In the dream, Joel stands on the deck of a ship, and the ship begins to drift from the dock on which he, Dewey, stands, and slowly the watery gap between them grows and grows. 'And I wake in anguish', he confided.

I encountered in Dewey, of course, several persons in one – the tender man who befriended me; and also the man who loved literary feuds (or was able to persuade himself that he did); who could say to me one day that the real fun to be had in giving parties was in choosing whom *not* to invite; who loved 'camp' and loved to play mischievous tricks. As a child, he told me, he had delighted in calling up stores, assuming the voice of an adult and putting in huge orders to be delivered to this neighbour or that, down the street – then peering out the window to watch the confusion of the person receiving the unwanted goods. Or calling some house and giving the maid the message that So-and-so would just love to come to dinner, and delighting in the imagined scenes of bewilderment caused by this news. And that child lived on in him. I was to hear him muse, one afternoon, over drinks, upon a whole series of pranks he'd like to play upon someone in town with whom he was annoyed. He could tell that I failed quite to enter into the spirit of this 'fun'; but in one of his other persons forgave me.

I finished my poem one day:

Love shakes me.
Love has its hand upon me and with
Obstinate motions
Unmakes what I am.
It circles its seven times round me:
I am down.
Who says that love has gentle ways?
Awakened out of all order,
I am fire air earth water!

Happy to have completed it, I decided to knock on Dewey's door, though it was early afternoon. He came out, looking rather dazed. He was reading, he told me, and it would be hard to put the book down. He was like an addict about his reading. But he gave me a long close stare – as though to make sure that all was well with me; and told me he'd see me later, in town.

I decided to climb a nearby hill to the ruins of Castel Mora, up above the small settlement on that hill's flank that bore the castle's name. I was getting my strength back and thought I'd test it. I didn't take the highroad, which wound round and about, but one of the several paths that climbed the hill more directly. I followed two boys riding on a slow donkey who, watching me begin to drag my feet, asked would *I* like to ride for a while. And then I gladly took a turn on its broad scuffed back – to a spot not far from the ruins. As I approached them I noticed a raven perched on the broken battlements. I sat at a distance and watched it for a while – watched it hop to the ground, waddle among the stones, then return to its parapet. I decided to see how close it would let me get to it – began to move, as one can, a careful inch, another inch, breathing very gently. To my surprise the big bird let me draw close and then still closer, and – holding my breath – I reached out my hand, just barely moving it, slow as slow, and – stroked the top of its glossy head. At which moment, as it looked me in the eye, the thought abruptly came to me that I had succeeded too easily. The bird must be a tame bird. Which was confirmed for me later, by one of the people who turned up at drinks time at our table. Yes, everybody fed this raven. The look it had given me had declared in effect: 'If I *chose* to be wild . . .' I wrote you this tale, too.

I took another path down the hill, the light beginning to fade now – or rather, the land beginning to darken, but the light still seeming to hang in the air like scattered dust that would take till the day's very end to settle. And round one bend of the path I came upon a slim little girl, in a ragged dress, a white headcloth on her head, neatly tied. And she asked me: 'Taormina?' I answered: 'Si' – yes. And she held out in her fist a scrunched bouquet of roses and small daffodils. 'Prendali' – take them. I smiled at her with a question, for I wasn't sure whether she meant that she wanted to sell them or to give them. Both, I guessed. So 'Quanto?' I asked. And she said 'Come vuole' – whatever you want. So I gave her I forget what, but it pleased her, and we said goodbyes, and I continued on down the sometimes zigzag rather rocky path – a flock of sheep scrambling below me, the bells round their necks shaking out an airy music. And then as I was turning a bend in the path, that curved me for a moment back along the mountain side, I heard a small cry in the air. From far up the hill, someone was calling: 'Hello – o – o!' – the sound very clear but very small. And I peered up and saw that it was the little girl, standing now in the upper window of one of the houses way up there -- waving. Yes, hello, little girl. I wrote you that night about her, too. I wrote: 'And hello to *you*, Lottie.'

You had told me that the town of Noto – beyond Syracuse – was said to be full of marvels, so I decided to take a couple of days off and go there. One morning I took an early train. It was crowded. A sailor rose and gave me his seat – introducing himself: Frederico. And as we passed through the beautiful countryside – orchards, farmland carefully irrigated – he very eagerly began to tell me about himself. He had just been released from the Navy after a two-and-a-half-year stint, and was going home – yes, to Noto. I wanted him to explain certain sights along the way. For example: What were those little piles of stones I kept seeing in the fields – one stone set very carefully on top of the other? He didn't seem to hear my question. An old man who shared the compartment with us spoke up: 'Fatto di Dio' – an act of God. And that's all that I ever learned about them. For Frederico had opened his wallet and wanted to show me photographs of all his relatives – as well as a photograph of Ingrid Bergman and one of Lana Turner. When we reached Noto, he wanted to take me home with him at once – to show *me* to his relatives. I suggested that the family might prefer to greet him first alone. So he named a hotel I could afford and said he'd meet me there, then, at tea time.

I began to roam the town. And you were right – to tell me I should come to stare here. It was a town that shone a beautiful pale orange; for most of the buildings were of that colour. And a town leafy along every street – its trees clipped carefully to spread their branches in particular shapes. There were many balconies on the houses, and as I began to look up at them, the most amazing sculptured faces looked back at me from under them. I had a camera with me and began to snap pictures. Where are those photographs now? I can't seem to find one of them. But some of the faces still do look at me in memory. Faces with tongues out, with cheeks puffed, with eyes rolling – faces, I noted in my journal, that reminded me of the faces my brother Ben used to love to make when we were children – to make at me or to make at himself in the mirror. To work what elemental magic? Sometimes half-bodies leaned out, high up, as I recall, near the eaves. Sometimes the sculpted figures were of lions or of horses – strangely contorted always, whatever they were. And above the highest of them the clouds moved – assuming their forever changing, sometimes mocking shapes. I stared and stared. And then began to realise that I was being stared at, myself. Not merely by the stone faces, but by nearly every townsperson who passed. Frederico would explain that few tourists came to Noto. In my memory, they approached to touch my camera, touch my clothes, but I don't say this in my notes; so it must be simply that they stared so hard I felt that they were touching me. I tried meeting their stares with smiles. The children would giggle, then, but the adults would just look very confused. They were of course confused above all by the fact that I was a woman travelling alone. 'What would you have done if you hadn't met *me*?' Frederico asked, when I found him again, back at my hotel, at tea time.

He took me first on his own tour of the town – showing me all the new construction, which was quite ugly, though I kept trying to explain that buildings with some history to them interested me more. He spoke no English, and having noted that my Italian was scanty, decided to simplify the information that he gave me as he showed me about. With a wave of the hand at a sculptured lion, he would tell me solemnly: 'Questo, leone' – This, a lion. Or, with a broader gesture: 'Questo, Noto.' That particular piece of information he kept repeating. I soon began to wish that I were still strolling the town on my own. And then he took me to show me to his family.

They sat round me in the small parlour, which was furnished in wicker, a very large radio featured and a very large electric clock, and on the walls chromos of Naples and Marseilles – for that was where his father and mother had taken their wedding trip, I was told. The father was an accountant; and that's what Frederico would now learn to be. His mother and sisters and several aunts seemed all to be teachers – 'maestre'. They studied me as though I were a difficult lesson. Their stares at first I felt as hostile. But I decided soon that no – like all the others, they were just deeply puzzled. Alone? I was travelling alone? And how much did the trip cost? Was my watch gold? (My watch, an inexpensive one, had a coppery tint to it.) They stared at my clothes. At my camera. Passed it round. And passed round my dictionary. When was I to be married, the mother asked. Frederico, during our giro, had asked would I like him to come to America, so I had thought it just as well to tell him that I had a fiancé. I forgot this for a moment, but recalled it just in time, and told them that a wedding day had yet to be set. How far had I gone in school? they asked. 'Colta', cultured, they nodded at one another. Then one of the sisters asked me would I sing an English song for them. At my request, she sang first. She sang 'Vien, Vien' – in Italian; and she sang 'Lili Marlene'. One of the aunts then sang two Sicilian songs. I sang 'Auld Lang Syne' – the first song I could think of the words to. And we began to smile at one another now – the music dissolving the awkwardness between us. The mother brought out the family photograph album, and began to share in this way a little of their life story. She handed me picture after picture. There was the town's big school, in one early picture, all the children out in the yard giving the Fascist salute. She handed me a snapshot of an American soldier who had become Frederico's friend during the war; a young soldier sitting at the wheel of a truck, smiling a boyish smile. And she turned it over, to show me that he had written something on the back. The smiling boyish man had written: 'This is for your sister. Tell her I'd like to shove it up her.'

I glanced in horror at Frederico – but he looked back at me blankly, and I decided that he really didn't understand what his friend had written. I wanted to scratch out the words. I wanted to tear up the picture. (And if it were today, I would.) But I didn't want to have to explain my action. The mother tucked the photo back in the album.

Someone asked could one of them use my camera to take a picture of all of us together. One of the sisters hurried off to remove the curlers from her hair. And then we should go, Frederico said. But I must come back in the morning, the mother insisted. There were other relatives who would want to meet me.

Frederico walked me to a small restaurant and sat with me while I ate – hunting through my dictionary for words with which to try to converse a little in English. He confused the word 'amor' with the word 'amaro' somehow, and began to mutter about growing bitter, when what he meant to be saying, I finally did figure out, was that he was falling in love. But I managed to turn the conversation to some other subject. Then he walked me to my hotel – crossing the town square on our way, lovely in the evening light, shadows of palm fronds fluttering against the orange buildings. And he returned home, to eat with his family.

I rose early in the morning, to wander again – and again drew a great deal of attention. Frederico came along and found me and, with an air of impatience, led me back to his house. And there once more I sat surrounded by his relatives – who kept arriving in new relays. It was clear that Frederico had brought me upon his mother's orders. He kept muttering, 'Andiamo', Let's go. But his mother would say each time, 'Aspetti', Wait. She served me white wine, now, with biscuits to dip in it. The father kept strolling in and out of the room, and the brother, in his undershirt, strolled in and out, too, but each woman who joined the group sat concentrated entirely upon me. One of the aunts recalled our singing the day before and asked couldn't we sing again. And once more our singing put us at ease with one another. One sister asked eagerly whether, if she came to America, I thought she would be able to find a job teaching Italian. I wasn't sure how to advise her. Another sister asked me in a low voice whether I thought that in America they would know how to treat her skin condition. She had a bad rash on her face and neck. The mother wrote down their address and said I must write them. Before I left, she gave me a violet, which she had drenched in very sweet perfume. And the sister who was worried about her rash gave me a carnation. 'You have made us very happy', the mother told me – hugging me to her.

I kept musing about her words, as the afternoon train bore me away. How exactly had I made them happy? Was it simply that I did travel alone – though a woman – and now they could, if only in fancy, travel a little with me?

On the way home I paid a certain tax for this freedom I enjoyed. I stopped off in Syracuse for a few hours to stare at that town, too – at its ancient Greek theatre, its baroque palaces. Waiting then at the station for my train to Taormina, I sat down to have a hot chocolate and a middle-aged Sicilian with amber eyes sat with me and insisted on making the drink his treat. He then walked the platform with me, trying to persuade me to return home not by the train but on his motorbike. He tried to kiss me as I mounted the train, saying my 'No thank you's, and did succeed in grabbing and kissing one of my hands. I had thought I was climbing on to the third class carriage, but I'd climbed on to the wrong one, in my haste, so I had to get off again for a moment – at which he rushed forward, grinning: he thought I'd decided to rejoin him after all. When I hopped back on to the next car, he hopped on right after me, to my astonishment, beckoning for me to stay, and kissing the air – but hopped off again just before the train pulled out.

And I had to deal with another like him before the day ended. As I was walking from the home station to my hotel, a man on a Vespa pulled up next to me to ask how to find a certain street which I just happened to know. He didn't seem able to understand the directions I was giving, and asked would I ride there with him. So as it was on my way, I climbed – without a thought – on to the back seat of the scooter. Even as we sped away, he began to try to fondle me, one hand behind his back. The street he had asked for was nearby, luckily. I took my angry leave of him and he, too, stood kissing the air as he stared after me.

Dewey wanted to hear every detail about my trip. And he decided that he and I and three friends from town should make a day's trip to Catania – 'richest city in southern Italy'. A car was borrowed and we set off together very early one morning. I remember little about the two men who came with us. One of them (my notes do remind me) had funny little ears that curled forward. The third friend I remember much more clearly: Laura, an amiable dark-eyed woman I had met several times with Dewey at the drinks hour; an illustrator who made delicate, spirited drawings. I liked her and felt she liked me, but we were shy with one another. (I have wondered since: were we shy because she too was a lesbian and uneasy about the fact?)

Catania was, yes, rich and also rather ugly. But very lively – with great numbers of people hurrying about in all directions. Everybody in our party had special shopping they wanted to do here. Dewey wanted to shop for brown velveteen for a smoking jacket, and I went along with him. He persuaded me to buy some of the same thick beautiful stuff, myself. As we were choosing it, he asked me why I didn't have my hair dyed red, and told me of having his dyed silver once. Suddenly he gave me a little hug and a tender kiss, to my surprise.

After lunch with the others, he asked me to join him in a carozza ride. We drove through the Bellini Gardens, where the lawns were cut to form shapes from Italian operas – elephants for *Aida*, swans for *Norma*. I had brought my camera, and sat crouched forward, trying to catch the best glimpses. After too long a while, I noticed that Dewey was looking a little sulky. I realized with a pang that he had been feeling affectionate and wanted this ride to be a sharing of feelings. There was I, just looking about for good camera shots.

On the way to meet the others again, we stopped at a food store, and I bought him strawberry marmalade, which I knew he loved – but it was poor amends. Most of the way home he fantasised more pranks to be played upon acquaintances in town. And the two other men joined in the game with glee. One of them should tell Carlo that he'd seen Elinor at the doctor's office, and she had blushed deeply. Or – one of them should tell Paulo that they had seen Sheila. She hadn't left Sicily after all; they had seen her with another man. Count Roccafurgalo, Dewey decided his name could be. And on and on and on – while Laura and I sat silently, faintly smiling at one another now and then.

'Went to bed early', my journal says. 'Why am I so depressed? Dewey's moodiness? No letter?'

I meant by 'no letter', no letter from Nell. You had by now written twice – to say you were at work again, to thank me for 'making' you take the trip south. 'It brought me back to life.' (Curiously, your letter didn't mention Leonard.) But Nell had not written in many weeks. She and my brother had sent a loving cable after I'd written about the operation. But with the exception of that cable, she'd sent no word since she'd written two letters in quick succession about the birth of her daughter. Before Nan's birth, she had written frequently; followed my every move about the continent – with questions, comments, and endearments. Many days ago I had written her at length about Pete. I'd written, 'For the first time I can begin to conceive of marrying someone whom I do not love as I love you.' I think that – in spite of my reasoning self – in spite of her marriage to my brother – in spite even of the child she had now borne – some stubborn part of me half-hoped she would write back: 'Oh don't, please, think of making such a move. For *our* lives are knit together still.' But in all these weeks no letter had come from her at all.

A few days later the letter was there, at the hotel desk at the morning's end – the familiar wide-looped handwriting, the familiar blue envelope. I carried it back to my room and lay down on my bed to read it, feeling suddenly frail. Nell did write, 'Write me more of Pete. You must be loved, and if you embarked on an unloving life, I should be sick indeed' – adding: 'If you were happy, I too would be.' She didn't of course write that she felt she and I were still bound in a kind of marriage. Most of the letter was an apology for not having written sooner. The baby had had a series of ailments, and that had kept her anxious and distracted. 'Caring wholly for a baby is a strange thing,' she wrote, 'with enormous burdens of care and responsibility and cherishing and absolutely no ego – so it is a draining thing too the way no other connections are. I've even become a cry baby. I just cry instead of react, and each time I cry I surprise myself and yet I can't stop – and can't wholly tell why.'

I remember that I read and then reread the letter. I remember that I told myself: 'Try now to really read what it says – and what it doesn't say.' I walked up into the town and had lunch at one of the small outdoor restaurants, and then sat on; took the letter out of my pocket and read it still another time. A fine fine extraordinary rain began to fall out of a sky clear pale blue – the drops so small and light and scarce that their delicate touch was like a caress. Some young boys were playing a variation of marbles nearby, with coins. One would cast out his coin, the others would try to flick theirs as close as they could to his without touching it. When the rain began, they paused in the game and all turned up their faces. Now a playful wind began to blow. It flapped the tablecloths on all the small tables. I was having coffee, and it blew the sugar off my spoon. I sat on but then began to feel a little chilled and returned to the hotel – the words of Nell's letter still touching me like the delicate rain, still blowing against me like the brusque wind.

Before it was quite drinks time I decided to visit Dewey. Walking down the path to his house I could see the sea far off – like the sky, clear blue today. A bright rainbow flung its arc there. I stopped to stare.

Dewey answered the door with a smile, peered at me and asked me up to his room. He had a small fire going, and drew up two chairs to it. Again he peered at me, his smile very subtle. He looked to me in that moment like a wise old crone, rather than a man; and I decided to reveal my heart to him. I told him I'd just heard from Nell. I began to speak about the unreasonable hopes to which I had been clinging, all these months.

He listened in utter quiet – slowly nodding his head.

'Yes,' he said finally, 'I could sense that a little when you spoke of her before.' And then he said, 'I'd like to shake you.' And at my questioning look, 'I'd like to shake you out of that dependency.' He said, 'You can go anywhere you want in your life, you know. Joel said that about you the first night he met you. He said that you were like somebody's dream of the beloved.'

'Joel said that?' In spite of myself, his words thrilled me of course. But I shook my head. I was not able to think of myself in that way.

He chided me, 'It's crazy to feel that you must cling to this one person.'

I did really know that this was so, I told him. And then I told him that the direction I had been feeling it was perhaps time for me to move in was marriage, and I spoke a little about Pete.

He was staring at me, his eyes growing round. 'Ridiculous!' he pronounced. 'Marriage! For you! Ridiculous!' And he began to tell me of one person after another he had known, or known of, who was really homosexual but had tried marriage – with life consequences that were miserable, and absurd. And this Pete Bannigan – what made me think I had even half a chance of being happy with him? Our ages were so different. Our outlooks, from what little I'd told him, so very different.

True, I admitted. And I sat musing – while he stared at me, waiting, cannily, for me to catch up with my own thoughts.

It was strange, I said finally. I knew that I could make a very foolish union with a man. Whereas I *couldn't* make a foolish union with a woman. I had sometimes felt myself attracted to women whose ways were incompatible with mine, but I'd never dream of actually joining my life to any one of them.

'Aha', he said. 'That's because your relation to women is serious, and the other relation is not.'

Well, I tried to argue, the one relation was known to me, the other was unknown. He just looked at me – again holding his tongue.

I mused: The kind of knowledge of my heart that I had was strange. Just for example, I told him: I knew a woman with whom I would never let myself fall in love because I knew so well that it was impossible to hope she could return my love. But if I thought it *were* possible, I'd fall in love with her in a minute. And though I couldn't predict the shape of a life we might make together, I knew without question that I'd want to live it, whatever shape it took. Whereas if I married Pete I did know I'd be walking into the marriage blind.

'You're talking about Lottie, of course', he startled me by stating at once. 'I thought at first when I saw you together here that you *were* lovers. Not for any coarse reason', he added quickly. 'But then I decided that it wasn't so.' He looked at me, shaking his head. And then I heard him say, very quietly, 'But of course it's *not* impossible.'

'But of course it's *not* impossible.'

'Of course it's *not* impossible.'

I kept hearing these words over and over. I can hear them now again – said so quietly. Dropped into my life like the very small drops a chemist adds to some mixture that will now be utterly changed by those small drops.

'She could love you easily,' he was saying, 'and be very happy with you.'

Could easily.

I spoke my unbelief: 'Oh, I don't think she could love a woman.'

He folded his hands. He smiled his crone's smile. 'You can't fool your uncle Dewey.'

He jumped up. He said, 'I have a letter I should get into the mail.' He snuffed the fire, and we headed together back up the path to town.

Magical path. My feet wanted to leap. My throat wanted to shout. My breath wanted to burst through my ribs.

I said, 'If I could believe you – oh then I *would* feel that I could do anything in life, anything.'

And I did believe him. I did believe him. (My feet wanted to leap along the path.)

But in the next instant I realized that I couldn't believe him. (And my feet were leaden.)

I said, 'The truth is, I'm afraid, that someone has just proposed to her and she's going to accept him.'

'Who?' he asked. And I told him a little about Leonard.

'Ridiculous!' he said firmly. 'She won't. It's just a despairing thought. She won't do it.'

We had reached the town, and a friend was hailing him. 'Come back for dinner', he said gently.

At dinner Joel was full of a story he had just heard about some young man they knew who had slept with an older woman they knew to try to keep her from sleeping with the person he was really in love with – who was of course another young man. I couldn't listen very well. I kept wanting to get up and move around the room.

As usual, Joel went upstairs early. I asked Dewey, 'Dewey, how can you feel so sure that she won't marry Leonard?'

He told me, 'I'm not really what's known as intelligent in the ordinary way, but I know things directly – I have feelings that are accurate, that tell me truths.'

He said, 'It's the only true answer for her – to live with you. I thought this, actually, the very first time I saw you together, several years ago.'

He said, 'If she had stayed on – it just would have happened of itself, inevitably.'

At these words, of course, I felt a sharp pang.

He was saying, 'You perfectly complement each other.' I turned to him. 'I've been writing her a letter in my head. But perhaps I should wire her?'

'Wire her and it's sure', he said. 'It's even unfair.' Now he grinned. A little boy's grin. I was suddenly filled with panic. Could this be one of Dewey's mischievous pranks?

He sensed that panic, perhaps, for he gave me then a very gentle look. And he assured me, 'If I were a woman, I'd marry you in a minute.'

When I left the house at midnight, lighted fishing boats were on the sea. The sky was a strange sky, my notes recall – quite bright but with dark blotchy clouds.

Just before morning I dreamed of you. You opened your arms as you had after our climb from the beach, and we kissed most tenderly. But then you pushed me away. Angrily. You complained, 'How utterly digusting!' I woke in alarm.

I walked out on to the balcony. It had been raining again and the first double rainbow that I had ever seen gleamed above the water. I laughed like a child. I believed again.

I took my sunbath and composed as I lay there several variations of a telegram to send to you. I did some laundry and made myself write two letters that I owed and I walked up into the town. And there was Dewey strolling down the street. It was an unusual hour for him to be there, but he had just finished a chapter and, to celebrate, had come to town to have a fitting for his velveteen jacket. He joked, 'Should you have your suit made up too, now? Shall we work a tailor to death?'

I showed him the wire I had composed. He made some comment and I changed the wording just a little.

He nodded, 'Send it.' And he walked with me to the post office.

I wonder if you remember the wire. It said: DEAREST LOTTIE LIFE IS AMAZING MAY I COME ANTICOLI PLEASE WIRE YES LOVE BOBBIE.

Dewey engaged in some spirited teasing of the young official who took down the words. 'Can he count? Why, I didn't think he could.' And the young man replied in joking kind. But as we left the building, we both grew sober.

'So I'll be leaving,' I said – 'if all goes well.'

He said, 'And I'll miss you.'

'And I'll miss *you*, of course', I told him – feeling tears rise up in me.

Dewey left for his fitting. Restless, I started off on a walk through the town. A little ahead of me soon I spotted a young American who had once sat down at table with me and chatted for a while – Eddie. Blond and athletic. I was walking more rapidly than he and drew abreast of him. Nodding a greeting to him, I saw that his face was darkly flushed and his eyes exhausted. I asked, 'Where have *you* been?'

He startled at the question. 'I've been to Castel Mora', he answered.

It didn't seem a climb that would have put that strain on a young man. I said, 'You look as if you'd been walking through the desert.' And I asked, 'Are you all right?'

His face flinched slightly. 'Not really', he said. Then he was silent. But then he glanced at me, as if to appraise me. 'I've had news', he said at last, tapping his pocket.

I tried to guess what kind of news it could be. 'The Army wants you?'

'No, not the Army,' he answered. 'Well, it doesn't matter.' But though he avoided answering still, I felt his inward being turn slowly toward me. And I continued to walk along beside him. Then he said through his teeth, 'The prosecuting attorney of my home town is after me. Do you understand?'

'I think so', I said – though I wasn't yet sure.

'Will you have a drink?' he asked. We went into the back room of one of the cafés – empty at this hour. And he showed me a letter from his cousin. A teenaged boy had complained to the police that Eddie had made sexual advances to him. The cousin wrote asking him please to give him all the facts so that he'd be able to help.

'There was no act. Thank God, eh?' he said. I can remember still the sharp shrewd though panicky look in his eye as he uttered that 'Eh?' The *boy* had made the *first* advances to *him*, he told me; but then had asked for money, and so he had told him to go to hell. He knew for a fact that others – several others – had had that boy. He'd done this simply for revenge. And then Eddie drew out a second letter – from his mother. She didn't refer directly to the unpleasant subject. She chattered on about family news, about a new china set she'd just bought. But at the very end of the letter, she asked him please to trust his cousin and do what he advised.

'My poor mother, she's been noble', he said – with a voice of pity that masked, I thought, anger. It wasn't the first time he'd been in trouble. He'd been kicked out of school, kicked out of the Navy. 'It's always with minors', he confided. He was the family's disgrace. 'We're the oldest and wealthiest family in town', he said –

his tone sarcastic. So people pretended they didn't know. But of course everybody really knew.

Others were beginning to come into the bar. He'd finished his drink and I suggested that we go sit somewhere outside. 'Should I tell my tale to Dewey?' he asked. 'Do you think it's amusing enough?'

Dewey didn't require amusement, I told him. But perhaps he *should* ask his advice.

We walked to a small square at the end of town where there was an ancient fountain, and we sat on the fountain's stone rim.

He asked me, 'What do you think I should do?'

I said it seemed to me that the thing he had to fear was not scandal. He himself had said that everybody really knew. The thing he had to fear for was his own life. For was this really the life he wanted: sex with these youths who were strangers and who didn't give a damn about him? I asked, 'Have you ever thought of looking for love?'

'I couldn't take love', he said, emphatically. 'I want meetings in dark alleys.'

When I was silent, appalled, he confided: He had a friend back home who had told him he was sick and should see a psychiatrist. But the day after he told him this he'd gone not to the psychiatrist but to a travel agency. He'd flown away here. Here the encounters he wanted were easy. Italy *was* Sodom, just as they said. He spoke with no pleasure.

If his friend thought he was sick because he was homosexual, that was nonsense, I assured him (as I had learned to assure myself). But if he was afraid of love – perhaps his friend was right. 'Isn't that perhaps a sickness?'

He sat considering my words. And then – I can remember the look still – he glanced down at himself, down at the full length of his graceful body, and an expression of utter disgust twisted his face. He whispered, 'I wish this body didn't exist.' He whispered, 'I wish it weren't here.'

Then he turned to me with a beseeching look, as though I could somehow unwish his wish.

I don't know what words I found to say after that. But I remember that after a while he shook himself, as though he were trying to shake himself awake. And he said, 'Yes, I should return to the States. Time to go home.'

And the next day he was gone – just like that.

But not gone from my consciousness.

Did you ever learn to look for love, Eddie? And did you ever learn to conquer that self-disgust – whose shadow I know, too?

The next day I walked to the post office several times, hoping for an answering telegram from you. But there was none. I decided in spite of this to buy a ticket for Rome on the following day's train. I must have sent you a second wire about this.

In the late afternoon Dewey went with me as I said a shy goodbye to Laura. And he cooked a farewell dinner for me. I can remember of that evening only the moment when we stood at last on the terrace outside the house to say our goodbyes. 'I love you very much', he said. I said, 'I love *you* very much.' He kissed me on the mouth.

And now I suddenly felt panic at leaving him. He had spoken the magical words 'It is possible', and emboldened by these words I had dared to admit to myself that I loved you. But would I dare to continue to believe what he had said when he was no longer nearby?

11

And so, my heart in my mouth, I took the train back to Rome. I tried not to think too much during that trip. There'd still been no answering wire from you. I'd asked the hotel could they page me at the railway station if word arrived after I'd left, and they'd agreed to do this; but no call came. I wondered: Could it be that Leonard had arrived? I can dimly remember a laboured fantasy I had of meeting the two of you together, drawing you aside, declaring my love in spite of the fact that he was there already. A slight rain was falling as the boat train crossed the straits of Messina. But I climbed out of the train anyway and went to stand near the front of the boat. My notes speak of our passing on the shore some sculpted monument which, through the rain's blur, I could not quite make out. 'An angel?' my words ask hopefully. I needed a blessing.

I stared out the window as the train travelled back up the coast you and I had stared at together. At the small crowded fishing boats with their patch-on-patch sails. At the family groups on shore setting out nets, or dragging them in, or squatting on the sand to mend them patiently. One ragged family walked single file, a caravan, bundles on their heads, along the long beach. Where were they walking to? I remember that I stared after them as though the answer to this question could tell me my fortune. Their small yellow dog ran alongside the train for a long while. It was sundown when we reached Paestum – with its quick lovely glimpse of Greek columns against the shining sea. It was dark by the time we reached Naples. Dark and cold. Peering out at the people on the station platform, I saw a young man who looked surprisingly like Pete. He met my eyes, then turned away. I felt very tired. I pulled my coat over me and napped fitfully the rest of the way – and awoke in Rome dazed.

I called my old hotel from the station, to reserve a room and to ask – my heart in my mouth – whether there was any word from you. There was no word. I called one of your friends at the American Academy. She said you hadn't been in Rome for days. There was no way to call you in Anticoli. I found myself a cab.

The familiar city streets seemed unfamiliar. 'Cold. Strange', say my notes; 'The light gone.' These buildings that had always seemed to me to glow even after sundown looked dull now and blackened – strangely stained, as though after a despoiling fire. Even homeground, the Piazza della Rotunda, looked strange and cold and black.

The manager was glad to see me, but had no outside room that he could offer, unless I wanted an expensive one. So I took a room that looked out on the bleak inner courtyard. Then I called Aaron and Peggy from the hotel's phone, to let them know that I was back and to ask their news.

'You at last!' cried Aaron. 'Where are you? You have a telegram here.'

I had a telegram there.

'Shall I open it and read it?' he was asking.

You had wired: PENNY AND CHILD HERE FOR LONG WEEKEND SORRY CAN YOU COME TUESDAY WRITING WONDERFUL LOVE.

So you were there still on your hilltop. Leonard hadn't carried you away. After I'd hung up, I walked out into the city again, to find a bite to eat. The piazza was alight. I laughed to see it. 'Bella Roma!' – a passing woman was humming the popular tune. Down every street I walked, the buildings shone in lamplight, their tawny colours fiercely glowing. I hummed my own song: Lottie, Lottie.

The next day Aaron came into the city. And he brought a letter from you which you'd sent at the same time you'd sent your telegram. You were sorry that I had to wait till Tuesday. You wished you could say 'Come at once!' But there weren't beds enough. '*What* brings you home! Will be marvellous to see you. Rushing to the post . . .' Your silence was explained, for the note began, 'Your telegram just came.'

Aaron asked me home with him and he and Peggy and I shared a meal at a little restaurant nearby – where the cook and the waitress could be glimpsed dancing in the kitchen to the music of a friend's accordion. Your letter of course had lifted my spirits and my heart danced with them. But then as the three of us stepped out of the restaurant and looked up, we stood stock still. 'What's the matter with the sky?' Peggy asked. There was a blackness that was like a hole directly overhead. We stood and stared, and superstitiously my heart stood still, too. 'What does it mean?' Peggy demanded of Aaron. 'It means that in a few minutes more the sky will be a simple blue again', Aaron said. And in a few minutes it was so.

Back at my own piazza, I watched an old woman feed the cats who lived in the dry moat round the Pantheon. She worked out of a large shabby old bag that had many packages protruding from it. She spread out newspaper at different spots, dumped spaghetti on to the papers; then she'd scoop up this cat or that cat and carry it over to the feast meant particularly for it. She worked stooping over, so I never could see her face. Finally she climbed back out of the moat – with some difficulty – and with a nod of satisfaction, left.

I felt better for watching her. I assured myself again: All will be well. I glanced up at the sky and it was now a beautiful dusty pink.

In the morning, suddenly bold, I decided to buy a bottle of champagne to bring with me. And I sent you a wire, asking you to have ice on hand. You had written careful instructions about which bus to take and which not to take; for there was one that came all the way up the hill and one that didn't. I was half an hour early for the bus that left at four o'clock. But it did at last begin its journey. My notes recall the 'rusty winter hide' of the hills we passed; the 'ragged towns' on those hills, and the 'strange beauty to this raggedness'. They speak, too, of 'belief and unbelief alternating'. Yes, that is how I rode: belief at one moment alight in me; at the next dull and trembling – an ash; then abruptly a glowing ash that gave off sparks.

The bus finally climbed your winding hill. It entered the lively town piazza. And there you stood awaiting me. There you stood. At this first glimpse of you, a profound sobriety touched my spirit. When I stepped out of the bus I noticed at once that your face wore a look of strain and anxiety – though you were smiling at me, too. You looked startled when you saw my suitcase: it was a large one. I quickly explained that this was because I'd remembered how cold it could be up here, and I'd packed the down quilt my father had loaned me – the quilt he'd always taken on trips to the north woods. It took up a lot of space. Two girls were there with you – girls who'd been posing for you. They immediately grabbed the suitcase and insisted upon carrying it for me all the way to your studio.

We hadn't gone far when someone came running after us to hand you a telegram. It was the telegram which I'd sent many hours ago, asking you to have ice on hand. As you read it, your eyes grew wide. I explained that in the suitcase there was a bottle of champagne, too – wrapped in the quilt.

'What *is* happening?' you demanded.

I said, 'I'll tell you, of course.'

But I couldn't very well tell you there in the middle of the street.

I couldn't very well tell you in front of Pepinella, either. And she was there back at your rooms, making supper this evening – in and out of the kitchen, darting at me her searching glances. When I unwrapped the champagne, she at once snatched up the bottle. She knew how to cool it, she declared. (Happily, there was some ice.) You snatched the bottle back. You knew how to cool it, too; and you'd do it in the bathroom sink.

There was a bright fire in the fireplace and we sat in front of it, and began to talk of I don't know what.

'Dewey sends you love', I said at one moment.

'He does, eh?' you asked – with such an odd intonation that I suddenly guessed: You thought I was engaged to Dewey! I'd written you of course that we'd become dear friends.

'Pronto!' called Pepinella. Dinner was ready.

She didn't sit with us; she was expected for dinner by her family. But she did keep finding one excuse after another to appear in the room and study us – where we sat nervously putting the food into our mouths. And once the champagne was cold she sat to have a glass with us.

Dinner over, 'We'll clean up, Pep', you told her. But she said: No – there were only a few dishes.

As she moved about the kitchen still, humming rather loudly, you asked me abruptly, 'Are you going to get married?'

I shook my head.

You asked, 'Has it something to do with me?'

I nodded in Pepinella's direction and promised, 'Soon.'

And then we both sat staring into the fire, waiting for her to leave.

I put more wood on. Fire, don't go out. Fire, speak for me.

Under your breath, you asked, 'Why do I have her? It's coocoo, of course. She tells me that I need her.'

'Buona sera!' came a shout from the kitchen. Then Pepinella stuck her head in one final time – cast at me one final penetrating stare. She knows, she knows! I thought. She loves you herself and her jealous heart knows! But does she know what it is that she knows?

And she had left.

I looked into your beautiful eyes.

I had drunk two glasses of champagne by now. But again I felt sobriety touch my very marrow. I felt still as still.

What words did I find? I had probably been rehearsing them on the bus. I don't know how I began.

But wait – I have found some scribbled, just-legible notes among the letters we exchanged later, and I do begin to remember some of the words.

I told you, 'A very great deal has happened to me since you left.' I told you, 'I've made two discoveries.' I'd discovered that I couldn't really marry Pete – if he were ever to ask me. And I'd discovered that, though I didn't think I'd ever stop loving Nell, nevertheless I *could* fall in love again – I meant utterly in love, not the way I loved Pete but with all my heart and all my mind and all my soul. I'd made these discoveries while talking with Dewey. But no – it wasn't with Dewey that I had fallen in love.

You sat very still.

I said I'd started talking with Dewey about Pete. And he'd been angry and argued that it would be absurd and worse than that for me to marry him. I'd then admitted – to Dewey and to myself – that if I married *any* man, I would be walking into the marriage blind. It was strange: I could see that I'd been capable of making a very foolish marriage to a man. One I'd regret. One in which I would become a stranger to myself. I never would have joined my life to that of another woman in the same blind way. One couldn't know the future, but I did feel that, when it was a woman toward whom I was drawn, I could know quite clearly in advance whether I'd be able to live a life with her I'd rejoice in. I could know certainty here.

I said I'd started to talk to Dewey about one woman, whom I didn't name to him. I'd never allowed myself to fall in love with her because I'd sensed that it wasn't possible for her to fall in love with me. But if it were . . .

You sat very still.

If it were possible, I'd told him – if she *could* love me and choose to live with me – I'd join my life to hers in a moment, and have not one doubt that I'd want to live with her always. Even if our life together turned out to be hard. I could know with certainty that it would be a life I'd rejoice in struggling to make.

I said, 'He knew at once that I was speaking of you, Lottie. And then he astonished me by saying, "Of course she *could* love you – and be very happy with you."' I hurried on to say that I didn't at first dare to believe him. But he had repeated it. He'd said that the very first time he'd seen us together he'd thought that we belonged together.

You asked softly, 'Did he say that?'

I said, 'Yes. Yes. And so I have taken my courage in my hands and come here to tell you that I love you, Lottie. And to ask you: Will you make a life with me?'

Then I saw that your eyes were shining with tears.

You said – very softly still: 'I thought of it, too. The days we spent together down there were a kind of marriage.'

'But' you said – I had heard the 'but' in your voice before you spoke the word – 'I'm sorry, it can't be, dear Bobbie. I did ask *myself* the question. But it wouldn't be right for me, I know.'

I asked, 'Are you sure?'

You said, 'It is too easy. I think there has to be more struggle between two people who live together.'

I cried, 'Oh, Lottie, I think you would find that there was struggle enough between us. We are very different people, after all.'

But you said – firmly: 'It can't be. You mustn't let yourself think there's any hope.'

I then tasted in my mouth the very peculiar taste of hope that is spent. My journey had come to an end.

I was sitting in a studio chair that was as wide as an armchair, but had no arms. You got up suddenly and came over to me and slid on to the chair beside me – though there was hardly room; it was an awkward fit. We had to be careful not to fall off the chair. And you put your arms around me. You said, 'Now I have to take care of you.'

I was startled by your saying this.

And then you asked me, 'Do you want me to go to bed with you?'

And I asked, 'Would you just lie next to me?'

And you said, 'You don't even have to ask it.'

I think back to my feelings then. What did I want?

I wanted to join my life to yours. I was confused by your offer to come to bed with me, when you had just said no, we couldn't join our lives. In what sense was it that you could imagine our bodies joining?

You had some knowledge of the ways of men, I assume, and took it for granted that I would be aflame with physical desire. I wanted your close presence. Closest presence. But I felt confused about what *your* desires were, and so I felt confused about how to bring myself truly into your presence. My body was no, not aflame. It was now dumb.

We got ready for bed. It was cold in the bedrooms, away from the fire. No doubt I unpacked my down quilt and spread it on my bed.

You slid in beside me.

What can I remember? I can remember the sweet distinctive smell of you. I can remember your mouth hard and sweet against my mouth. I think it was you who kissed me. I lay in awe of you.

Then you said, 'Do anything that you want to do.'

I think you sensed my awe, and intended that to set me free.

But I wasn't free.

I remember that I kissed your breast, then – taking one of your nipples in my mouth. And you said, 'Oh – sweet.' But I wasn't quite sure that you had said it. I asked, 'What is it, Lottie?' And you said again, 'Sweet.'

But instead of feeling free to continue, I remember, I felt overwhelmed – and began just to hug you and hug you, murmuring your name. Afraid to have you vanish in my arms.

It's hard for me to remember as clearly what happened next. My hands must have wandered your body. Your hands must have wandered mine. Yours were the bolder.

I do remember clearly that when you finally fell asleep, we were holding hands. A little later, I tried to take my hand away, without waking you – so that I could turn in bed. But in your sleep you held to it fast. So I lay without moving. And, wakeful, I lay dreaming. If you had touched me as you had, and if you now wanted to keep hold of my hand, perhaps – I dreamed – perhaps your answer to me was really 'Yes', in spite of the words you had spoken. I lay reinventing hope. I lay, even, writing in my head a letter to Nell, telling her of my happiness.

Near morning, I was half-aware that you slipped from my bed and went to your own – muttering to yourself, in sleepy alarm. (Pepinella might arrive.) I woke later to find you sitting on the edge of the bed, beside me, fully dressed.

'Were you happy last night?' you asked gently. And as I nodded, in my dream still, and held out my arms to you, you said quickly and firmly, 'I shouldn't have. It can't happen again. I'm not in love.'

'I shouldn't have', you repeated, shaking your head sadly – as you saw your words strike me.

I leaned my head against your breast, then – not crying, yet crying; and you stroked my hair, as a mother would caress her unhappy child.

'Come have breakfast with me', you said.

We had breakfast together, and then you went to your easel and I sat out on the terrace of the bedroom with my journal. That journal tells me now that the air that day was soft, though cold – the sweet wood-smoke from the chimneys drifting out over the valley. And it speaks of birds (swallows?) 'softly thudding up through the air'. It began to rain, and I took my work into the kitchen. Pep had not appeared yet – or had appeared but then gone off again. We had lunch at a very late hour. For you just went on painting and painting, as though hypnotised. When you finally noticed the time, you asked me why on earth I hadn't called. I had of course been afraid of being seen as an interruption to your work. I can remember moving about on quiet-as-cat feet. You were to tell me later – near the end of that week I spent with you – that I'd been really *too* quiet. The sense of my keeping more quiet than was natural – *that* had disturbed your concentration.

Mid-afternoon Pepinella appeared, with a friend, Antoinetta. And the four of us set out on a shopping trip – to Subiaco, the town across the valley I loved to stare at from the terrace. One had to look at it twice to be sure it was a town, not just a line of the rock on that hilltop. We needed charcoal for the stove. And certain food supplies. And Antoinetta needed material for a new dress. The errands seemed to go on and on – Pep and Antoinetta taking an endless giggling time to perform the simplest operation, such as getting out of the car. It began to rain again, which didn't speed things up. We decided finally to have supper there; and Pep made an elaborate drama out of what to do with the large bundle of charcoal that we had tied to the back of the car. First she decided it should be taken back into the shop where it had been purchased – for safeguarding. The shop closed for the day before our supper was over, so then she had to rush out with Antoinetta to haul it to the entrance of the restaurant. All this done somehow in the spirit *both* of a desperate anxiety and a reckless merriment. And all done for you. Her glance always returning to you. Frequent giggles punctuated supper. A nice old dog with whitened brows who for some reason reminded me of my father stared at us from across the room.

'Home finally', say my notes – 'the little towns like Pleiades in the night.'

At Pepinella's insistence we stopped to pick up her brother, Pietro, so he could help carry in our bundles. And this meant of course that he had to be invited in for a glass of wine. He – and Pep – stayed on and on. Or so it seemed to me. But at last we were again alone.

And now *we* sat on at the table. And – in answer no doubt to the look of love I at last felt free to turn on you – you talked again of how it could not be. How it was too easy, our being together; there was no conflict – which gives strength. 'Love is pure', you said, and last night had seemed right in its way. But it couldn't be repeated. Your words bewildered me, and I think I had little to say in answer at the time. Though no doubt my eyes protested, and this is why you kept looking for words.

We went to our separate beds. My journal notes: 'Hellish cold night.'

At the time – do you remember? – you were not only painting but teaching yourself to work in copper and silver; hoping to add to your income by making jewellery, or belt buckles, or the like. You'd improvised a small forge at which you heated the metal, and then impressed designs. The craft was called 'sousing'. Hot pitch was involved. The next morning you worked at this, and you let me watch. As I watched, I tried to do some drawings of you. I still have a sketch of your profile – mouth half open as if in exclamation as you concentrated upon the work; and a sketch of your left hand. Then one of the children who posed for you appeared – Lorenzo. And you moved to your easel. He was late, you teased him. He'd not been feeling well, he said. He took a weary pose, his head leaning against his hand. But he was very graceful in his lassitude. You began eagerly to sketch. But then you grew worried about him. 'Are you really that tired?' And you sent him home. You returned to 'sousing'. Pepinella had turned up and moved about in the kitchen, strangely quiet. None of us said much all that day. Toward the day's end, Pep's brother turned up to take her home and started shouting that the place was full of poisonous fumes. It was the pitch you'd been working with. You should have kept a window open, it seems. We'd all been walking around half asphyxiated, without knowing it – no doubt each one of us supposing that her own mood had put her in that odd state. Now we ran to open windows wide. Then stood shivering, and smiling at each other shyly, as if waking from a dream.

Before we parted for the night, I asked you, 'Would you kiss me good night?' And gave me a quick but tender kiss. Then you exclaimed suddenly, 'Oh I know it's terrible. I do love you.' 'But' was unspoken but clear. And you told me softly, 'You're very beautiful. I keep noticing.' And I remember just looking at you dumbly. And we went to our separate beds.

The next day was a rainy day. My journal surprises me by noting that I began to work again on my poem 'Love shakes me'. I've written already that I finished the poem in Taormina. It must have been an earlier version that I finished there, and now I began to work on its final wording.

After lunch Lorenzo turned up, with his tiny brother Luigi, and proceeded to teach him how to pose. You watched enchanted – sometimes rapidly sketching, sometimes just standing and staring, as if to memorise them. Posing, for these children, didn't mean taking one position and then stiffening into it, eyes glazed. They moved whenever they began to want to; then would relax into some other position that felt natural. There was a lovely grace to them – their relation to their bodies always simple and free, in their baggy mountain clothes. Meanwhile their eyes glanced everywhere – taking *your* portrait, too.

After they'd gone, we took a walk down the hill, though there was light rain in the air still. And picked some little plants and ferns to make a sweet-smelling bouquet. Sat at tea and talked about the children, and the grace of them. Then I went into the kitchen to do a few chores. We had been having roast potatoes at almost every meal and I decided, while I was at it, to wash not simply enough for supper that night but for several suppers. When Pep turned up, she cooked every single potato that I had washed. Served us perhaps ten potatoes apiece. 'Pep, have you lost your mind?' you exclaimed. She opened her black black eyes wide and pointed at me: 'The signorina washed that many.' She just barely managed not to burst out laughing aloud with delight.

That night was another cold cold night.

Toward morning I had a puzzling dream. I dreamed that a young man was saying to me – lightly: 'As a matter of fact, I haven't read the letter.' At which I cried out, 'Then you can go to hell!' Adding, 'For the moment, anyway.' But then: 'No, you can go to hell!' – cried it out in weary despair. When I woke, the dream was still vivid to me, but I could make no sense of it. Then midday a letter arrived from Pete – the first in many weeks – forwarded by Aaron to the Hotel Bristol in Taormina, and by the Bristol to Anticoli. It was the letter in which he apologized for his long silence, explaining that he'd tossed his address book back on to his desk before setting forth on the training cruise; shouldn't have, 'But wot the hell?' He wrote, 'Three letters from Ned which are also unread. A tough man that. I suppose you're pretty unhappy about the whole thing. Well you've cause to be. But don't ever forget that that's the way he wanted it.'

'A tough man that' seemed inanely inaccurate words with which to describe Ned. A man longing to be tougher than he was, perhaps. And why had Pete put off reading Ned's three letters – quotes from which I would have especially welcomed? It was several hours later before I wondered suddenly: Was Pete the young man in my dream I had told to go to hell? Waking, I didn't allow myself to feel clear anger at him. Did my dreaming self allow it? But how had I managed to dream about a letter he'd left unread the night *before* receiving his admission about leaving letters unread? I showed you his letter and told you my dream. You sat shaking your head. Yes, it was strange, strange. The feelings men had about war – these were strange, too. Of Pete, 'He doesn't really know what he's feeling about anything', you hazarded. 'He's in a state.' 'Hateful war!' you exclaimed.

This day was a quiet day, for you'd decided to ask Pepinella not to turn up until late afternoon. We both worked hard. I finished the final revision of my poem.

When Pep did turn up she brought with her another towns-woman, who fixed for us an electric switch that wasn't working; then showed you how to make a mixture of vinegar and salt and clean the copper designs on which you'd been working. She also, to Pep's delight, mended the fire I had done a poor job of getting to blaze. And we all had tea. Then Pep and her friend left and you fell asleep by the fire. And I sat staring at you. Tried again to sketch your portrait. Talked to the fire.

Fire – why wouldn't you blaze for me?

Fire, fire – cast a lover's spell for me.

After a while, you woke, startled. We made and ate a simple supper. And then as we sat on at the table, by candlelight, I began to batter at you. Began, foolishly, to try to argue you into falling in love. You almost were in love with me, I argued. You had said as much. I argued that you wouldn't *let* yourself love me, that you hadn't tried just letting yourself feel what you felt. I said that you reminded me of a story my oldest brother liked to tell – about a man who wouldn't eat spinach. A friend told him that if only he'd eat it he'd learn to like it, but his answer was that he didn't want to learn to like it, because if he did learn to like it, he'd eat it – and he didn't like it.

I'd hoped to make you laugh, but you didn't laugh at this. You looked pained. You shrugged your shoulders, grimacing – as if to shrug out from under all the difficult feelings. You told me that I mustn't do this. And you told me then, too, that I mustn't stay on. You weren't able to work well with me there, you said. You said you'd be driving into Rome on Tuesday (this was a Saturday) to run some errands, and you'd drive me back to my hotel. 'I don't believe in half things', you said firmly.

At which all my words were gone. We both sat in silence. The candles guttering. The fire making small sounds as it died.

As we stood up to go to bed, you suddenly looked at me with sad gentle eyes and asked, 'Should I come in and make you warm?'

But I shook my head: No.

We went to our separate beds.

The next morning, when I awoke, a bitter childhood rhyme was ringing in my ears:

Rain, rain, go away!
Come again another day!

Yes, Love, love, fly away – that was the spell you sang, I told myself.

After breakfast (fried potatoes, says my journal – we were trying to use up the many left-over potatoes) – after breakfast, the words of a new poem began to come to me – the words with which I seemed to hear you warning yourself. I listened for these words all the morning, and by lunch time the poem had its shape:

'Rain, rain, go away!'

If I love her lightly now,
Who knows how love might grow?
If I know not how it grows –
And know not where the wind blows
And know not where time goes
And know not why love chose
This time of this day
And this unfamiliar way –
Then I am love's, and not love mine,
And here is endless wondering.

I decided not to show you the poem.

Toward the middle of the afternoon you suggested that we take a drive. So we set off in your little car to see some of the hill towns beyond Subiaco. The hills this winter day had 'the look of scuffed leather', my notes say. They add that I was 'silent and unpleasant'. The first town we came to was quite beautiful – set high above a winding river, its ancient houses the mellow colour of its rock, except for one pink house which shone out from among the others. We drove on. The buildings on the outskirts of the town were ugly – new construction. (To replace houses destroyed by bombing, you said.) How could they build such horrid new houses, I complained, with the beautiful old ones there before their eyes. You noticed an edge to my anger, and turned on me a look that was dour, harassed. The climbing road we took now became just loose rubble, across bare slope. We laboured up and up it to a very high-set village which was grim and bleak. The stone of which everything was built here was a peculiarly grey-whitened stone as though all spark had been chilled out of it. Or so it seemed to me that day. And the town was strung out along the hilltop without the grace of any central piazza – the town fountain just there by the wayside. 'They have no piazza', I complained. There were a few beautiful carvings, though, in the stone lintels above doorways. This was sheep country. We kept having to stop for slow-moving flocks along the road. The shepherds wore puffy sheepskin leggings against the cold, and carried those big Robinson Crusoe unmbrellas. Large white dogs that looked like polar bears helped them keep the sheep from straying. It was much colder up here than in Anticoli. And the shadows on the ground were a cold cold blue. 'Depressing', you muttered. But I think we both felt a kind of awe, too – that people did make their lives up here. At one spot where the road was being mended, there was a small improvised tent with a regular bedstead set up inside it. As we headed back for home now, I kept remembering that little tent, that cold, cold bed.

We made our own supper again. And somehow in the course of the evening we became at ease with one another once more, and began to talk about our lives. I think you told me a little about one man with whom you had been really in love – but without hope. And I think you questioned me about Nell and our life together. The fire died down. It was bedtime. We got ready for bed. You had questions still to ask. And somehow it ended with your sliding into bed next to me, just to continue the talk. I remember that I had told you of the one time I was unfaithful to Nell – spent one night with an older woman by whom I had been fascinated. I still felt a lot of anguish about that – which surprised you. It seemed a rather innocent event to you. Which surprised *me*. As we lay next each other now, I began to talk a little more about that time. My desire for the two women had been so different, I said. When I was with the older woman, I felt as though I were on fire – burning up. When I was with Nell, I felt as though I touched the sweet ground, and knew who I was again. I had barely spoken these words when you suddenly turned in the bed and pressed your mouth hard against my mouth, your body against my body. Then you drew back, startled at yourself. 'How does this happen?' you asked; and then in a small voice, 'Shall I stay?'

And I said, 'Oh stay, yes, stay.'

You said quickly, 'This doesn't mean that I have changed.'

'No, I know', I said. 'But stay.'

So you stayed. Though it was shyly that we touched. And you slipped away soon, didn't stay the night.

Next morning, at breakfast, just to make sure that I'd not begin to hope again, you asked me what I planned to do once I'd left Anticoli. I didn't know. Perhaps I should go to Greece, I hazarded. And you urged me, 'You should.'

You went to your easel. And I sat out on the terrace, wrapped warmly, and stared out across the valley. A new poem began to gather in me. It wrote itself:

Let us touch, love
Let us go
If that much, love
Frightens you
Turn aside, then
Hide our eyes
And in parting
Sigh our sighs.

I copied it out. And sat on.
Another poem began itself:

An eye for an eye, love
A mouth for a mouth
Next me lie, love
I'll give you both

You called to me that it was lunch time.
After lunch the rest of the words burst in me:

Next me lie, love
Limb by limb
Each take the other's
Life from him.

I was very tired and lay down by the fire to take a short nap.

The mail arrived. You had a letter from Leonard. I studied your face as you read it. It didn't seem to me a happy face. You saw me watching you and gave me a strained smile.

The day had turned balmy, and we decided to take a walk. Our goodbye walk. We walked up the hill behind the town. On our way we met your landlord, who began to walk along with us. And he couldn't stop talking. He was telling us for some reason about how nervous he had been for at least two years after the late war's end. He'd kept taking his temperature (he made the gesture of sticking a thermometer under his arm) and he never had a real fever, yet he'd be turning hot and cold in turn, and the thought of performing the simplest task would throw him into a state of acute anxiety. You listened to him patiently. I had a hard time pretending to. This was to be our last walk together. In the morning you'd be driving me back to the city.

There were early violets along the rock-and-mud path we took. I stooped to pick them. The hills were wonderfully beautiful this day. In one direction, they were the shadowy delicate colour of these violets; in another they held a fire-lit glow, cast by the rosy clouds that drifted above them. The whistling of birds was in the air. At the end of our climb, we stood and gazed.

The landlord pointed to a distant spot. There was a grotto in that mountainside, he told us, to which the village made a pilgrimage each year. Once, long ago, a farmer had been ploughing up there and his oxen and plough had fallen off the cliff. But he'd prayed to the Trinity – and when he opened his eyes and looked, there the plough hung from some out-bending branches, and far below the oxen were peacefully standing. The people of Anticoli would start off at midnight – some time in June, this was – the young and the old, on foot, making their slow way single-file along a narrow mountain path over there. They'd reach the sacred spot by afternoon. 'Stanca, stanca' – tired, tired – but exalted, he said.

'Some of them more tired than exalted, I bet', you said. And he laughed.

He said, 'E vero. And when they get to the grotto, they want to stop for a while, of course, but there's a priest with a stick who keeps them moving.'

You groaned. 'Just a peek, after all that!' And you both laughed.

We walked down the hill again, toward the town, which was smoking and seething now, its charcoal fires lit. It was seething at all its cracks. The moon was up and the first star out. Goats were picking their way back down the mountain paths, sheep were crying out from their folds. A crowd of people was in the piazza, making a lovely racket.

Home, we found Pepinella bargaining with a boy for some small trout he had just caught. Blessedly, she left soon after and again we cooked the meal ourselves. Then you went back to work on one of your copper pieces – for what seemed a long long while.

But at the evening's end you came into my bed again. To say goodbye. To say goodbye. I didn't know how to say it. But you knew. Your hands spoke to me. To my confusion, they seemed not to say goodbye but to discover and greet me. I can remember your asking, 'Shall I stop?' – and remember breathing, in ecstasy, 'Never, never.' For a sweet brief eternity you never did stop, but touched and touched and touched me, till you touched my very life, and I cried out your name from somewhere outside of my body, which had swooned.

I woke next morning to hear you and Pep shouting at one another. She, too, had errands to run in Rome and was here early, to be ready to drive in with us.

You came into my room, then, and sat down on my bed, and hugged me in your arms and whispered, 'What can I say? Such loving! Wonderful girl! Thank you! I'm happy that you came!'

Your words thrilled me and stunned me. I heard you in a daze. You were happy that I had come. But you must send me away.

Pepinella made us all a hearty breakfast of kidneys. For the road. She was in high spirits. 'The signorina is leaving and it's the first beautiful day we've had', she announced – not able not to sound jubilant. It was, yes, a particularly sunshiny day. Roof tiles shone like gold. The view across the valley was clear as clear. 'It's not as much a thing to paint, though – these clear days', you said, scowling at Pepinella.

And away we drove, back down that beautiful winding steep hill my hope had tried to climb.

As we started down, 'Dewey will be sad', you said.

'Yes,' I said, 'Dewey will be sad.'

12

'I'm sad, too', you told me as we parted that day. We'd dropped off Pepinella with some Roman relatives, had lunch together and sat on over a bottle of wine at an outdoor café in the brightly shining day. And then you'd dropped me off at my hotel. You had decided to stay in the city for a couple of days, but made some phone calls and said you'd be seeing other friends that evening.

I settled in again at the Sole. To my relief I was given a room that looked out on the piazza. I went out and found a florist's and sent you a dozen roses. And then I went to Cook's to ask about boats to Greece – and learned that the first boat wouldn't be leaving for eleven days. But before I went out, I sat down and wrote you a letter:

'Lottie, Lottie – I have promised. I won't batter at you again. I write this gently. I just whisper it: Do on odd rainy afternoons – sunny afternoons – just think of it? For love is not familiar. I fear only that you will hurry in some other direction too fast. And I remember your saying one night, "What makes this happen?" And if there is this "why" . . .

I am too filled with wine, and too filled with sun, to speak. But here is something I want to say – though it may make you smile: I would support you, Lottie, if you wished. *Could* support you. In no great style, but I could support you. Well – you *are* smiling, but I must say this, for you may need this kind of peace. And it is not that I am full of wine that I say it. I say it soberly. For myself I may do a lot of fearing. But with you to care for, I would be capable.

However it turns out – I love you, and am only happy that I do. And I remember you, and because I can, I again know life to be generous.

Work hard – or rather, happily. And then maybe come to Greece? Or if you ever feel that perhaps you might dare just to *see* if . . . write me, wire me, and I'll catch the next boat, plane. Even if you should wish just to look at me again and then decide to send me away after all.

And so, and so, Lottie – I do hope, because that is the nature of love. But quite beyond all hoping, I look at you.

Keep well. And *you* hope all good things. They are intended for you. Do nothing in despair. You won't, will you? Because – because at *you* God does not smile at a distance. His *hand* is on you.'

(It jolts me to write 'His'. But that's how I did think in those days.)

When I went out to mail the letter, I ran into a friend of a friend, who asked me to join him for supper. Luckily he was in a mood to ramble on about his travels and didn't expect me to say much. I made some excuse for cutting the evening short, and went to bed early. And dreamed.

I dreamed that I was on a wide staircase, that mounted the open air. And a large tawny lioness had just passed. Very close. Close enough for me to smell her vivid lioness smell. And to feel the small hairs stand up on my skin. And then someone nearby said quietly, 'There is another one.' I saw another great beautiful but scary lioness approaching. Then rebellion stirred in me. I had felt helpless awe as the first beast drew near. I decided to refuse to feel that helpless again. And I summoned more strength than I had and I grappled with the great animal – and just managed to throw her from the stairs.

When I woke, the dream was still vivid to me. I can, in fact, still clearly recall what it felt like to dream it – recall how it took every bit of strength that I had.

I decided to mail you the three poems I had written in Anticoli. Then I spent the day running errands, passing the time until the evening, when you'd said we could meet again.

When you turned up, you thanked me almost formally for the roses.

'You are welcome', I said.

We had dinner together across from the Pantheon; hurried off to see a performance of *Romeo and Juliet* – 'not well done', say my notes; and then we decided to drink a little wine together in a nearby 'cellar'. And there I stared at you with love.

You told me in a tense voice, 'You mustn't look at me like that.'

And I was abashed by your words – sat fighting off the horrid feeling that I should be ashamed to feel toward you as I did. I remember that several couples were on the dance floor, dancing out an easy-going lust. And I felt a sudden rage at them. Their lust was permitted. My love was not. I was filled with confusion.

I began to tell you my dream. 'The first lioness was of course my love for Nell. The second lioness is my love for you. And it is scary – to feel so much and with little hope. But I'm not going to let it destroy me', I told you emphatically – struggling for my pride. You were looking at me with an edgy rather baffled look, and I lost all my words then and couldn't say more.

The dancers surrounded us with their noise and their motion. We sat without talking for a while. You glanced about you uneasily.

You said, 'I know – you hate me now.'

I repeated your words stupidly: 'I hate you? I hate you, Lottie?' And then I could only shake my head. 'But I do hate it here,' I told you – 'let's not stay.' And you nodded quick agreement.

So we walked about the city a little. I wanted to ask you to my room, but I didn't dare. Hunting for the words, I searched your face, and your face told me 'No' without my asking.

As we paced, you began to speak about Anticoli. 'It's a funny place,' you said, 'magic. It can make things seem possible that aren't really possible.' You stopped, stood where you were, and looked at me squarely. 'You mustn't think of it as possible, Bobbie. Let's say goodnight now.'

So we said goodnight, and I went to bed meek and dispirited – all my stubborn life spirits rebuked.

But in the morning I was surprised to find – when I looked for them – that these spirits were still in me. I sat down and wrote you another letter:

'Lottie – I love you so very very much, so wonderfully much. So extravagantly much, you think I might add, but you are wrong. So much loving, you are thinking, and what in return? Save it, save it. But money is to spend, Lottie. Love is to give. Now here is what I say to you: Be delighted. Is it such a disaster to love, and is it such a disaster to be loved?

As for loving: If I wake up in the morning and know that I could lovingly care for you a lifetime, and whatever came along, find some answer to it, and whatever adversary, cope with it – is this nothing? Just to know it. Is it nothing just to know that it *could* be so? That one can be possessed of – force? – I do not know what word to use.

As for being loved: I wonder do you believe in prayer. That one person praying for another can be in some strange way effective – sustain the other? I do believe this. And one person loving another – why is it not a little the same? "I know you hate me now", you said. But this was foolish. I love you beyond any wish to possess you – simply love you, bless you, hope all things for you, believe all things of you. Is this nothing? I think it cannot be quite nothing.

As for me: In that dream I dreamed I did not throw love out the window, but its power to destroy me. And had to decide. "I can let it eat me – why not?" I thought. And with a kind of pang. But decided not. Beautiful though the beast was. Not my love for Nell nor my love for you. (It was a startling moment when someone said, "There is *another*".) I am not in a mood to die. And I shall go on loving you, and I say to you: Accept it. It can do you no harm. For it thinks no harm. It does wish to persuade, but not by force. So if I look at you with love – don't wince. If I write you of love, don't wince. Nothing is asked of you. Except that you not be distressed. Except that you not fear that love, despise it. You said to me once, "Love is pure". And so – how can it work injury?

And, Lottie, if you think of it in this way, and do not turn aside from it, and – still do not find one day that you *could* live with me, that you would *like* to live with me – well then I know that this was not to be. But if you turn aside – then until the day I die I am unable to believe it.

Because it was, it *is* a close thing, Lottie, a near thing. It is *not* that that house in Anticoli is a funny place, a magic place. It was you and I. And those days together may be all there is to that story. (That is much.) But whatever was, was you and I. Deny this and you are – wrong.

I am not a presumptuous person, I think. Yet here I am speaking to you boldly. But love is not one's own, anything that we could ever have invented. It is a gift. And to disdain it – this, I think, is presumptuous. And once I would have disdained it. But no longer. I will not disdain it or despise it. I love you. I shall love you until I die – Lottie, lovely wonderful knowing unknowing bending unbending girl . . .'

I decided not to mail this letter to Anticoli, but to show it to you that same day when we met. You had stopped by, in the middle of errands – as I was writing it – and suggested that we meet for lunch. I wanted to eat at the café on the Piazza Navona, where I could stare at the fountain that always gave me heart. But they hadn't yet set out the tables there. So we returned to the café across from the Pantheon. I gave you the letter and you read it, very slowly.

You said – carefully: 'I *don't* disdain your love. I woke up this morning thinking how wonderful it was to have such a friend. And more than a friend', you added.

You smoothed out the pages of my letter, your fingers gentle on the paper. I felt it as a caress.

But then you looked up at me with a lift of your head that was almost a start. And you said, 'I have a confession to make. I wrote Leonard just before you came back from Sicily, and I told him that I would marry him.'

As I stared at you – stared a thousand questions – you said in a voice so quiet I could just barely hear it, 'Love is something very rare – momentous.' You told me, 'This is for the best, I think.'

We ate our lunch. I didn't put my questions into words.

I felt quite blank and listless. You took charge then, rallying as though to care for a bewildered child. You told me that you'd found a tailor who could turn the velveteen I'd bought in Sicily into a beautiful suit. You sent me up to my room to collect the material. You walked me to the tailor's. There you leafed through patterns with me – 'This?' 'How about this?' 'Or here, this?' I agreed finally on a suit that was casual enough for my taste, elegant enough for yours; and you watched, nodding, as the smiling nimble-fingered man took my measurements. 'You're going to look just nifty', you said. 'Don't make a face. Isn't she?' you demanded of the tailor.

You were then due to pick up Pepinella at the house of her relatives; for she had stayed in town, too, and was waiting for her lift home. You let me drive with you to that door. Just before we got there – 'I'm sad, but I'm not going to let myself be', you said. You stopped the car. You gave me a quick little goodbye peck on the cheek.

Home again, I lay down on my bed for a while, dazed. But then I got up – to write you still another letter. You may be feeling: 'Stop, stop – not still another?' But to be faithful to that time, I copy all these letters. For then I couldn't stop. I had to write them. Yes, in this way I struggled with the awesome beast who had drawn near me in my dream.

'Ah, Lottie – You have written Leonard that you will marry him. May I whisper to you how my heart receives that news? For I wonder: Why does it not alarm me more? Why am I not more despairing? And this is why: Lottie – if you wrote him this *before* I came, made this decision, faced this way (and with that way of looking which you do have – for when you turn your eyes, one knows it) if this was so, and yet, and *yet* you then moved toward me (as, surprising us both, you did) is this not truly strange? I whisper this.

Ah, Lottie, how queer it does seem to be going to Greece – to be moving *away* from you whom I love. You do know that I go not to forget you – would not wish to forget you even if you had told me today that you were already married. Do you truly know that I mean it when I say that I wait to return at a moment – after only one day there – if you should feel even for a moment that *perhaps*. . . If I go to Greece, it is still you I go seeking. And would that you would ask me not to go. You see, I ask you not to fear how I would feel if you should give me a little hope and then withdraw it – ask you only not to turn aside if in your own heart such a possibility might begin to suggest itself, and to be not careful at all of me. For you cannot hurt me. I am happy in loving you, even if I do not win you. And to try to win you is in itself a happiness. And so you see that you cannot hurt me. Do, do, Lottie, sometimes look my way – forgetting that you have set yourself in any other direction.

I will stop, let you breathe. But not before saying that I write presumptuously when I say to you "Life is to live, love is to give" – for why do I love you? Because you know this, and live this. It is just that I fear your thinking: I must now look not to left or right or I will be lost! But I think that you can now, of all times, Lottie, turn yourself three times round . . .

I do batter at you. But – read it lightly, Lottie. (Which perhaps is like the request I once heard a friend of mine make of the telephone operator, when he called his mother rather late at night, didn't want to wake her if she had gone to bed – so asked the operator would she ring lightly.)'

The next day I wrote again. You had told me that you wanted to see me off when I left for Greece – put me on the train I would take to Bari, where I'd get on the boat. The boat was to leave the day before Easter, and the best train to take left early in the morning of the day before that. I wrote:

'. . . Or – I wouldn't need to go at all. And then you wouldn't have to get up that early to see me off. I have a lovely sunny room at my albergo now, and I could see you weekends, or simply Sundays, or simply when you chose to come in. And then when you finished your canvas we could go to Greece together.

Lottie, love *is* momentous. And God knows it can cross spaces, but God knows too that it can work more peculiar wonders when it need not do this.'

At day's end, I wrote you again:

I think I have written you only one letter today. And what are postmen paid for? Just to wander about the streets? So I write to tell you that I love you. No – what can I tell you *new*?

It would be news to you, strangely enough, to learn that you are terribly beautiful – that every move you make is startling, because you move in a way no other person moves.

But here is news, too, Lottie. I have been out walking about, and here is my news. A grey evening, too – a grey day – not even able to rain much, just holding it over one's head. And at my albergo, no hot water. And the lights in the room are very dim. Though I've now bought a huge bulb. No, it's not the spell of my surroundings. But here it is, darling: It is wonderful, but I think you are going to marry me.'

(It jolts me to copy the word 'marry'. For marriage means ownership, I now believe. But that is the word I wrote – feeling at the time that only this word could make clear the solemnity with which I asked you to live with me.)

I wrote: 'I think you are going to marry me. I do, Lottie. I believe it with all my might. And truly I don't believe things easily. And when I took that train, I didn't believe it. When I saw you in the square, I didn't believe it. And even when you kissed me – Lottie – I didn't believe it. Though . . . And even when your sleeping hand didn't want my hand to leave. But now I believe it.

And I can tell myself why I believe it. And have written you *some* of the reasons why. But 1 2 3 4 5 6 reasons aside – not aside, but all in one, and so no longer to be numbered – I believe it. With my heart, with my head, with my liver and lights, I believe it. Believe it, too? I mean believe it today instead of next week or next month, or even next year? Because – then it can begin.

You'll be staring at this letter, I know. And will put it down and frown. And pick up your metal-working hammer (and your neighbours below lift up their heads), and you will say: "No, Bobbie – you must stop." But I believe it. Because, Lottie – I think you love me. And I mean as I love you. If less – which is proper enough – still as I love you. And when you write me, or say to me when you see me, "*No*" – I shall still believe it. And I have never felt more sober.

Here, you see, *is* a new ending to my letters. For I do repeat myself. But here *is* a variation: Lottie, I think you love me.

'And if you do . . .'

When I woke the next morning, there was suddenly again the

taste of spring in the air. Outside my window a little girl in a bright pink dress rode an electric blue bicycle round and round the fountain. Now and then she would disappear down a side street – but then would reappear and make the round again, her joy in this circling and circling apparently inexhaustible. Watching her, I began to try to write a poem about spring.

That night I looked up Aaron and Peggy. They were on their way to attend a lecture about modern music at the Italo-American society, and I went along too. Kurt was in the audience, and we sat down next to him. He was whistling softly to himself the theme of one of his own compositions.

'Back from Greece already?' he asked me.

'I haven't left yet', I told him.

'Lottie told me you'd left.'

I suggested that you must have said, 'She's off to Greece', and he'd misunderstood you.

But 'No,' he said, 'I complained, "How could she leave without calling me?" and she just smiled a Lottie smile. I guess she wanted to keep you for herself.'

As he spoke these words, the day, though at its end, burst into springtime again. This smile of yours which he reported released in me a smile of my own, which started to grow and grow. I had to turn it somehow to a smile for Kurt.

At the lecture's end he asked me whether I'd like to drive out to the beach at Ostia with him the next day, and I said yes. So the next afternoon he picked me up in his tiny car – and sped off with me, as though we were in flight.

'Could we go a little slower?' I asked.

'Trust me', he said cheerfully. 'This is the tempo the car likes.'

It wasn't the tempo that I liked. But I guessed from the tone of his voice – the tone of one cheerfully The Master – that further appeal would be wasted effort.

We strolled up and down the wintry faintly-glittering beach, while he discoursed with a good deal of wit and feeling on one subject and another – pausing at intervals to note whether or not I seemed to feel as he did; head thrown slightly back at these moments, as he glanced at me, down his long nose, out of his rather beautiful grey eyes. I think he liked the way I listened. And he liked some of the things I said. But – something about me disturbed him, too.

'Why do you wear that beret?' he asked.

I pulled it off and held it in my hands. 'It's warm. And comfortable. And I can put it in my pocket', I said.

He grunted.

A little later: 'You talk kind of tough,' he said, 'why is that? I don't mean the words you choose. I mean something in your voice.'

'I wasn't aware of it', I said. In confusion. I wished both that I was a tougher talker and that I could talk just as he would like to have me talk – however that was. I also despised myself for holding either wish.

There was a small restaurant nearby, with a glassed-in porch from which diners could stare out at the quietly hissing sea. And here he led me after he began to tire of walking. Now by a strange coincidence he began to discourse about unrequited love. If it was hard on the one who loved, it was hard on the loved one, too, he philosophised. It was very unpleasant to feel more loved than loving. 'Poorly live the loved ones', he quoted the poet Rilke. Was some poor woman madly in love with him? I wondered. From his look of affliction as he rambled on I gathered this was so. And had he asked me out because he was hoping to be able to replace her? If he had, I guessed, he was already beginning to wish that he could find in me a bit more of just what he scorned in her. For could he really be happy, I wondered, with anyone who didn't love him more than he could possibly love her? My guess was that it was only his music that he could love without reserve. He was humming a very complicated and rapid melody again as he rushed us back into Rome.

I went to bed this evening, too, in low spirits – still confusedly despising myself.

But in the morning, after a struggle, I found my cheerfulness again. I wrote you that Kurt had mused aloud that you wanted to keep me for yourself. And I found the impertinence to write, 'Lottie, do you see how all the world informs us that it is so?'

Mid-morning I received a short telegram from you. You would meet me Thursday evening for early dinner; and put me on my train the next morning. Love. I decided then that I had better pick up the tickets I'd reserved. But at the travel agent's I learned that – because of some special Easter weekend pilgrimage to Greece which hundreds of tourists were planning to make – passage would be impossible now until the weekend was over. So I quickly sent you a return telegram – telling you that I'd not be taking a train till Wednesday next, and asking 'WHAT ARE YOUR WISHES? I COULDN'T VISIT YOU EASTER COULD I? WOULD BRING YOU CHOCOLATE RABBITS CHICKENS LAMBS DOVES AND MYSELF AS MILD PLEASE SAY YES.'

Yes, I could visit you on Easter, another short wire came back. Though you would be having other company, too. You'd still keep our original Thursday evening date.

I bought a Greek dictionary and a grammar, set about practising the Greek alphabet and memorizing a few key words. A travelling Greek who was staying at the Sole noticed the grammar I was holding as I sat out in the piazza trying some words on the cats who basked nearby in the few streaks of sun. And he volunteered some lessons. A kindly plump-chested man, Stramba. I'm pleased to report that he never made a pass at me, seemed simply to enjoy giving the lessons. I made him a list of some of the phrases I'd decided I might be most in need of, and he wrote down translations for me – in large block letters, as though for an infant, and in phonetic spelling.

WHERE IS THE TOILET? I can still ask this question in Greek. Can you? 'Poo eenay ta mera?' (Yes, that's the phonetic spelling.)

I NEED A DOCTOR. (But I forget the word for doctor.)

STOP! – Stamata!

PLEASE – Seegnomeen.

WONDERFUL – Calla!

THANK YOU VERY MUCH

I'M SORRY, I DON'T UNDERSTAND

I AM LOOKING FOR AN INEXPENSIVE PLACE TO STAY

I AM LOOKING FOR AN INEXPENSIVE PLACE TO EAT

CAN YOU TELL ME WHERE I COULD SEE DANCING?

Stramba was greatly amused by my list. He added a few 'necessary phrases' of his own:

A BOTTLE OF RETSINA, PLEASE

I WOULD LIKE TO ORDER SOME BAKLAVA (This was his favourite dessert.)

And he taught me a few Greek gestures. For example: How to say 'No' – I'm sure you'll remember this – by tossing one's head back and clicking tongue against teeth. A gesture I could easily have mistaken for a flirtatious 'Yes'.

These lessons were a welcome distraction. I'd been sending you one bold letter after another – somehow finding in myself each day, after a search, the pride to do this. But except for your two clipped wires, I'd had no word from you at all. One morning I found to my dismay that I couldn't write another word to you. Pride had abruptly deserted me. I could now only wonder with a dull ache what you were thinking and feeling.

That very day a letter from you arrived. I opened it shaking. You had written it after sending your first wire. You had just received three of my letters – in the same mail. (I groaned then and I laugh now to think of this.)

But you thanked me for the letters. They were sweet and wonderful, you wrote. And you liked the poems. You'd speak of them when you saw me; you couldn't say what was in your mind about them in a letter. You told me that I should leave for Greece as planned. You couldn't go with me. But you hoped with all your heart that you could join me later for a little while. You were working hard, trying to finish several canvases. You didn't know, though, whether or not you could finish them and have time enough left. My letters were sweet, you said again. You didn't deserve such complete and deep love, but it made you happy and blessed all the same. 'You are a wonderful girl, and grow more so every minute. Be happy, dearest Bobbie', you wrote. And you would see me on Thursday at six.

Kurt had suggested that I might like to visit his studio that afternoon. A young singer was going to begin rehearsals of a cantata he had written. When I got there, he told me the singer had phoned to say she would be several hours late; but he invited me to stay, if I wanted, and listen as he worked on the piece himself. He was still making changes in it. So I stayed. It had begun to rain on my way there and my shoes were wet through. I set them to dry on a ledge of the brick stove in the corner of the studio, made myself comfortable in a dilapidated armchair, and listened hypnotised for the next hour or so – forgetting my shoes, which dried and then fried, the shrivelled toes curling up at their ends. Kurt had to loan me some old bedroom slippers to wear home.

These hours were worth the price of the shoes. When Kurt was concentrated entirely upon music – and forgot that I was even there – I found him a joy to be with. His fingers revelled across the keyboard of the big piano; his head he cocked first to one side, then the other, as he listened to the notes in the air; his skin grew ruddy, glistened; his eyes were alight with a love freely given. He wasn't worrying now about who loved whom more – whether it was the music or the musician. I felt my whole being ease, as I watched, listened. And I reminded myself: Yes, the love we give to our work is always love requited. I promised myself that afternoon not to forget this – to hold always, above all, to *this* life thread.

I nevertheless awaited my next encounter with you, my heart again in my mouth.

When you turned up at my hotel, you began quickly to chatter along, giving me news from the hill, putting questions to me – had I had a second fitting for my suit? (yes, I had); had I bought a ticket yet? (no); how much Greek did I know?

'I know how to say "I love you",' I said – 'S' agapo'.

You quickly asked the next question. But as we began to walk toward a nearby restaurant, you fell silent. And when, after a few steps, I glanced at you, you stopped in the middle of the sidewalk – I remember, still, the other walkers pushing past us as you stood looking at me with wide eyes – and in a voice that trembled slightly you said, 'Nobody has ever written to me like that.'

At which my heart began to pound against my ribs like a caged creature. My tongue stuck to the roof of my mouth; I couldn't speak; but my eyes must have been saying more to you than you wanted to hear. You shook your head, back and forth.

'But no,' you said, 'no, you mustn't hope, Bobbie. It's *not* possible.'

And then, in still another voice, strained and harsh, you said, 'When a woman comes too close to me – I resent it.'

So we stood there, with others pushing past us, staring at one another. And then we walked on to the restaurant. And we had our supper together. You left the table several times to phone the friends you had asked for Easter – two Roman painters, man and wife. Their line kept being busy. When you had finally completed the call, and I thought there was some chance of your hearing my words, I must have tried again to argue with you. For here is the letter I wrote you the next morning:

'Lottie Lottie Lottie Lottie Lottie – what more, you will wonder, can I think to write.

It is queer. I still do believe it I still do believe it. I also most terribly do *not* believe it. I will confess that. Because if I cannot speak the truth, then I am a poor thing. And yet and yet and *yet*, Lottie – in spite even of my disbelief, I still do believe it. And this is why I believe it more than ever before. Because it survives even this disbelief.

You say that I mustn't think that it's because of my fears, because I have been unable to draw near you without fear – without dreaming that you might withdraw. But Lottie Lottie Lottie Lottie Lottie – I do think it.

Do you know what I remember? I remember lying next you – It was the night of the day I had been so grouchy – and we had been talking, and then you turned where you lay and kissed me. How can I write this? But I do. And you said should you go – or should you stay? "What makes this happen?" you asked. And I said "Please stay". And you stayed. And I touched you in some way – but I don't remember what way – but I remember, lying next you, seeing your face suddenly, and you were staring at me hard. And I remember it, Lottie, (I write presumptuously, but forgive me) I remember it as a look of surprise that – that truly you did love me. But it was the look of one who didn't believe what they saw, and who was about to turn and run from it – Lottie Lottie Lottie Lottie – You then did turn – and my hands my mouth became fearful and I couldn't call you back.

I don't write it correctly even. Because I remember – Oh I remember that first night – your asking did I want to make love to you – and I moved toward you – and I can remember my heart failing – my spirit standing still – truly, Lottie, like an enchantment in a myth, where one turns into an object not oneself, a tree, a stone – and I feared to touch you. That dream I told you about revived in me: "How utterly disgusting", your voice saying it very casually – and it was as though a terrible lethargy came over me, a weariness, dumbness – and I couldn't speak – though I tried – and couldn't find you. And I think that it was after my own spirit failed me in this way that you turned from me. I do think so, Lottie. And that second night, too. Because for a moment that second night I did touch you with love and then – try to remember – didn't you for a moment *not* turn from me? Please please remember. And then again I remember that fear – and always I felt: Ah it is in this moment only that I *can* speak. And if I don't now – If I violate her, trespass . . .

Lottie – lie next me one night more?

Ah you see that I persist and persist . . .

But I still believe I still believe, Lottie. That it is only strange to you. And that you don't want it to be so. And because a man is protection, one thinks. And so I myself when I think in the abstract of getting married, always choose a man. Yet when I fall in love, it is with a woman.

Lottie, you say that when you turn from me, it is "psychic". But – this is not a simple answer and – could mean *anything*. So many things do press upon one. But the pressure may be one's very nature – or may seem so and not be.

Do you know what I remember, too, Lottie? I remember your saying to me, when I spoke of Pete, that the feeling of being strangers that I described is always there between a man and a woman. But if you say this . . .

Here *is* a presumptuous letter. And yet I send it. Because I did write it to you.'

Easter weekend I remember in disjointed fragments. I remember how the bus trip began. You had told me to come on Sunday, but I had pleaded with you to let me come on the day before, so that you and I would have at least a little time by ourselves before your other guests arrived. And you relented finally – agreed on condition that I promise in fact to behave as mildly as a chocolate rabbit, a chocolate lamb. I could come on the four o'clock bus, you said.

I arrived at the depot early, as my habit was, but found a small holiday crowd there already. I sat down quickly in the last empty seat left on the bus. More and more people kept climbing on after me. Everybody chattering, shouting, in excited feast-day spirits. The driver got on – pounded the horn to get attention, and announced that he couldn't drive a bus with people standing in the aisle. Another bus would be arriving, and those who were standing should get off and wait for it. But no one made a move. All the people standing fell silent – as though they figured that, silent, they might just become invisible. Clearly none of them believed in that other bus he promised. The driver folded his arms and just sat there.

A few people began to speak again, in whispers. But still nobody budged. The man next to me muttered:

'Just like my goats! Stubborn as goats! They need a Mussolini to handle them – not one but two Mussolinis!'

'So *you* can get off and wait for the other bus!' a woman who was standing told him; 'Follow your Duce off the bus!'

'Yes, follow your Duce off the bus!' another woman echoed her. But he didn't move, of course.

And the bus didn't move. The driver took out a newspaper and began to read it.

And for nearly an hour we stayed there, the hubbub of voices again rising, not one passenger doing as the driver had asked. He never bothered to threaten – knew it would be useless, I suppose. When he had finished reading his newspaper, he stared out the window.

At last somebody came to that window and told him the second bus had arrived, was round the corner. He pounded on the horn again, and made this announcement. Group by small group the people standing began to get off. Slowly and suspiciously – for the bus wasn't actually in sight. And finally just one man remained in the aisle. If he would get off, the driver told him, the bus could start. But now this one man would not dismount. Knew better. Wasn't going to be fooled like the rest of them. He was a small man, in shabby clothes, with a yellowish complexion, bad teeth, little quick blue eyes. He held a small paper bundle in his arms. He stood there rooted – and grinning. 'I can't be fooled', he insisted, as the other passengers began to shout at him. He stood there and stood there, facing them all, wonderfully pleased with himself to be so canny. I can remember across the years the glint in his eye as he held his ground, as he faced them all – master of his fate, the One who Could Not Be Fooled – on the bus that didn't move.

At last a young couple rose from their seats, in exasperation, and climbed off. And at this the small man, for some mysterious reason, instead of taking one of the seats they'd left empty, hopped off too, laughing, and ran quickly round the corner after them, hugging his bundle to his chest. And our bus pulled out.

Some of the passengers began to sing. I dozed off, soon. And dreamed. You were peering into my face, speaking loving words to me. I woke with a start. A woman in the seat just behind me was murmuring a tender ballad to the child in her lap.

It was dusk by the time we began to climb your winding hill again – that hill that was my glass hill. (You remember the fairytale hill which the lover climbs and climbs but always slides back down.)

My notes say 'Cleaning house'. You left no time for any too-intense talks that evening. You'd like the place to gleam for your next day's guests, you told me. 'Pep has done her usual once-over-lightly.' So we dusted and polished and tidied. And went early to our separate beds.

Your guests were there soon after breakfast. He, Paulo, a lean intense man in middle age, rather brooding but with pleasant manners. She – a woman I had to tell myself not to stare at. Elena. There was about her a beautiful amplitude: her figure full and graceful, and her hands strong; her brow very wide and flat, and her eyes, brown satin, set far apart; her mouth wide, too. And there was a lovely stillness to her, none of her motions hurried – each waking of itself out of that quiet. I felt irresistibly: I wish this woman would give me her blessing – without putting these words to the feeling; I put the words now.

After they had looked at your recent work – with great respect – and gazed at the town from the terrace, and then chatted with us a little in front of the fire we'd built, she dozed in her chair for a while. They'd risen very early to catch their bus. She wasn't embarrassed at all just to doze off like a cat. In sleep, though, I noticed, the corners off her mouth turned down, revealing some disappointment she kept hidden when awake. I would like to have known more about her; and wished very much that I could see what the work she did was like.

Some time after lunch, talk turned to Greece. You told them that I was about to travel there and, spreading a large piece of paper on the table, began to draw a map, marking places that had seemed the most remarkable to you.

I asked you to tell me which places you would want to see again when – if – you came to join me. And now I became aware that Elena was watching us – looking from one of us to the other, very quietly, appraising what was between us. She can see, I decided; she can see that I am in love with you – and that I am trying, by wishing it, wishing it, to conjure you into joining me.

I was finding it hard to hide my feelings. In a matter of hours now we would be saying goodbye. For my travel timetable had changed. At the week's end, Aaron had brought me news that a boat for Greece left from Brindisi as well as from Bari, and a ticket on this boat cost much less than on the other; if I went as a deck passenger I'd pay almost nothing. The agent at Cook's pretended not to know of its existence, but a phone call confirmed that it did exist, and its next sailing was Monday. So I was going to catch a train south this very night. I'd told you not to see me off. I'd rather that you work without interruption – and then follow me.

Yes, I was trying to conjure you into following me. By believing that you would. Let the place names you were writing on the map act as a magic to draw you back there. Let my believing that you would follow me draw you.

Elena was seated again in the big chair by the flickering fire. And her satin-brown eyes were on us. My notes contain the brief jotting: 'Elena's eyes.' Yes, I thought, she can see into my soul. But her glance didn't contain the blessing I had wished for at first sight of her. It wasn't a hostile glance, was perfectly kindly. But it was the kindly look that one would give an awkward or a faltering child – a child perhaps who had entered a room in which adults are talking of serious life matters which the child, it's assumed, cannot understand. I experienced panic. I felt my belief in the magic I was invoking evaporate. Elena had been to Greece, too, some years before. Though he had not. You began to compare notes as you went on drawing the map – the two of you very much at ease with one another. And 'she should' see this perhaps or 'she should' see that, you'd agree. I felt myself become a small distant figure the two of you moved across the map of Greece. I think that you felt this happening to me. At one moment you looked at me with a quick painful grimace – that seemed to me to signal 'I can't help it'. Yes, I felt myself become light as the paper on which you drew the map – paper thin. You and she – and Paulo, too, there in the background – were real people in the real world. But I was not quite real.

Before it was time to climb on to the bus that would take your guests back to Rome, we all went for a short stroll though the village – Elena and Paulo walking a bit ahead of us, out of delicacy I think, to give us a little time together. During this time that we were alone – or half alone – you thrust into my hands a small square of copper, about the size of a buckle, in which you had worked the design of a flower.

'Here, for a good luck charm', you said.

'If it's a good luck charm, it will bring you to Greece', I said, grasping it.

And you replied quickly, 'You mustn't count on that.'

But as I closed my hand about it, hard, the four edges of it sharp against my palm, I felt belief in that possibility revive for a moment.

As we stood by the bus, though, finally saying goodbyes, I felt belief again evaporate. It was as you and Elena were saying goodbye. The simplest of affectionate goodbyes, it was.

'Ciao, cara', she said. Goodbye, dear.

And you repeated, 'Ciao.'

You had just given me a quick but strong hug, and a kiss on the cheek. And then you nodded at the two of them, and they at you.

And 'Ciao, cara', she said – looking with simple respect into your eyes. And you returned her look.

And again, at this glance she gave you and you returned, I felt myself become an awkward child in the company. Above whose head the grown-ups, the real-life people, exchange their real-life messages. And though it would be hours still before I would be on the ship to Greece, I felt myself already miles and miles away, again at sea.

13

'Although it is you who have sent me away, Lottie, it's to you that I address this book: a book of travel. Of travail. Spell that either way. You don't wait for me to return. Nevertheless it is you I go seeking.' These are the words with which I began this book years ago. Then after writing a first chapter, I set the book aside, for the friends to whom I showed it looked at me – this strikes me now – with glances rather like Elena's glances. And belief in the dignity of the work I had begun failed me – just as belief in the dignity of my wish to live with you failed me on that Easter Sunday. I knew better than to doubt, both of these times. But I didn't know that I knew. Even today I take up again each morning the labour of learning to know what it is that I really do know.

I wrote in that first chapter: 'God grant me only that I not forget you.' I think now that I meant by those words: Help me to refuse to forget the truth of my deepest nature – a truth I experienced most intensely in your presence.

I wrote you from Athens:

'Lottie – filos (which, if Greek to you, means friend) –

This in a delirium of weariness, so if you make little sense of it, no matter.

It is seven in the evening. But six where you are. A difference which nearly lost me my ship Monday. Six I'd been told, so came back at 5.30 from wandering the town – and whistles were blowing and smoke was up and I full of wonder – and six o'clock Greek time had been meant, and the chief engineer – fortunately my friend (we'd talked when I left my stuff on board) – he'd been holding the boat for me! Which, yes, was nice of him.

So it's seven in the evening, Wednesday now, and am sitting

finally in a hotel room – but had rather thought to be wrapping my blanket round me up on the hill of the Acropolis. Rooms are rare. We docked about nine this morning and I've been looking ever since – with a couple of hours out I took to climb that hill. For then I figured I wouldn't care where I slept. But in the end I did find a place. Meanwhile a jaunty elderly Greek I'd encountered on the street had asked me home to *his* house – or rather, found me again to tell me his *wife* had asked me – and I had been wavering between yes and no – but decided that coffee with him tomorrow morning might be better. For I'm not even a fit guest to drag into a house. I must write Ned that I smell, I think, even higher than he does. Or did I read you his last letter from Korea? Haven't changed my clothes – well, since I left you – or done more about washing than hold my hands under a spigot and then sometimes wipe them across my face. For there was no 'ladies room' on board for deck passengers – just one washroom for all, with a couple of toilet stalls and the aforementioned spigot just outside them. And have been sitting about with the chickens and the goats. And every time the ship has touched land have been getting my hands into sticky pastry. And – draw your own conclusions. I might be worse, I guess, for I *have* been out in the fresh air. The place provided us to sleep was a cave with great double-decker shelves – and here everybody else did choose to curl up. But I couldn't figure how I would breathe. The engine room was near, and the kitchen, and the toilets, and the stink from all three – and from the chickens tethered under the bottom shelf, and from the humans too, for some of them, alas, were seasick. So I slept out on the little slatted bench that runs round the deck. Half the crew told me that I mustn't for it was stormy. But I disobeyed them – and wrapped my hot-water bottle inside my coat, and then the both of us inside my quilt – also the brandy bottle – and pulled the quilt right up over my head, and arose now and then for a brisk walk about the deck to work up a little extra heat – and partook steadily of the bottle – and survived very happily. The ship rolled wonderfully and I had to wind my arms and legs about my bench not to fall to the deck – and the boards shivered under me – and we hissed our way along – And it seemed a good way to be travelling. There was no doubt that I was on my way. So be it. That has an odd sound, but you know what I try to say by it, Lottie.

The next night was less good, though the night itself was

warmer, and the sea calm. A lot more people had come aboard – at Corfu – and spilled out on to the deck with me (some of them wrapped in thick striped rugs which I envied). The cook went to bed early and I had no hot water for my bottle. (Or rather, I went to bed late, for I went ashore at Patras with some soldiers for a beer.) And there wasn't much room left on my bench. Nor much quiet. So I went to the deck above, which was deserted. Except that one of the soldiers kept waking me at intervals. He'd come up to say "Hey, I couldn't sleep with my head in that direction or the blood would run into it and I'd be dead in the morning", or come up and wake me to ask wasn't I too cold, so I finally gave up the idea of sleep which was just as well, for it was nice to watch us go through the Canal.

I think of you, Lottie. I also keep seeing your paintings.'

A letter came from you quickly, care of American Express. Welcoming me to Greece. Saying once again that you were sad, sad. Saying that you thought of me, admired my courage, thanked me for the strength I'd given you. And you asked me to forgive you for the 'bad temper and petty spirit' you'd sometimes shown. You wrote: 'So dear girl, be free and happy and bask in the sun and dry sweet air of that island strange world while I struggle in this bird cage with Pepinella and/or myself . . .'

I wrote back:

' . . . You are not petty with me. Forgive you? You were weary, you were on edge. I was not gentle with you. I battered at you. At the end, I was hitting out without even taking aim – so damn monotonously – because despairingly – and how could you be other than distracted by that? But you were not petty. I love so how you are. I fear only, out of cowardice, to try to forget you. But I will not. I do go seeking you, Lottie. As my friend only, if you will – which is no light search. But in my own heart, as my love. For you *are* my love and ever shall be – even as my friend.

You were never petty, Lottie. You are hard. Which I love. Although I suffer from it. You are not mild. And I love it that you are not. And one who was mild could never be tender as you are tender when you are – for that is a motion that takes my breath away and more delicate, ah than that Sicilian rain I tried to tell you about. You are hard because you respect yourself – and respect your work – and are not willing to be destroyed – or to have your work destroyed – and this is *good* – though yes, I suffer from it – and dream still that I might not have destroyed you – but that was for you to say.

Did two large ragged crows live in the Pantheon when you were here? And a small hawk live in the cliff?'

You had given me a letter to your friends Russell and Lisa and after looking them up, I wrote again:

' . . . They took me out to dinner – to the Bateau Ivre. And there, as every table was taken, we sat down with a Greek poet and his wife and his friend – the poet a man with a shaggy beard and great soft eyes. And drank much of that resinous wine together. He read palms, it turned out. And read mine. Stared at it an endless time. Had I been married or engaged, he asked. And I said no. And then he stared at me softly and told me: "You have left somebody." To which I said nothing. Then he asked me was I worrying about somebody in my family, and I said yes. Of course. Ned. Had I had a pain in the left side of my body lately, he asked. And queerly enough the last few days I have had a stitch in my left side. (I do call it queer, that he knew.) And then returned to his first remark and "The one you have left," he said, "you are not really severed from." And then he put my hand down. The subtle Greeks!'

It was a few days later that I took a ship with Lisa and Russell to the island of Mykonos. As my first chapter has already told. And there met Cyclops, the fisherman who knew how to 'live like a king'. His friend the doctor liked to make this boast about him. At a small feast which the doctor gave, I watched this barefoot king spill wine and spill songs. And leap from the table to spread his arms and dance – dance his very soul. And I was smitten with awe of him. I wrote in my notebook:

'How to dance one's life? How to celebrate it? This is what I go seeking.'

This is what I went seeking – in awe now and in confusion. When the doctor asked me to go with him on an evening visit to a patient – a boy with tetanus, who couldn't speak again yet, who tried, but couldn't speak; and when on our way back to rejoin the others, he told me how alone he felt; and when he stopped me in the garden of his house, his hand reaching for mine, his eyes asking 'Wait' – I let him pull me down among the flowers. Hearing from the open windows the thudding sound of Cyclops dancing still, I asked myself: Mustn't I, too, affirm life – by this act of assent? I felt no pleasure as the needy man entered my body – but tried to tell myself: I, too, spill wine to the gods.

And here is where I ended that first chapter.

As I take up the story again – and think back to catch up dropped stitches – I can remember, by trying, those moments in the garden. But I can remember more sharply my feelings the next day – as I lay on the deck of the ship taking me back to Athens, doubt troubling my mind. I had affirmed the doctor's life. But had I affirmed my own? As the ship moved through the afternoon and through the star-bright night, this question plagued me like a dull ache. And another question, too: What if I found myself to be pregnant? How would I dance my life then?

Back in Athens I found a second letter from you. You wrote:

'Your letter was generous, Bobbie, truly and I thank you for it. I know how painful it must have been for you to write but it has helped me a great deal opened up my heart again so that we can be friends and I won't be uneasy worried and a whole complex of feelings I don't understand myself but I know aren't good and so wherever it is we meet again in Greece or wherever we'll have fun together and be free and easy and I'll be more myself. So I hope anyway and if I don't it will certainly be my own doing because *you* have given already everything humanly possible to me in your love. Please don't feel you can't write me will you Bobbie – *that* would be wrong.'

You wrote that you'd let me know just as soon as you'd come to a decision about whether or not you could join me for a few days on your way home. And you astonished me by saying how tempted you'd been just to leave *with* me. 'It seemed so simple to go and so hard to stay.' But you had started another large painting, you wrote – 'and I have the right thing finally'. And you were going to start still another large painting.

You wrote, 'I'm having a picnic with all the little boys and girls. They are a delight. They woo me for their reasons which is all to my advantage because they are so much children when they do and I have dark plots brewing – posing for instance. Had a gay whirl this evening at dusk skipping rope with a gang of little girls in front of the church while the Padre paused and paced and read his evening bible – hat and all.

Lots of love thanks and thanks again for everything for your letters for you . . .'

So you might still come.

I wrote in my journal: 'Oh it does revive, darling – my belief in a life that we could have together. But I stamp on it. Like a snake. For it bites not me but you. But yes, it does come out again in the sun. I think: it was to be, it should have been. If only . . . But I stamp on it.'

What I went seeking now was how to stamp on it without stamping out, too, my own life fire.

Lisa and Russell had told me I could stay with them any time I wanted. I left my suitcase at their place and – carrying just the striped wool knapsack I found the second day I went wandering through Athens (I have that knapsack still) – set forth on a series of journeys, to visit the places you'd marked on the map. Returning at the end of each journey to see whether there was any word from you.

These were wondrous trips. Today, I suppose, buses are sleek and the highways smooth and the time it takes to get from one place to another fairly predictable. But back then – the roads were a succession of potholes and the buses ancient noisy wrecks which their drivers swerved from one side of the road to another to avoid the deepest of the potholes. Sometimes they'd break down several times a day. When this happened, we would all climb out and sit about in field or olive grove or wherever we'd come to a stop. If we'd arrived in a village, we'd sit down at one of the outdoor tables and have coffees, while the driver tinkered with the motor. Sometimes one or another passenger would help with the tinkering. Nobody showed impatience. This is what it was to travel. And the stops were occasions for talk and for catching up with news of what was happening in that particular place. Sometimes, in fact, in the villages, even if no one had to get on or off, the driver would slow to a stop and have a brief chat out the window with some acquaintance standing by the way.

Though I had only a few words of Greek, I was often included in the conversations that went on. Words weren't considered necessary. They could be translated into gestures. I remember a bony old woman across the aisle from me on one trip who spoke and spoke and spoke to me, without once saying a word. She'd waggle her eyebrows at me as she'd see me staring out her window at a bright field of poppies. Or when we'd jounce into a pothole, she'd clutch her stomach and wink at me. Sometimes, catching my eye, she'd just shrug her shoulders or jut out her chin in a friendly way. Before she hopped off the bus, at a stop before my stop, she turned, looked keenly into my eyes, and nodded her head – as though to bless my journey through her country. Thank you for that blessing, old woman. It did help me on my way.

One of my first trips was a trip to the temple at Sounian – set on its high promontory above the sea, and distant misty blue islands. Its original shape was clear, though many of the stones had fallen or were askew now, one upon the other. A temple of beautiful simplicity. A dazzling white. Yet a white that was all colours – as you have painted it – the colours of every delicate flower that had sprung up among the encircling grasses. I was shocked to find initials carved in the ancient stones. Shocked especially to find the name of BYRON scratched in letters larger than any of the others. The temple itself, placed as it was, invited one to muse on all the natural world surrounding us, mother to us. But the name-scratchers had felt a desperate need to insist that we not forget *them*.

I sat on the flowered ground at the verge of the cliff, listened to the bees in the air, listened for the far-below-me voice of the sea, and stared about me. A sickle moon was in the sky. I wrote in my notebook: 'The broken temple. And above, the moon – a fragment too. But it is really whole.' With this thought I fell into a kind of trance. During the trip to Mykonos the four of us had taken a small boat to visit Delos, too – the island famous for its row of sleek stone lions that look rather like seals ranged on the shore, staring across the years. And we had roamed among the ruins of the ancient houses there – small rooms clustered round sunny courtyards, the mosaics which formed their floors often still intact, each floor holding some beautiful geometric pattern at the room's centre. Some of the patterns shifted as we stared, playing tricks with our eyes. This began to play tricks, too, with my sense of time. In which century did we now breathe? The guide who had brought us there in his caïque stooped, at one point, and picked a small stiff yellow many-petalled flower, and with a smile held it out for us to see. It was the very flower that was a figure in one of the mosaic designs. I'd felt a quick joy flare in me as I recognized it in his outstretched hand, and I hadn't known quite why. But as I sat now staring up at the moon that one could think was only a fragment of itself, I understood that the small persistent flower had been a sign to me. It told me: What I had just lived through so intensely with you – I needn't fear its loss. What has so intensely been can't be taken away. Can seem to be taken, but in fact persists. I wasn't at all sure how to act upon this thought. I nevertheless sat holding to it, holding to it. A breeze was blowing and the flowers all about me bent on their slight stems, trembling, but didn't blow apart. I sat on and on, staring at the flowers, staring at the temple, staring at the gliding moon.

On another day I took a bus to Elevsis. And on that day I fell into a dreaming state deeper still. My first feeling was a shock of disappointment. I found little more than three columns upright there. A peasant woman who saw me staring about made a rolling motion with her hands – 'Bomba'. Here was a jumble of fractured stones and pillars and bits of ornament. The site was on a small hill above a town that was now a factory town. Townswomen were gathering some edible weeds among the ruins. And a few chickens hopped from ancient stone to stone. I wandered along the hilltop, among the marble wreckage. No shape of what once had been was still discernible. Here was just the rubble of it. But I can remember still my disappointment changing to a deep surprise, as I stood among those scattered stones. Smoke rose from the chimneys of the town just down the hill. Its factory whistle shrilled. There were bursts of popular music, and a continual seething of voices. But these sounds which were the nearby sounds of the present day seemed to me curiously remote – even illusory. Whereas the jumble of tumbled stones at my feet seemed electric with life – subtle, undeniable. I stood for a long time in a state of surprise. The factory whistle shrilled again. It was as though the sound struck against my body but fell away. My inner ear brimmed with a gentle humming. In fact my whole body seemed to hum. It was as though the soles of my feet picked up vibrations from the ground. I wrote in my state of wonder: 'These ruins are more live than the present life.'

At the time I found it strange that I should feel it to be so at that particular site. I no longer find it strange. For I have come – as other women have – to muse at length about the rites that once were celebrated just there – the Eleusian Mysteries. Rites in which Persephone, who has been carried off by the Lord of the Underworld, is reunited with her mother, Demeter, and with her own stolen-away self. Rites acted out in a time when women had begun to lose their strength to the patriarchs, but here affirmed the truth that it could not be taken from us once and for all – will be found again.

As I write of Persephone's abduction there floods into my memory a dream I dreamed as a young girl. Which has remained for me down through all the years of my life sharp as though I had dreamed it yesterday – its imagery distinct, and the feelings, too, distinct that cast their net over me. I dreamed it at a time when my father used at bedtime to play with my brothers and me a game he called Daddy Wolf. He would hide in the parlour with all the lights out. We would creep together down the long hall that led to the room, and then – venture into that dark. He would jump out of the shadows, catch in his arms first one of us and then another; tickle us until we screamed with joy and terror. It was play my mother pleaded with him to give up. For she would have liked to put us to bed in a calm and drowsy state. But my father loved the game. In the dream: I am on the back of a large silvery wolf. Seated there, captive. Not able to slip off. Not bound in any physical way, but passive, accepting – that I *am* the captive. It is this resignation that is the dread feeling that fills the dream. The wolf moves with awesome dignity slowly down the hall and toward the front door –

passing in this motion the open door to the dining-room, where the rest of the family sits. They see us pass and with helpless looks they raise their hands in sorrow and then bow their heads. Yes, I belong to the Daddy Wolf. He will bear me wherever he wants. And it is for me simply to be his quiet passenger. At the front door, I wake from the dream. Though I don't wake entirely. For its feelings hold me still.

A net of feelings in which I struggled all through my youth. As an adolescent I began to feel that net give. Began to feel I had the new weight and new impulsive motion to break it. This was a delicious feeling. Which persisted during my four years at an all-women's college. There we young women stared into one another's eyes and saw each other as strong and beautiful. But as soon as I graduated and was attempting to make my living and my way in a man's world – I could taste in my mouth again that familiar earlier taste, of captivity.

Nell's kisses could dispel it sometimes. And her assuring glances. But too often I could catch in her own eye the look of one being borne in a direction not her own. She did have about her a lovely air of capability. Of gaiety too. That could seem to assert: Oh our lives belong to us. And yet – I could see that she too sometimes doubted it. Or doubted at least that two women hand in hand could find their way. And finally of course it was a man to whom she had turned. Would the woman I loved always finally turn from me to a man? Probably. And what was I then to do with all my feelings for her? Or rather, if I stamped out those feelings, stamped them underground, what was to become of me – whom those same feelings had first brought alive? As I stood there among those tumbled shining stones, all my feelings for you circled through my body as though they were my blood. And the humming in my ears asserted: This is more real than that 'real world' nearby in which you must make your way. The world which will ask you to deny what you are feeling. How was I then to make my way? But this question only flicked in and then out of my mind. I was listening to that humming. Which my feet picked up from the ground. And which circled through my body as though it were my blood.

I think again suddenly of the myth of Persephone, and of my long-ago dream. In the dream it occurs to me now, there is no figure of Demeter, angrily demanding her daughter's release – refusing to let there be summer, going on strike, declaring winter until her daughter has her liberty. My mother's glance, meeting mine, despairs of my release: names herself a captive too – pained to see me caught up now as she has long been. She is herself Persephone. Her glance declares: 'I know, I know too well. No, we cannot belong to ourselves. It is his kingdom here.' She does not show fear for me, exactly. This wolf as she knows him in her own life does not bite or snarl. He simply carries us in a direction that is not our own – is his. Her look is awed and bitter, her anger masked.

My beautiful and bitter mother. At this point in my life I was trying not to think of her very often. I feared to have her captive glance take away my strength. And yet – any bold or near-bold gestures toward freedom I had been able to make on my own she had always given her astonished blessing. She had seen me off on my ship to Italy, and left in my stateroom a long box of flowers (mountain laurel she had picked) and a note that had made me cry. We were shy with one another, she had written, but she wished she had the words to tell me her pride in me – and in the book I had just finished, and the poems she had seen. 'I can never talk to you about your poems', she wrote. 'To me they are so very personal it would seem a sort of intrusion. But my admiration is very deep.' Some of the poems of course were about Nell – as I knew she knew. Her note ended with the sudden cry: 'Feel free!'

I stood among the fallen stones of Elevsis, and I listened to the humming in my ear. It seemed to be telling me that I was in fact free. However, the hubbub of voices from just down the hill seemed to be warning me that I was not.

Soon after, I took a trip to Delphi. I rose at dawn to catch that bus. It took a long time to load it. A large brass bed had to be tied on back, and a variety of smaller household objects. We hadn't been riding long when a metallic clatter startled us all out of napping. I thought that the bed must have fallen off – in spite of all the rope I'd seen being looped about it. But no – a spring beneath the bus had broken. The driver with a sigh pulled off the road. The passengers climbed out; a few crawled under the bus to give advice, and the rest of us stretched out in a sweet smelling field to continue our naps. But soon both driver and helpers gave up; he called us back in; and steered us – slow-motion, springs dragging – the few miles to the next town and a garage. Two hours later we were on our way again.

I was now awake enough at last to look at the countryside through which we drove. Black huddles of goats under trees. And huddles of sheep – the peasants tending them stretched out among them. The land had been close-cropped by these flocks, and the day's drifting clouds cast clear clear shadows of themselves – the motions of grasses and the motions of clouds colliding on the ground in a lovely way. And such a light! It rinsed everything, leaving it shining-bare. The raw earth often showed in gashes of red – the rusty red of the shoeshine I'd been given back in Athens. Or it showed a startling pink. (I remembered that pink from your sketchbook.) We entered hill country, and ledges of rock shone – sometimes greenish, sometimes bluish, sometimes a white-grey, mysterious as water. Many tall white-grey flowers had sprung up that were the very colour of this rock – as if rock had exploded into blossom, I mused. And I mused that really *anything* could be struck from rock by this light. No wonder the ancients here had worshipped a *god* of light; and had seen spirits in rocks and in trees and in streams.

I was making this particular trip in a mood of anticipation I only half acknowledged. At Delphi was the site of the ancient oracle. I knew that it was not said to be speaking to anyone any longer. And yet I couldn't help asking myself whether it might not give me just a hint as to how to take my bearings now.

We did arrive in Delphi finally. The driver honked our way through the town. For everybody was in the street – it was Sunday. The hotel in front of which he stopped the bus was an expensive one, placed strategically at the foot of the hill one must climb to the ruins. As I walked off to find a cheaper place, the manager called after me, wagging his finger, 'Wrong way!' But at the furthest edge of town I found a room I could afford, and then returned to make the climb.

To the small treasury – this one building carefully reconstructed. To the theatre. To Apollo's temple, and Athena's. Climbing from one to another by steep mountain paths. Birds singing against the cliff.

A few other travellers were wandering through the ruins, too. But this site was so extensive that we rarely came face to face. At the wide theatre I noted, 'British voices, and butterflies.' And I wrote, 'Always an amazing setting has been found.' These ruins faced from their heights not the sea as at Sounian but 'a sea of land' – a wide valley and what seemed an endless grove of olive trees streaming through that valley, in leafy flood.

I wondered where the site of the oracle might be. And went clambering around, searching for it. Goats took these paths too. And their keepers had improvised shelters for them here and there among the rocks. They gazed out at me from these refuges as I passed, with their shiny wild eyes. I asked directions from one young woman who was watching her herd, but she didn't understand my question – just smiled and shrugged. I should have gone up to one of the English tourists, I realised. Any one of them would probably have known. But they were nowhere about now. So I just kept clambering about. Finally as I was wandering again near the temple to Apollo I encountered a young Greek who did understand what I was asking – and he led me to the spot where, he told me (in French), the oracle used to speak. He stood there for a few minutes, staring at the place himself, with a dreamy look, and then – to my relief – strolled off. There was just a low grassy pit here now among tumbled pillars – the grass long and curly. I waited until the man was out of sight. And then I jumped down into the curly grass. And stood very still. Bringing all my being to attention. I will hear you, I breathed. I am ready to hear you, whatever you say. The sun beat on my head. The light shimmered in front of my eyes. Nothing spoke. But then from just over the nearest hill came a speaking. A long-drawn-out speaking. A half-groaning half-laughing paroxysm of speech. That most irreverent of sounds – a donkey somewhere braying its heart out.

This answer, yes, took me by surprise. And yet, instantly, delighted me. I couldn't tell why. (I think I can now tell why. What better counsel – than that a good measure of irreverence is required if one is to find one's way?) I can remember that I stood there lightened in spirit. Smiling foolishly. Refreshed. And then I heard again the birds singing and singing against the cliff.

The next morning I rose again at dawn to take a bus to Amfissa – where I hoped to catch a bus to a town from which I could walk to the mountain monastery of Hossios Lukas. Russell had told me there were wonderful mosaics there. Our road ran through the great valley aflood with olive trees, for mile after silvery mile. I had time to waste at Amfissa. Always in these little towns, as you know, there'd be at least one Greek who had been to America and then returned – and so spoke English. Here there was an old man with several silver teeth who had run a cigar store in New York for many years. He sat down with me as I had a cup of coffee, and told me the story of his life. Other villagers gathered and listened. And they discussed my trip together – decided it was a bus to Itea I needed to catch next. I had time still to visit the church there – where two women were shining the altar candlesticks, and turned to stare and smile. I heard a hammering down the street, followed the sound and stood at the door of a forge to watch the making of sheep bells – one man at the bellows, singing, three others hammering, shaping the bells. Then the bus rumbled in, and I jumped on.

Itea was a seaside town. After finding a room, I walked along the shore. Sat for a while near some women who were mending nets. We made a few awkward attempts to speak together. Some small goats browsing nearby poked their faces into mine, curious about me.

As I wandered on, past a little house set back from the beach, a woman who was standing in the yard of the house peered at me, then hurried forward beckoning for me to come near. Then: Wait, she gestured. Hurried into the house and brought out a chair for me. Vanished again and reappeared with a sweet to offer me in a spoon. Then she taught me a little Greek. Pointed to one of her flock of chickens and named it. Pointed to the sea. The chair I sat on. The spoon I held. And then she brought me a photograph of her brother, who lived now in Connecticut. She gazed at me as though to learn a little more about the country to which she had lost him.

I wandered back into town and into a grocery store to buy some cheese to eat for lunch. The owner of the store asked me to sit and talk – for *he* had lived in the States for many years; had run a restaurant there. I climbed the hill behind the town to visit a church atop it. From this hill I could see the olive groves flowing back between all the hills beyond. The whole town made its living from these olives, the grocer had told me. As I walked back down, two women I had noticed on my way up came out of the yard of their small house and beckoned to me: 'Ella' – come. As they led me into their yard, they picked almonds from one of their trees and held them out to me: Eat. The nuts tasted quite green to me, but I didn't want to refuse them – and ate. At the steps of their house, one of them spread out her coat and gestured: Sit. The other darted into the garden and plucked a few beans and held these out to me. Again, when I tasted them, they didn't seem quite ripe, but the woman held them out to me so eagerly, I didn't want to refuse her gift. And ate. Then the other hurried into the house and brought out a chunk of bread with cheese on it, and that I ate thankfully. We stared at each other shyly. They knew no English, but one knew a little French. 'Que voulez vous?' she asked, with eager sweetness, peering into my face. What do you want? I remember searching for the words with which to answer. And remember her waiting, intently – almost as intently as though it were her own self she had asked the question. What do you want? I was just travelling, I answered clumsily – and looking. 'En regardant.' She nodded slowly, and wistfully. Translated for the other. Who stared, wistful too. The one who could speak French then shyly offered me a bed for the night. I told them I had a room. Wishing that I could stay with them instead, but not quite having the daring to change my plans.

Back in town the grocer hailed me again and walked with me to the town's dock. And now he began to speak of the time when the Germans had been here – burning burning everything. His niece joined us – and he changed the subject. They both sat with me as I ate dinner at a small café. He insisted on paying – the young woman nodding that yes, I must accept. And they walked me to my hotel.

I was up very early to catch my bus. And there were the two of them to say goodbye to me. The niece had picked some lilacs ('aprili' – she told me the name for them) and put them into my hands. 'We are glad to know you.'

The grocer had spoken to the driver. Sometime mid-morning he pulled up at a crossroads and gestured that this was my stop. Pointed the direction I should take on foot. To Distomon.

I had begun to feel a little queerly. It was the raw almonds and beans I'd eaten the day before, I figured. My guts were now in revolt. I walked the mile or so to Distomon slowly. It was a small village with a pleasantly assymetrical central square with a war monument, two small cafés, assorted animals running about.

Groups of men were sitting at the outdoor tables, twirling in their fingers those strings of beads – 'worry beads' – Greek men are seldom without. While the women of the village plodded past on their way to or from the fields, or carrying spindles, or washing, or bundles of sticks they'd gathered. My notes add, 'Let it be said: a few men did pass with farm implements in hand – riding on mules.'

'Poo eeenay ta mera?' ('Where is the place?') I asked the first woman I met – an old crone with a load of sticks on her back. I had dysentery, it was clear to me by now. She led me to an outdoor privy around the corner. When I emerged – from behind the dirty fluttering curtain – she grimaced at me sadly, clutching her stomach in sympathy. And she came and sat with me at one of the outdoor tables – to find out a little about me. With few words and many gestures she managed to question me and I to answer. I was headed for Hossios Lukas. Yes, on foot. I was an American. Yes, alone. She grinned at me, amazed but glad about all this. But – she patted her stomach – she was sorry I was having this trouble. She left me to gather more wood. Returned after a while, leading by the hand a little girl – her granddaughter – who wanted to meet me. Left again, work to do.

Meanwhile of course several of the men had crossed to my table. I had ordered tea, taking out my dictionary to find the word – for I'd learned over the years that this was good medicine for what ailed me. The men passed the tiny book around, flipped through it, put their own questions to me. I drank the tea quickly, asked for a second cup. The more I could get down, the better. The waiter seemed puzzled. I'd used the words for 'another, please'. Asking for my dictionary, I found the word for 'again'. The word for 'more'. Held up the cup, pointing at it – 'Tea'. Yes, tea, the men agreed – and took turns saying the word in English. I held up two fingers for the waiter. He stared. I held out my cup to him – 'Please'. He took it from me then – tentatively; left, and returned with it full. I wanted this second cup? I wanted this second cup. I thanked him. Drank this, too, as quickly as I could. And asked for a third cup. This time it took me longer still to make it clear that I really wanted it. And when I held out the empty cup to ask to have it filled a fourth time, they all grew silent, silently gaped. Women alone – look what happened to them. The waiter ran off as if to hurry to serve one who was demented.

I started off down the rutted road the old woman had pointed out to me. Which soon became a path. The path led me, after a mile or so, to another smaller town – Styros. Or the remnant of a town. The Germans had burned most of the houses that once stood here. And killed most of the inhabitants. I learned this from an English-speaking old man who ran the dilapidated tavern. He sat down with me while I drank still another cup of tea. He started to say more about those terrible times. Then decided not to. Just shook his head. He said he would set me on the right path to Hossios Lukas. Walked with me to the edge of town. Scratched in the earth a map of the way to take. Gravely waved goodbye.

This path led me up into the hills – hills with deep gulleys of reddish soil. It was a rubbly path and the ground sometimes fell away from it sharply. I had to be careful not to let my foot slip. From the slopes above me came the cries of shepherds calling to one another or to their flocks. And the teasing will-o-the-wisp music of sheep bells. I kept climbing. But my insides were in a strange state still. I began to feel almost dizzily tired. And to wonder why I was taking this walk. I felt my feet begin to drag. I stopped, disheartened. I lay down on the ground next to the path.

At first as I lay there, I was aware only of my own exhaustion – my own discouraged body. But slowly I began to be aware, too, that the ground against which I was resting was warm. With the warmth of new-baked bread. And, like new bread, sweet-smelling. This sweet-smelling warmth began to warm me, too – to spread through my body, slowly easing me. My guts began to stop their writhing. I lay there quite a long time. Then stood up, astonished and refreshed.

I walked on. The terrain altered. Grew wooded. There were torrents of daisies among the woods. After a mile or so, I began to tire again. Rounding a corner, I stopped and leaned against a large rock by the side of the path. I turned my head. And to my relief just ahead of me, down the path, stood the monastery.

The monks were accustomed to visitors. An English-speaking Greek had been hired especially to cope with them – a man who'd run a restaurant for some years in New Hampshire. So I was shown to a neat room with bed where I was told I could spend the night – the walls covered with photographs of monks, two large books about the monastery on the reading table. And I was taken on a brief tour, to see the mosaics. Which were indeed very beautiful. I was allowed then to wander about on my own. Sat out under a plane tree and admired the terraced gardens. But when I re-entered the church, to look again at a particular angel I had liked especially, a dark-clad woman whose relation to this place I never did figure out, decided she should take me in charge. She began to escort me about in a peremptory way – making, as we went, multitudinous signs of the cross. To cross out our female presences? – decontaminate the spaces we mere women were daring to enter? She led me to a chapel in which a service was about to begin. Fell to her knees, touched her forehead to the floor. And again. And again. Glanced at me severely. So I knelt, myself. But couldn't bring myself to knock my head against the floor. She scowled. And now she beckoned me to a seat over on the side, up against the wall. The monks began to drift in. In dirty vestments drawn over work-ragged pants. Monks all ages and sizes. Drifted in and began to chant. Quite beautifully. Sometimes taking turns. And sometimes all together. A few in deep concentration, but some – I noticed – yawning, between times, distracted. My mentor continued to cross herself. And to go down on her knees, rise, then go down again – twice as often as the monks knelt and rose and knelt. Wanting me to copy her, I could see. But I pretended not to notice this – knelt only when the monks did. After they had all shuffled out, she darted forward towards some golden pictures that surrounded the altar – an array of holy males, figured in gold leaf. On her knees again, she kissed the golden hems of their garments. Then gestured for me to do the same. I pretended not to understand her gesture. Just nodded my head – as if I had been asked simply to admire. She gestured again. Her glance commanded: 'Do as I do, woman. You are a woman, too. Or don't you know it?' I pretended stubbornly not to understand what she asked. At the time, I was surprised at myself. Why couldn't I make the motions she was asking me to make – just as a courtesy? At my heart's core I experienced the most stubborn refusal. I would happily have knelt to kiss the warm earth that had nestled me that afternoon. But I was not going to kiss these golden hems. She shrugged, disgusted. Soon left me. Let me go my own impious way.

My original guide brought supper to my room: a boiled egg, which I gratefully ate, and some fried potatoes which I wrapped in a handkerchief as soon as he'd left, and hid in my knapsack, afraid my stomach couldn't handle them. I washed in the glass of water he'd left me (there was no wash-basin in sight), and went to bed early. For he had let me know that the proper time to leave the next day would be at 5 a.m.

A small sad-eyed man was returning to Distomon, too. We walked the way together. I was sorry not to be alone, for I would have liked to stop often and gaze about. We left by starlight, the hills black, but the stones underfoot queerly alight, with the look that ashes can have, in which fire still lives. High in the hills sparkled camp fires – fires kept by shepherds, my companion let me know, by giving a noisy imitation of sheep. The hills turned slowly blue, a lighter and livelier blue, then, as sunrise burst the night, a glowing purplish pink. When we came to fields and vineyards soon after day, we found the women of the nearby villages already at work. In the vineyards they were shaking a yellow-green fertilizer out of tin containers. A few men were riding about on mules. Walking briskly, We were back in Distomon by seven. I was greeted by the old woman I'd met the day before. She was out gathering wood again.

During the bus ride back to Athens I sat wondering whether or not I'd find a letter from you waiting for me. And wondering whether you'd say that you'd join me for a little while. And dreaming in spite of myself of what those days might bring about. I recalled to myself the words of the man who'd read my palm: 'The one you have left you are not really severed from.'

In Athens a letter was waiting. You wrote, 'This is going to be a perfectly horrid depressing annoying letter because it's about my plans and/or lack of them. First of all I cannot come to Greece. This probably won't surprise you!'

It did surprise me. When one falls downstairs, even the last step is a surprise.

You wrote:

'This decision you do, I hope, realise is not based on any personal considerations – believe me. Solely work and last days Panic. My head is so full of a jumble just thinking of *one* trip that it is all I can do to keep some kind of perspective as it is. I'm even in a state about leaving here on the 26th, still have no reservation, trying to convince myself that I must. If I wait and leave on the 10th of June I will have just one week before leaving for my Boston summer teaching job which is ridiculous if I am going to Face This Business with Leonard. That's a rather cold way to put it – sounds like an execution! But you understand me so well by this time that nothing could shock you. Will you Bobbie do me one more very great favour – send me a *cable* (one or two words) giving *your* opinion on the boat business (26 May or June that is!) – moral support for me in need – but more important cold reason and wisdom – yours. It is ridiculous and shameful to ask this of *you*. Then why do I? One reason you saved my life once remember and you are my dearest friend *and* I am getting to be a real Dostoevsky character and that about covers Everything!!! Please do try and forgive me if you can Bobbie. I don't want to hurt you but that seems to be all I do.'

I can remember sitting with your letter in my hand, both grimacing and smiling now, not knowing whether to laugh or weep – my feelings whirling.

You wrote, 'I'm perfectly willing to swallow the Greek fortune teller analysis whole. That's one of my vices, believing in palms, even my cousin Nita's tea leaves – though that is going a bit far. I am sorry about not coming, you know *I* have thought of it for the past twelve months (only!) but can't decide otherwise because my work has to be solved by just sitting and within myself at least for now . . . When will you be back? Are you coming to Italy before you leave or don't you know? I guess the latter!'

You wrote, 'Painting children all week. Hope I have got something. Pepinella has had the flu thank heavens and is home.'

I read this letter a second time. And a third time. Sitting at a small café where I'd stopped to have my medicinal cup of tea. Making strange faces, I think, as I read it – for I can remember that several people as they passed slowed their steps to look at me with curiosity.

I walked back to the American Express and sent the only cable I could in conscience send: EARLIER DATE BETTER IF YOU WOULD NOT GO INTO IT BLIND MUCH LOVE.

And then I wrote:

'Lottie – rope-skipping girl – Dostoevsky girl – my more than dear friend –

Do *me* a great favour – or – your*self* (in what I am about to write count me not a dramatis persona) – please. It is this: You are reluctant to leave the 26th – because of your work – but also – ?? – because you are not altogether sure what your meeting with him will be. More than that, what a life with him will be. And so – you'd postpone it – isn't this so? Promise only this: if when you meet him something in your heart tells you that here is *not* the life you want – do not feel EVER: here is the last chance for me, it is this life or none – please, Lottie. Because this would be wrong. Because for you choices need never be narrow, Lottie – need never – much as you may have felt so in recent months.

If choices have not presented themselves in *multiplicity* in the past, it is because you have not – have you? – been altogether seeking them.

Yes, of your sailing date – a week is not very much, is it, in which *both* to pack for Boston and – well – to look quietly at this man, just a few times, before marrying him?

Ah, Lottie – so – God bless you. (And who is this God it is so easy to name? But – may you be blessed, Lottie. May God bless you.)

And here is a question:

Ah, what I wish you would do is leave from *Greece* for the States – fly here at the end for just a week (and call the difference a gift) – and have the travel agent put your things on the ship at Naples – which would make only one motion of packing (you would bring to Greece a satchel, just what you would travel with) – and – before moving toward this new life take a deep breath here. I know the answer to this is no, but say it.

Here is my question: If I came back to Italy just before your leaving – a week, ten days before your leaving – could I come and stay with you – to say face to face God bless you – and – just to be with you again – whom I may not see again for – what length of time? Where will you be after Boston? . . . Or – would you rather that I didn't?

Of asking me to send that cable – of hurting me – don't ever be afraid of hurting me, Lottie. Be bold with me always. Speak what comes into your heart to speak, and make that move that it comes into your heart to make, and you touch my life as I would have you touch it, and it doesn't hurt to be hurt.'

I decided to visit Crete while I waited for your answer. But I stayed on with Russell and Lisa for a few days, first, to let my guts quiet down. Not that theirs was a quiet household. The simplest activities in which they engaged became dramatic events – as when they washed each other's hair one morning, rinsing with water poured from a large pitcher, each of them uttering wild screams. And Russell hadn't run out of questions to put to me; he hadn't run out of elaborate theories about life and art he'd want me to listen to – for if I'd not hear him out, how could the world hold together?

They took me to the ballet one night; took me on another evening to a tavern where ordinary working men (but not women) came to drink beer, and after drinking up would rise and, solo, improvise what seemed to me even more wonderful dance. I went back there several evenings on my own to watch this again.

The men sometimes wavered on their feet at first, from much drink. But every one of them I watched took the dance with great seriousness and – however tipsy – would find within it slowly a solemn grace.

I remember especially one small man in worker's boots, worn pants tucked into them like knickers, a loose jacket, a work-soiled cap. Who always turned toward the small orchestra an almost winsome smile as he'd get up from his table and move out into the dancing space. With a high-stepping walk – his steps then hesitating as if he listened for something; then quickening; but then again hesitating. He spread his arms out like tentative wings. And then turned these curved arms from side to side – slowly – as if testing the air, as if seeking his way. But then with the most delicate and tense motion he'd stoop suddenly and touch the ground. His hands hovered over it – then touched it again: I don't forget you. He made then a series of amazing light little jumps into the air, turning quite round. But then touched the ground again. Kneeling on one knee and shifting his body so as to touch the ground with the other knee. Again. Again. Earth, I am of you.

As he danced, I remembered the ground on which I had stretched out on my way to the monastery. Remembered how it had given me back my strength.

He danced a prayer, it seemed to me. And danced my prayer. Help me to know my way. Help me to remember where it is my strength comes from.

I was grateful to have him dance this prayer for me – and grateful, too, to see a man dancing not a dance of war but a dance that touched the earth. I also couldn't not feel jealous that men only were allowed to dance here. Except for the waitresses. Sometimes, though not often, they would dance. With one of the men or – more likely – with each other. I remember two of them suddenly putting their arms round one another and whirling and whirling and whirling round the floor, as in a waltz, except that with each whirl they made they'd turn in almost a complete circle – whirling quite fiercely round and round and round the floor. As if to assert: Women are alive too.

With one of the waitresses I talked when she had moments to rest. For she knew a tiny amount of English, and wanted to learn more. We told each other a little about our lives. It was lucky for me that I had made her acquaintance, for one night a policeman came and sat down at my table and started putting stern questions to me that I couldn't understand. My friend came running over, talked to him rapidly, and he stared at me and left. She explained then that he had been about to arrest me as a prostitute. Which he assumed I must be – for women who were not prosititutes never came to this place unescorted.

Though unescorted, I went night after night to this taverna, until I left for Crete. Just before I left, I wrote to you again:

'Lottie – sweet friend – brow-contracted friend –

I know the answer to this letter and yet I can't help writing it. And write it out of quietness – sitting in a little triangle of blowing grasses above the sea. And sit very still and write it – write to say: in spite of everything I think you should fly to Greece for at least one week before you go. I still do think so – and respecting your work, as you must know that I do, and respecting your panic, still do think so. Think with *reference* to your work you should stand here again – think with reference to your life you should stand here. Ah, Lottie, throw this letter over your left shoulder if you wish. I can't help writing it. But can't write it well. Because it is not even words in me – but conviction – but a most intense feeling – which my feet pick up from these rocks (which are no ordinary rocks – but could strike sparks – could spark into flowers) – which my eyes drink in with this light – no ordinary light –

Ah Lottie, I could gesture what I would say, but can't write it. I could *dance* what I would say. It would be one of the dances they dance here and in which they touch their knees touch their hands to the ground again and again. I think you should come here. I do think it. Well I know you won't. But I say it.'

14

There was such a crowd at the dock at Piraeus waiting to board the ship bound for Crete that I doubted at first I'd manage to get on. In fact, the gates to the dock had been closed. And the ship appeared to me hardly large enough to hold the swarm already inside there – shouting and laughing and pushing toward the gangplank. But after a certain number had swarmed aboard, the gate was swung open again to my surprise, and even more of us were allowed to push in and aboard.

I like to remember that crowd – at first sight rough and careless, but in fact, I decided, a very safe sea into which to cast myself. I saw a father carrying in his arms a boy with both legs set in plaster, borne forward gently in that press of people – the child wide-eyed but smiling as he was bobbed slowly to and fro on the crest of the human flood.

Most of us were deck passengers. How even one more person could have been fitted on to that ship I don't know. Though I'm also sure that it would have been done somehow – if even more than one extra person had turned up. Parked in the middle of the deck was a huge truck. And there were people packed close together inside it, clasping small bits of luggage; people on the hood, people on the roof, people sprawled underneath it. And packed round it right up to the ship's railings.

There was an upper and a lower deck to the ship and I inched my way to the upper. Found a crate full of vegetables on which I made myself comfortable. My fellow passengers soon attempted conversation – a middle-aged man with a loud necktie; a soldier with a moustache too large for his thin face, who knew only a phrase or two of English, but was soon declaring, 'I love you!', and with the help of my dictionary asking would I take him to the United States. The man with the loud necktie moved off and then returned with a young friend who spoke English easily. Manos, he introduced himself. He worked for Shell. He too would like to go to the States. And there was a chance he could get a scholarship to study there – to study statistics, which he liked. He'd be risking his good job with Shell. 'But' – he gestured now, and raised his eyes – 'if I stay home, my father is the boss.' Yes, Crete was his home. When I mentioned the dancing I had loved at the taverna on Athinis Street, he began to speak of other tavernas and of the songs to be heard in them. Songs created under the Turkish oppression. And the government would like to suppress some of them, he said. For some were about opium. There were many places he could show me; maybe I'd like to spend the weekend with him, he suggested – 'If you are not uncomfortable with a man.' I thanked him but declined: I'd be more comfortable by myself, I said. The man with the loud tie laughed, and Manos sulked for a while. But was soon suggesting that we hunt for a cosy spot where we could stretch out for the night. I found for myself instead a tiny private space just beyond the tip of a lifeboat; wrapped my quilt round me and slept well – though waking now and then to listen to the mingled musics of waves and snores.

Manos shook me awake at dawn. Crete was in sight. My notes record my astonishment at seeing at its crest a delicate snow-topped mountain. 'Like a Japanese print!' Mount Ida.

Making my way through the crowd toward the ship's kitchen, for coffee, I found there were three young Americans on board – two men and a young woman, dressed in sturdy hiking clothes. They were on their way first to see the ruins of Phaestos, and suggested that I join them. I found the will to refuse them, too – knowing that I'd see more clearly if I visited the place by myself. But we took the bus together up into Herakleion. They walked with me while I hunted a cheap hotel. And then washed up a bit in my room. Checked again to be sure that I didn't want to go with them. 'Ah, you really *are* antisocial', the young woman laughed, with evident approval – as though she wished she knew how to be.

The hotel I'd found was the Olympus. On a street of butcher shops, Thaos Toy. This was now Good Friday, the start of the Greek Orthodox Easter weekend – which I was confused to learn fell later in the year than the Easter you and I had lately celebrated. The street of the butchers turned out to be the street toward which everybody in town was striding on that day, to make ready for

Easter feasting – carrying lambs they'd flung about their shoulders, or walking them upright on hind legs; an old woman dragging a goat by the ear, the goat bleating angrily; a fat-legged boy in rompers toddling along with them, gurgling with laughter. Some carried crying pigs, or bunches of upside-down chickens grasped by the legs. The butchers had their aprons on – large red aprons – and stood at the doors of their shops to receive the poor animals.

My notes recall: 'Shut your eyes and see blood! . . . Tangles of flesh on hooks and severed feet upon the kerb! . . . But at day's end the disjointed carcasses decorated with paper flowers!' I wrote to you, 'Lottie darling – What a murder here of the paschal lamb! What a bleating and what a bleeding! And the poor damned creatures lying on the curbs waiting their turn, their eyes already dead.' (They lay often, feet bound, under the long strings of blood dangling from those already slaughtered.) I wrote, 'But by evening cologne water falling upon us from the church dome. Well!'

Meantime, I fled this street and caught a bus for the nearby ruins at Knossos.

On the bus I sat next to a blue-uniformed Greek aviator with curly hair and a glossy blond moustache he kept stroking with pride. He spoke a little English, introduced himself (his name was George) and told me gallantly that he would show me Knossos. I tried to explain that I wouldn't need a guide, but his English was apparently not good enough to understand me. Once at the entrance, he paid the small sum for my ticket before I could stop him and – my guide he was. He'd obviously never been here before, himself, but was prompt to point out to me the clearly labelled statue of Sir Arthur Evans who had unearthed and reconstructed these ruins; and to let me know that all of this was 'four years away – no – past?' (Four thousand he meant, of course.) I liked to stand and stare at things longer than he was used to standing. At the beautifully simple downward-tapered wooden columns of the palace, for example. And I descended very much more slowly than he had expected me to the deep palace stairwell – the steps making repeated right-angle turns round that sunlit well, so that one felt one entered a downward maze. But he patiently adjusted his steps to mine. In the throne room and the rooms just off it he was at a loss for words – blessedly. Just kept nodding at me as we both gazed at the frescoes of griffins, of wave-leaping dolphins, of bull-leaping acrobats (two of the acrobats women!) But as we entered the small room with the centuries-old stone bath tub and ingenious drainage, he recovered his zeal to keep me informed – went through all the motions of scrubbing himself, lest I possibly mistake the tub for something other than it was. Then we came to an ancient store room, with rows of tall-as-we-were earthenware jars. They had many small handles to them – through which, I assumed, ropes were once slipped, to move them. He pointed at the handles and carefully explained: I could see what small hands those people had had. I glanced at him, but he wasn't joking; his face was solemn. And I didn't argue. For it seemed a thrilling thought to him that the human race had evolved since then so sturdily. He looked down at his own somewhat chubby hands with evident satisfaction.

As we walked toward the bus stop, I tried as best I could to forget that George was with me. For I wanted to take in the new landscape, undistracted. The light on this island was, if possible, even stronger, more transfiguring than on the mainland of Greece. A hillside stand of wheat shone as though on fire. A mule on the crest of the hill appeared to be twice as large as I would have thought it would appear at that distance. I glanced everywhere but at George. But he seemed unaware of my attempt to ignore him. 'Why you heart of gold?' he began to ask me. I shook my head, to discourage him. If he ever found a girl, he would want her to have heart of gold like me, he persisted. 'Look', I pointed at the shining wheat; I pointed at some shining clouds that seemed to leap above us like the leaping dolphins. I didn't want to lose that joyous sense of freedom of motion the frescoes had awakened in me.

Would I spend the evening with him, he was asking. I shook my head again: No. He looked confused. He couldn't believe that I meant this. I seemed in a lively mood, and if so – surely I was in a mood to say 'yes', not 'no'. He repeated the invitation during the bus ride. Back in town, he walked me to my hotel. Again, his face was unbelieving as I told him thank you but goodbye.

The street of the butchers was filled with villagers come to collect their butchered animals, all prettily wrapped now in white paper. The blood had been washed from the kerbs, and there was no more bleating in the air. I sat for a while at my hotel window and watched the passers-by. Then I went out to wander, and soon followed a crowd into a church for Good Friday services.

There were no pews in the church. All of us stood. Bunched

together. I stood among a group of women, in a part of the church where a great dome rose above us. There was chanting, which the dome seemed to swirl round and round above our heads. The service went on and on. And on. I began to tire. Began to feel that I was swaying on my feet. I had dressed as I always do to be ready for any sudden drop in the day's temperature. Had on both a sweater and a light coat. Now I felt stifled by all this clothing. But there wasn't room enough in which to take any of it off. I became afraid that I might faint. But just as this fear began to agitate me, I felt a hand on my shoulder and then found myself sitting in a low chair that had been slipped under me. A woman was easing me out of my coat, while another woman fanned me – then handed me the fan. After I could stand again, I saw chair and fan passed along, through the crowd, to be there for somebody else unsteady on her feet.

Toward the end of the service, cool holy water was sprinkled upon all of us from a little balcony in the dome. As though to remind us that it was from on high that blessings came. But I carried away from that afternoon the sense above all that one's own kind here on earth could bless one. I can remember, still sitting there slowly reviving, staring at the sturdy legs and hips and bellies and backs of the women close around me, and smelling their warm scent. I was flooded suddenly with a very simple but quite overwhelming love for all of them. And the experience of this love was so sweet that I had to fight back tears.

Now everybody flowed out into the street, in procession, and then flowed down the street and through the town. As I was following along, I noticed George among the throng. He noticed me, too, and joined me, with a little cry. We walked along together for a while. He suggested a coffee, then, and I agreed. But over coffee, as I should have known he would, he renewed his invitations. 'And if you have no place to sleep . . .' he ventured. He knew that I had a room, for he had walked me to my hotel earlier in the day. I decided to ask, 'How would your sister answer?' (He had mentioned a sister during our talk.) He flushed. And I had brains as well as beauty, he told me glumly. And glumly walked me again to my door.

The next morning he found me somehow at the Herakleion museum. I was delighting in the many delicate gold ornaments that had been found in the earth at Knossos and at Phaestos – their intricate patterns drawn from flowers, insects, sea creatures. And in the pottery, its designs, too, celebrating the natural world – even the octopus drawn not as a monster (as it would be today) but a graceful being. Delighting in a small carved ivory figure of a bull leaper. And in two goddess figurines. This wide-eyed goddess wore a long ruffled skirt, with apron, and a little jacket, but was bare-breasted. And she held a lively serpent in each hand. One of the figurines had a small proud cat sitting on top of her head.

I looked up and George was standing there, holding a piece of paper in his hand. He began to read from the paper. He had prepared a little speech. He was sorry about last night. But we are not only pupils, he pleaded with me (he meant people); we are also animals. He was sorry. And he wanted to be my friend. He would not put a hand on me unless I wanted him to. And would I come and have a beer with him now?

I told him I had looking and looking still to do here. Good, we were friends. I shook his hand. But no, I couldn't leave with him. Could I have lunch with him, he asked. Or could I have dinner? I told him I'd made other plans for the day. Could he see me tomorrow? No, I'd be going to Phaestos, I said. He stood there staring at me – like a big dog who wants something and can't understand why you won't understand, will just stand there until you do. Why didn't he give me his phone number, I asked. If I found I could meet him for a coffee at some point, I'd call. He just stood there. So I began to move round the room again, looking at things – as best I could. He followed me for a little while. And then suddenly he wrote his phone number on a piece of paper, handed it to me and left – to my relief.

I never did call him, for the rest of the day I was on the move. After lunch I started looking for a shop where I could buy for you one of the turbans the old men of Crete wore – those who still dressed in the baggy pants that gave them the shape of roosters. You'd asked me to find you one. A stocky middle-aged man saw me peering into one store after another and asked could he be of help. Introduced himself: Acratos. He directed me to the right shop and then offered to take me to see the raisin factory he ran. And I accepted the invitation. The factory, at the edge of town, was closed for the holidays. But various friends of his were sitting about in the office, passing the time of day. He showed me around. Then back in the office again showed me, laughing, the contents of his desk: brought out a copy of *Life*, a copy of *Ladies Home Journal*, snapshots of himself in his younger slimmer days. Would I have known him, he asked; then answered himself, glumly: 'Our faces change.'

He had to be home for dinner, he said, but after dinner, if I'd like, he could drive me to several different churches, so that I'd see something of the service in each one. 'You'll be safe with him', one of his companions assured me. On the way out of the building Acratos pointed to a large boat in the yard he'd begun to build before the war. But – it sat there half-finished. He shrugged. He'd drop me at a restaurant, he said. He entered with me, gave the waiter an order: boiled potatoes and snails, it turned out to be. And when I tried to pay, later, I found that he had paid *for* me.

'You are in Crete', he told me simply, when I thanked him. He picked me up at the little café across from my hotel. Carefully introduced me first to some people he knew at another table, then rushed me off in his rather battered car through the town's narrow stony streets – making sudden stops whenever he sighted still another friend along the way. Again he would introduce me, chat for a minute, then rush on. He drove then out of the town and, fast, along rubbly roads, into the countryside. To visit one church after another, and also to knock at the doors of several more friends. He was showing me the churches and he was also showing *me* to his friends. I was not the only American tourist in town of course. But I was apparently the only woman who was travelling alone. 'You are the talk of the town', one friend remarked – as we sat with the family in their wicker-furnished parlour, eating Easter candies.

At the country church we visited next, people were gathered, but no service had begun. For the priest was late. Outside the church, little boys were tossing firecrackers. We entered the church, but Acratos immediately decided to leave and head back to the cathedral in Herakleion. There the service had begun some time before. A great chanting billowed forth. And as we came walking up, the congregation surged out on to the front steps, all holding unlit candles. The priest stepped forth, *his* large candle blazing. And then one after another all the people lit their candles from his – or was it first from his and then from one another? And now, Acratos explained, everyone would walk home, carefully keeping their candles lit; and, once home, would mark smoky crosses over the doorways of their houses. He'd drive me up a high hill so that I could see all the lights scattering. As we walked toward our car, the children here too began to set off firecrackers, tossing some of them at our heels, where they nipped like little dogs. 'Christos Anestos! – Christ is risen!' they shrilled – in the same tones with which they might have shrilled, 'I'm the King of the Castle!', faces aglow.

So we drove up a high hill, to watch the tiny lights of the candles moving through the night. I would have liked to have sat and watched this for a long time. But he wanted to take me now to a country church at a certain crossroads where a Nazi general had been captured. One of his friends had helped in the capture. There was very beautiful chanting at this church. I would have liked to have stayed *here* for a while, but Acratos was restless. He decided to take me to see (or be seen by) a nearby friend of his. So we drove now up a road that seemed sheer rock. And knocked at a door. The friend appeared in pyjamas, half asleep. So we rushed off to another house of a friend. But here too the friend had already gone to bed. Before he took me home we stopped at an inn for wine and boiled eggs – the red-dyed Easter eggs of Crete. He showed me the Cretan Easter custom of knocking egg against egg to see which ones will crack and which stay whole. His egg kept cracking, and he looked quite disappointed each time. But as we left the inn, he lit and threw back into the large room a few small firecrackers of his own, and now he laughed in a great fit of glee, like one of the little boys.

Though I had gotten to bed very late (the hotel doors were locked and I had to knock and knock to wake the proprietor – or rather, Acratos knocked, and shouted) – I managed to wake in time to catch the early bus to Phaestos. There wasn't time to stop for breakfast. But at the station was a man who sold biscuits and esquimo pies and of these I made a happy enough meal.

The ride kept me awake, sleepy as I was. For this was a marvellous landscape. Fields of grain – shining gold, shining green. In the midst of the fields sometimes a few trees – like grazing buffalo. A clear clear light upon them. And on thick vineyards. On groves of olives. The ground under the trees as in your drawings, pinkish. Their shadows sometimes a dusty blue I couldn't explain. And the hills, the hills! – of shifting shape and colour. We were climbing soon into these hills. Their shapes not awesome, like the Alps, but somehow familiar to me – though they were not in fact like any hills I had seen before. There were scattered whitewashed hill villages. We passed through, stopped briefly in a few. Passed finally through Miris. And soon after, the driver stopped the bus at a crossroads, and pointed for me – the path to Phaestos. A young Englishman alighted, too, headed as I was to visit the ruins. I was relieved to find at once that he was more interested in looking about him than in making my acquaintance. Though we did exchange a few words. By common consent we walked as it were together but apart. The path led through wheat fields, an olive grove, then climbed steeply. We crossed a stream. A peasant woman lay sleeping on the ground next to it, one arm under her head. We came to a rest house, run by an old couple to accommodate visitors to the site. There we each decided to stop for something to eat. Out on the wide porch we exchanged a few more words over the bread and oranges and coffee served us. And then went on – over the ridge, and down to the knoll where the ruins were.

Here there had been no reconstruction as at Knossos. The ruins had simply been laid bare: broad flights of steps in gleaming white stone. Doorways of large blocks. Intricate corridors that turned as in a maze. Into the ruins swallows dipped – as if into the ancient life these stones had once held. Dipped and dipped again. The Englishman hurried around, taking out his notebook. And I stood in one spot for a long time. There were the high earthenware jars here, too – one still half sunk into the earth, spears of grass leaning against it. I stood by this great jar. Below the knoll on which the ruins spread lay the Messara plain. And hills stood in the near distance. But what was near and what was far? Here as at Knossos I had the extraordinary sense that the rules of space had been broken. A group of trees on one of the mountain ridges seemed much nearer than they logically should seem. And the sky itself seemed nearer than I had ever known it. I had suddenly the queer sense not so much of being able if I wished to leap very lightly up into the air as of feeling almost unable not to fall up/down into it. To regain my equilibrium, I looked again at the hills, and their shapes recalled to me the outstretched sturdy dreaming figure of the sleeping peasant woman. My notes say: 'A wonderful stillness to the place. Sense here that all ends. No more.' Or all begins.

The Englishman finished his note-taking, said a courteous goodbye. I stayed on and on. I walked to the rest house for a drink of water. The couple there shared some raisins with me, and I asked them about Miris where I planned to stay the night. Then I went back to the ruins for a final long look. Sat this time on one of the ancient worn stone benches. When I started back, I found the caretakers heading for the town themselves, with their daughter. We walked along together. The daughter picked a sprig of mint for me. As we passed through the olive grove, the mother broke off an olive branch. We parted at the highroad. I hailed a ride to Miris from a passing jeep driver.

It was dinner time by now. I ordered something at the little outdoor restaurant. And the owner sat down with me – a stout man in patched white linen pants. He could speak Italian, so we managed a halting conversation. A rather bossy shopkeeper who spoke English sat down with us and told me about his brother in New York, but then had to leave. Meanwhile – the town was walking by. Family groups. Groups of young men, in riding pants and boots, their caps at angles. And – a group of little girls, who passed my table, then turned and passed again, then turned and passed again and again. Each time they went by they'd added a few more to their number – like one of those strings of paper dolls attached to one another by their arms that a mother keeps cutting and cutting to intrigue her child. As they'd go by my table, they'd stare. All except the littlest one, who'd pretend disinterest until the very last moment, when she'd turn suddenly and – startling herself in the act – give me a head-on look. I'd meet her eyes and smile. She'd look away. They all did slowly begin to return my smiles. But though I beckoned to them shyly, shyer than I they never approached my table. And as the light dimmed, they scattered to their homes.

I was sitting under a large just-blooming Eucalyptus tree which gave off a sweet slight smell. I had just become aware of this perfume and was only half looking at the road in front of me when I vaguely noticed two mules passing, noticed ragged trousers, then the motion of a flounced skirt, another, bare feet taking lightly springing steps. And then I took sudden sharp notice of two particular striding-along feet – of a woman, long dusty almost black feet. I looked up. A group of gypsies was passing. They walked quickly, without glancing about them. Had passed, with a windy rustle of the women's skirts, a soft pad pad upon the ground.

These are very simple words to have written. That a group of gypsies passed. That I took particular notice of one woman's long dusty almost black feet. But here is a strange fact: when there have been interruptions in the writing of this book, and I have asked myself: Will I be able to get back to it, and complete it? I have had only to think of those dark feet passing on that road to feel a quickening in me that was almost a shock, and to know that I couldn't not finish it and feel ever that my life had been spoken as a life needs to be.

Where was it that I thought those feet could lead me – if I let my spirit follow them? Somewhere blessedly beyond the pale – beyond the patriarchs' reach, I'd name it now. And where I'd fully dare to call your spirit to join me. At each of the ancient sites I'd visited I'd had the thrilling sense that a time had once been in which I would have been more free to be the self that I am. But now as I caught sight of those dusty striding feet, the joyful sense came to me that here within the present time it might be possible to invent such a world unlike the given world. I shut my eyes and see again the quick feet passing, and taste in my mouth again that delicious hope against hope.

I was staring at the dust of the road. A jeep drove up fast; braked. A young man jumped out and strode toward me. I recognised the pilot, George. 'I've found you!' he exclaimed. He'd asked for me at my hotel, he said; then at the bus depot; then he learned from the man who sold esquimo pies where I had headed. He thumped down into the chair opposite me. He beamed at me an energetically amorous smile. Would I go back to Herakleion with him? No, I told him. I wouldn't go back to Herakleion with him? No. The look of utter unbelief I had become accustomed to replaced the amorous smile. Would I go for a walk with him, he asked. I said, yes, I would take a walk with him.

We walked along the rutted road that ran toward Herakleion. He borrowed my small dictionary and flipped through it. Found the words to let me know that he was cutting camp to come and see me. Then couldn't think what to say next – just kept riffling through the pages of the little book as though hoping that a conversation between us could spill out of it. We walked on in silence. A little past the edge of town, some townspeople were standing at the foot of a wooded slope. I looked where they were looking and there on the slope I saw the gypsy camp – pitched among olive trees. Wide tents. Bundles hung from branches. The donkeys tethered together, and a few saddles on the ground. A dog kennel. Small fires before the tents. At the sight my heart leapt again. I glanced at George, and to my relief, he understood quickly that I wanted to linger here. We walked past the staring townspeople and began, slowly, to climb toward the camp.

As we drew near, there was a sudden hubbub. Two women were fighting – rushing at each other, with cries. And all the other gypsies rushed in, too, in a swirl – grabbing at them to pull them apart. All the while the villagers stood below in a line watching, but the gypsies paid them no attention at all. For a moment one of the two fighters broke away and stooped as if to pick up something from the ground to throw. But again the others had hold of her. And she sank to the ground, moaning and crying out in anger, as the others held her arms. Her hair was flying about loose.

'Let's go', George said.

And my first reaction was to want to turn and go, as he suggested. For I felt a pang of distaste and a painful disappointment. I thought: This life of their own that they lead is not the good life I had imagined. Look what they become. And I started to leave. But I found that I didn't want to, after all. And as I stood watching still – watching especially the young woman who was sitting on the ground sobbing now – my feelings suddenly reversed themselves and I felt a great wave of sympathy for her. And for the other woman, too, standing nearby now, trying to talk through tears. The others were clustered about in small groups, talking earnestly about what had just happened – talking among themselves and talking with the two who had been quarrelling. And then slowly they returned to their various occupations. The woman on the ground rose and shook herself and went into a tent. I watched one of the women who had been holding her go into a nearer tent and kneel to mend the small fire at its entrance. The woman moved about now on her knees, smoothing with her hands the bright blankets that were the tent's floor. Folding and stacking some other bright blankets. And as I watched the motion of her hands, I felt a sudden great homesickness – for a life I had still to find. And the life these people had found seemed to me again one that made my own sought-for life seem possible.

Someone had thrown more wood on to the main camp fire, and most of the gypsies were gathered now about the blaze – sitting about on blankets or on mule saddles, and still in lively conversation. I wandered with George up the slope in the dusk, toward the higher tents. And down below now, as I turned, a man was dancing there in the firelight – as the others clapped their hands for him softly. He was twirling and twirling and laughing aloud as he danced. And again I felt: Yes, here is how life should be. I felt: Here is a life from which we should never have departed.

He danced for only a few minutes and then sat down again among them. I said to George that I wished there would be more dancing. And he peered at me. We began to wander back down toward the camp fire. I was wondering: Could we draw near? Could we speak to them? Or must we keep apart?

George asked me, 'Shall I ask them would they dance for you?'

I hesitated to say yes.

Just then one of the gypsies' little dogs took notice of us and began to yap, and they all turned and saw us there. So we stepped nearer, into the circle cast by the light of the fire. And, pointing at me, George made the request.

They didn't have any music, one of the men answered. Someone had taken their gramophone. But as I stood there nodding, disappointed, one of the women stared into my face and then began to clap her hands, and then pulled toward her a big can and began to use it as a drum. A man brought a lantern and held it up high to cast a little more light – as another woman rose in a very simple motion and began to dance.

I can shut my eyes and see her still. A young woman with a worn scarred face which made me take her at first glance for an older woman. Her body lean and flat-breasted. She was barefoot, dressed in a long ruffled skirt and loose ragged jacket – both faded almost grey; her head wrapped in a faded cloth. An almost bedraggled figure. But as she danced a wonderful grace transformed her. She, too, twirled in place. Then gathered up the folds of her skirt into a kind of apron and bumped. I smiled at the motion, and she smiled back into my eyes, a wonderful delighting smile. She brought her hands together and raised them through the air, the fingers snapping. I couldn't at first imagine that it was her fingers making the sound I heard – a sound like crickets in the air. I can remember glancing about me, surprised. She shook her hips and shook her shoulders, her arms shivering, her feet tramping in place. I was watching her silently and she was watching me all the while too. As she danced her jacket fell open and I could see her breasts. In that moment she resembled suddenly the bare-breasted goddess figurine I had seen in the museum and my heart turned over. And now she smiled at me a smile deeper then words. And, ending the dance, she stepped forward. I held out my hands in a gesture to thank her and she took my hands in hers and held them. And as we peered at each other, I felt the dance she had just danced run through my own body. I could tell that she could feel that I was trembling.

Two very young women now rose and began to dance. They were not much more than girls. One of them, drawing near me, tried to show me how to snap my fingers. But I was slow to learn. Everybody laughed. A young man danced. And shyly, just outside the circle of lamplight, a tiny girl, in a raggedy dress that was like a long nightgown, twirled and twirled.

George was looking sideways at me. He must have guessed something of my feelings, for he asked me suddenly, to my surprise, 'Do you want me to tell them that you will go with them?'

It seemed time to say good night. I asked him to thank them for me. 'And you say it in English, too', he suggested. Which I did. Then he shared with them some cigarettes he had. One woman tugged at the strap of my satchel and with hand out whispered loudly 'drachmae'. But the others quickly shook their heads at her. And I was very glad that they too wanted our meeting to have had nothing to do with any exchange of money.

We walked off through the olive grove. I was in an enchanted state still. And George walked beside me silently for a little while. But he stopped suddenly in place and burst out:

'Miss Barbara, I love you! I love you! Kiss me, Miss Barbara, and take my hand! Because I have promised not to put my hand on you!'

And I had to rouse myself from my dreaming state and try to explain once again that I couldn't, that I had not the same feelings toward him. And again he stared at me as though dumbfounded. When we reached the little hotel in Miris, 'Where do you want me to sleep?' he asked. And I had to explain all over again.

He knocked at my door early the next morning. For he had a seven-thirty bus to catch. He wanted me to take it with him, of course. But I wasn't ready to leave. I had a coffee with him. And off he went – looking sad and puzzled.

Mid-morning I bought several packs of cigarettes and some oranges and chocolate and walked back down the road to the encampment. The woman who had danced for me the night before came forward, and I gave her one pack. Then I held out the other packs in what was meant to be a gesture that said they were for everybody; but another woman, whom I didn't remember, snatched all of them in a quick motion. Again I felt a pang of distaste and disappointment – and felt stupid, too, about the way I had held them out. But some moments later when I looked around I noticed that everybody now had cigarettes. The woman had quietly shared them. And my heart lifted again.

Today was Easter Sunday. People were gathered round the main fire where a lamb was being roasted. My friend led me to the fire and offered me a low chair. I was given wine in a metal goblet, and then bits of lamb handed me on a fork – by a man whom I took to be the gypsy chief. I shared the oranges and chocolate now.

The gramophone that had been missing had somehow re-appeared and my friend wound it up. It had a large green megaphone with flowers painted on it. Two of the women were nursing babies. One, when a record began to play, danced her small daughter on her lap. Both babies wore tiny dangling earrings and, round their necks, tiny charms. I asked could I hold the little one who was learning to dance and her mother set her upon my knee. She instantly wet me, and the mother rolled her eyes and took her back. I dried out soon enough in the sun.

Before I left them, I told them in halting Greek – with the help of my dictionary – that I would like to buy something from them 'na ochee lismoneeso' (to not forget them). I pointed at the bracelet one of them wore, at some simple beads round the neck of another, gesturing: something like this. One woman, who had a rather sulky and mischievous face, quickly took the necklace off one of the babies – who was not her baby – and handed it to me. The baby's mother made no objection, but looked sad, and I handed it back to her. The man whom I took to be the gypsy chief nodded at me. The woman who had danced for me handed me a tiny plastic turtle on a string, and asked a startlingly high price for it. I looked surprised, and placed it for the moment on the ground before me. Then still another woman handed me a simple bracelet of glass labyris-shaped beads – white, blue, orange, black, lavender – and quoted a more reasonable price and I bought it from her and put it on my wrist, happy with it. The woman who had danced for me, grinning, now named a much lower price for the little plastic turtle, and hung it round my neck before I could even answer, and quickly plucked the coins from my hands. I rose and they all rose too and I shook hands with each of them – the woman who had danced holding to my hand for a moment and peering into my eyes.

I'd decided to walk a bit of the way toward Herakleion, and to catch the bus at one of the small towns it would be passing through. So I slung my knapsack on my back and set out. I had taken only a few steps down the road when I asked myself: Why am I doing this? Why am I leaving this place? My rational self gave an easy enough answer, and I kept walking. But the part of me that had asked the question kept repeating it. And this repeated question like a knocking pain in my side.

When I was out of sight of the camp I sniffed at my skirt to see whether it stank of urine, but surprisingly it didn't. The strong Cretan sun had cleaned it – which was just as well, as it was the only skirt I had with me. As I walked, I fingered the bracelet on my wrist.

I had walked a few miles when a young man on a bicycle came along, riding in my direction. Seeing me on foot, he dismounted and walked alongside me. And finding that I spoke hardly any Greek, he began to teach me some words – pointing and naming: taught me the words for wheat, sun, tree, crow, flower. Then he began to urge me to ride the bike. He was so insistent that I finally did – though walking had been a lot easier, for I didn't want to get too far ahead of him, and it's hard to ride a bike very slowly. I tried weaving from side to side of the road. Fortunately the town of Agga Deka, where he was headed, was not far off.

At Agga Deka we both had lunch – Easter lamb again and wonderful Easter bread. When I tried to pay, I found that, like Acratos, he had paid for me. Various people of the town gathered round our table, and there was, as always, one who had been to the US and served as interpreter. He interpreted for the man with the bicycle when he suggested, toward the end of the meal that I marry him and take him back home with me; assured me that the man came of a good family (the others nodded their heads); and mournfully translated my polite refusal. The man, himself, remained cheerful throughout. He'd find a way to get to the United States some day, I was sure. I could hear lively music nearby, and when I inquired about it was told that, by coincidence, a wedding was taking place at the church next door. They all led me to see it. In a clearing outside the church the wedding party was dancing a circle dance – the lead dancer making wonderful jumps into the air, in which he turned all the way round, kicking his heels as he did so, his face grave. The just-married couple were still inside the church. Informed that an American was present, they sent me out a gift of two large white almonds. I entered the church briefly, to see them. But lots of people were gathered around them still kissing them and, afraid to miss my bus, I didn't linger to meet them

After I'd hailed the bus and hopped on to it, I began again to think of the gypsies. And to think of you, and to wonder what your reply to my letter would be. I rode, dreaming. I dreamed: If I put this gypsy bracelet round your wrist – might you decide that you wanted to live with me?

Back at Herakleion at my hotel I found a note from Acratos suggesting that I meet him at a certain sidewalk café just before dinner time. And as I was emerging from the hotel after washing up, there was George waiting for me. It wasn't yet time to meet Acratos, so I took a final walk with him. I set a fast pace, for I didn't want to have to try to converse. I had told him I was catching the boat in the morning, and he was of course trying to persuade me to stay. I was taking long steps. 'Open your feet small!' he requested angrily. But I didn't want to open my feet small. So he kept pace – eyes glowing.

Acratos was waiting at the café and I suggested to George that he sit down with us. So he did. Then suddenly he asked to see my address book, in which he had earlier written his address. He wanted to cross it out now. So I let him cross it out. He was muttering words that were unintelligible to me and I asked Acratos to interpret. At this George fell silent for a long moment, and then mumbled in less angry tones that he was glad to have met a girl of good character and with a warm heart. I asked Acratos to tell him that I was glad to have spent the time with him that I had. He gave me a long pained look, rose from the table, bowed to us both, and strode off.

213

I told Acratos a little bit about him. And then I told him about the gypsies. I was glad that I had, for he knew something about their lives, as it turned out – admired the democracy there was among them. Yes, technically there was a gypsy chief, he told me, but he had no dictatorial powers. Everything was voted on. And the chief, just because he was chief, was the one person not allowed to vote.

He wanted to take me across town to meet one more friend, and the friend's family. But I was tired, so we said our goodbyes. It struck me later that he never had asked me to meet his own family.

As I was having breakfast the next morning at a sidewalk restaurant, two gypsy women passed on the other side of the street, spotted me, and crossed to where I sat. One spoke a little English. Wasn't it I who had been at Miris the day before, she asked me.

'How did you know?' I asked – for I hadn't seen either of the women at the camp.

She raised her eyebrows as if to say, 'A little bird.' Then took out – as if from the air – a pack of cards. Would I like my fortune told? I agreed. And she spread out the cards on the table, fast. She could see my mother and my father worrying, she told me. And here was a young man who was in love with me. And here was a woman with whom I'd have a fight. And she could see travel – lots of travel. As I was putting down my money for the reading, the waiter passed by and exclaimed 'Polli!' – too much! But I gestured to him that it was the price I had agreed on. The gypsy cast him a haughty glance.

I was disappointed in the fortune. I'd hoped that she'd make some happy reference to you. But I was glad to have been hailed by the two women. It helped me to feel linked to that camp in the olive grove.

At the ship I saw them again. They were seeing off a woman dressed all in black and a little girl in pink. Each of the travellers were wearing several dresses, one on top of the other. Easiest way to pack. A skinny curly-haired man was there to see them off, too. There were kisses, kisses, kisses. I went on board, and stood at the rail. The woman who had told my fortune saw me and waved. The two travellers finally came on board. The fortune teller began to wave a little coat – the child's. It had been forgotten. The mother was distracted at the moment, straightening out the many layers of her daughter's garments; so the woman threw the coat to me to give to her. She now ran back down the gangplank to embrace the

214

three of them again. And to sob for a moment against the man's chest. The ship's whistle blew. She came hurrying back.

Dance music was playing over the loudspeaker system. And now the sailors began to throw off the ship's ropes. Just at that moment I saw George running toward the dock. He had decided to say a less angry farewell. The ship had drifted a little from the shore but now – as the sailors tugged at various ropes – it moved for a moment just a bit closer to it again. George stretched out his hand to me, and I stretched out mine to his – and our hands just touched for a moment. And he looked relieved. And made his little formal bow.

Meanwhile the man who had seen off the mother and daughter had begun to dance a farewell, in time to the ship's music. The woman in black was standing by my side at the rail, sobbing, and waving a large black handkerchief. I had to duck a bit not to be hit in the face by it. The man was crying too, I could see, for as he danced he now and then wiped his eyes with his sleeve. But he leaped and turned – arms held high, his fingers in rapid motion; took little jumps, clicking his heels together in the air. He climbed up on to the sea wall and danced there – slow-motion – as the two women with him clapped. Then sprang down on to the shore again, to have more freedom. Wiped the tears from his eyes again. Spun and spun in place. Threw his hat high into the air, caught it, and threw it high again.

I watched him and watched him as the ship drew away from the land – recalling to me, as it drew away, my parting from you. Remember this, I told myself. For yes, this is the way to say goodbye to one whom one loves. Weeping, but dancing, dancing. Weeping, but making a dance of one's love.

15

Back in Athens your letter was waiting for me:

'Dear Bobbie –
    Have been in bed all day trying to get over the exhaustion and
dry horrid temper three days in Rome produced. It was an
unfortunate break, all for this *stupid* wedding – some niece of
Pepinella's – she's been in a state about for months. She really
drives me Absolutely Crazy worrying. *Everything* becomes a
catastrophe. G– Damn.
    Your cable came Friday. The ticket home is bought. Your letter
was here yesterday. *What* a letter. What a girl. What a Friend. God
how can I ever thank you for being you. You're wise, you're
wonderful and I'll love you forever.
    As for coming back for a visit, of course. But I won't be in
Anticoli. Plan to be in Rome or Florence the last week before
leaving. Could you stand a trip there or running around Rome –
which will be shopping (horrors) and packing paintings and such?
    This is the calendar and I *must try* and stick to it – otherwise all is
lost! Absolute solitude, WORK, quiet, Anticoli until 15 May. 15
May move to Rome. Pack. On the 20th with everything done go off
for a few days' trip. And on the evening of the 25th get on the train
for Naples. How does this strike your fancy? I'll leave the decision
up to you.
    You are right, Bobbie, the answer is still no to Greece for me.
Just can't be done. It's complicated as it is. Too bad.
    So everything is settled finally and I feel much better – *very very*
glad that I am leaving early.
    Kurt is leaving the 30th so we can all say goodbye. Ah me –
strange words. So goodbye and very very much and many thanks

for being so good, for sending the cable and sitting right down to write me such a fine and generous beautiful letter, every word of which I appreciated – even the *mild* little scolding I understood very well indeed and agreed with.'

'So goodbye' – yes, strange words. But I decided of course to return to Italy to say them. To dance them in my own way, if I could find the spirit. Could I find it?

I'd had an experience on the boat returning from Crete that confused and *dispirited* me. I'd spent some time with the gypsy mother and daughter – conversing in gestures, sharing the food we'd brought along. But toward the end of the day two Greek soldiers who were fluent in English struck up a conversation. They then taught me the words of some of the Greek songs I particularly loved. First sang them – their voices raised above the complaining voices of a goat and two lambs tethered on the deck nearby. Then wrote the words down in my notebook for me. After night had fallen I said good night to them and to my gypsy friends and wrapped myself in my quilt on a sort of hatchway that looked like a good spot – just under the captain's deck. It was a chilly night. One of the soldiers came over soon and asked couldn't he share one corner of the quilt. It was such a large quilt, he pleaded. I told him no. And he lay down nearby. And then began to sigh to himself and to mutter, like a peevish child. Most of the other passengers had brought some kind of covering. I could see the gypsy mother and child across the way wrapped together in a bright blanket cocoon. His friend had a sweater, but he hadn't, he muttered. 'Listen to my teeth chattering', he said. The quilt *was* a very large one. And both of us of course were fully dressed. I had my coat on. I decided suddenly that it wasn't really fair that he should shiver. I lifted a corner of the quilt, moved to the far side of it and said: 'Here.' He quickly moved in under.

I heard a cackle of laughter from the captain's deck above. And a few shouted words. And then a second man's laughter.

'What is he saying?' I asked.

'He says if he sees any funny business below he'll toss a bucket of water on us', said the soldier.

'He won't see any funny business', I said.

I began to doze off. The waves hissed against the side of the ship.

The goat and the two lambs continued to complain. And then I felt a stealthy motion as the soldier moved just a little closer – and I felt his hand very quietly placed upon my thigh. And I sat up and pulled the quilt off him and wrapped it round myself and told him he'd better leave. And he left. I heard ribald laughter again from above.

The gypsy child woke me at dawn, and the mother suggested – in sign language – that we have some coffee. We stood in line for it at the ship's kitchen; drank it quietly, seated on her blanket. Then as I was leaving the boat, the soldier reappeared, stepped close to my side and suggested that we find a hotel room, where there'd be no ship's captain watching from above. And I had to explain that my letting him under the quilt really had been because his teeth had been chattering.

'Then you don't like men?' he asked me with an almost-sneer.

I believed in love, I told him. I added that I was sorry if he'd misunderstood me.

He gave a contemptuous shrug and strode off.

I'm sorry to report that I left the ship in a state of shame. It's hard to admit to this now. In what a criss-cross of bonds I allowed myself to be caught. I would have been ashamed if I'd continued to refuse a corner of my quilt to him; so how could I be ashamed, too, that I had offered it? But I was. I would have been ashamed if I had accepted his advances; so how could I be ashamed, too, that I had refused them? But I was. And ashamed – not for him but for myself – that he had made them. Ashamed to be a woman is what it amounted to. 'Unfair!' I can cry now – 'Unfair that women are expected always to feel ashamed that we are sexual beings – whatever our behaviour!' But I didn't know how to cry this then.

I think back to my earliest experience of my sexuality. I'll not count a few tentative childhood inquiries made of my body, of other child bodies. I am sixteen. In love with an older woman – Zoe. I begin to spill over with poems. Which I give to her. Poems which speak my love. One day I ask her, 'May I kiss you?' She tells me 'Yes'. I give her a childish kiss. 'That's not the way to kiss', she whispers. And then she shows me how to kiss. I drink sweetness. On a day soon after, we are lying alone in her garden. The sun high. The grass in which we lie warm. I have flung my arm around her, to draw her close to me – wishing for more kisses. In a languorous motion I can recall still she moves a thigh between my thighs. And magic travels across my body – wakes me now as if from long sleep. I give a small cry of surprise. She smiles at this. Her smile is summer. And shame does not exist. It is not shame that wakes in me with this wakening of sexuality, but my first vivid sense that I may be able to find a life that I want; that there are deeps in me from which I can draw. And poems, poems. Shame has still to be learned. Shame – that steals us from ourselves.

But I had learned it by the time I write of. And now when I thought ahead to seeing you again, in Rome, it was hard to imagine myself at ease with you, in equilibrium. The cackling laughter of the captain was in my ears.

By the calendar you'd drawn I had about two weeks left to spend in Greece before catching a boat to Italy. I spent a couple of days first with Russell and Lisa. And then travelled down through the Peloponnese. To see Olympia, Epidauros, Mycaenae.

The country round Olympia was lusher, less shorn of trees than the country I had seen until then. At the temple site, the many stone columns stood among living columns of tall pines. The smell of resin was in the air. And the shrill of insects. I wandered through the ruins, and then through the wooded hills behind them. Returned and sat among the grey pillars and wrote to you and to my family. Sat on past nightfall. An owl began to call with husky voice from high in the tree under which I sat. Called and called. I listened to it thirstily. Owl, call me back to myself. I watched the stars come out in their many delicate colours. Or rather, as my journal notes, I tried to but I never quite succeeded in seeing a new star appear – I could merely notice, of one after another: Now it is there. But as, one after another, they surprised me, the captain's hateful laughter faded from my mind.

I woke the next morning at dawn to catch my bus south, and so made the long ride through mountain country sleepily, though the jolting of the bus did awake me repeatedly from napping. At Argos I changed to another rackety bus which took me to Napflion. And at Napflion I changed to another rackety bus which took me to Ligorio. There I checked in my knapsack at the small hotel and decided not to wait for a ride to Epidauros but to start out walking.

It was a sparkling day and I began to wake fully. I had walked a mile or so when I saw a tiny figure ahead on the road. When I came up, I found that it was a little girl waiting there, clasping a bouquet of poppies and delicate delphiniums. She held it out to me with an eager gesture. And spoke – as a question – the beautiful Greek word for flowers: 'Looloothia?' I can hear again the sweet high lilt of her voice singing the word. She drew out the accent on the second 'loo' – 'Looloooooothia?' I took the flowers into my hands. Was she selling them or giving them, I had to ask myself – as I had asked when I'd met the girl on the path in Taormina. Both, I decided again. So I thanked her first. And then gave her a good-sized bill. She opened her eyes wide. And ran off licketysplit to a friend I noticed now, another girl, who waited for her under a distant tree. I walked on, feeling blessed by that meeting, but also wishing again with a pang that I had had something better than money to give. How could money equal poppies and delphiniums?

After another mile, a bus came along and I hailed it and hopped on. It was carrying a group of students and their teacher-guide to the ancient outdoor theatre. It was easy to keep a distance from them, once at the site, for they stayed together. I climbed way up to the highest row of stone step-seats – where the air was full of bird calls – and stared about me. Remembered the plays I had read that had once been staged here under the sky, the stories of Orestes and Electra, Oedipus, Antigone. I found soon that I was sitting there awed, the drama of my own life overshadowed by these classic dramas – of faith kept with royal fathers, faith kept with royal brothers. I didn't say it consciously to myself, yet sat there knowing that what seemed in my own life of the very deepest moment would not have found celebration here.

I started to roam about. The students began climbing up to the top and so I moved down and to another side of the immense theatre. Then they moved down the steps again, got into the waiting bus and went off; but I had decided to stay on. The birds called with sweet voices – across the bowl of the theatre and across the neighbouring fields. I began to wander through the fields.

There was a jumble of fallen temple stones here, scattered wide, lying pale in the fading light. A few horses were browsing, and I passed a tiny goat half-way up a tree, nibbling leaves. Overhead the evening clouds moved rapidly. I experienced now as I walked about the sharpest kind of loneliness. I remembered the soldier's contemptuous shrug; I remembered the bewildered look on George's face; remembered Elena's eye upon me; the words you spoke to me on the street in Rome: 'When a woman comes too close to me, I resent it.' I remembered Nell's leaving me to marry my brother. Had I the courage to be the sexual self that I was? To act out truthfully this part for which it seemed, no play was written?

Then staring at the lightly tossing many-coloured grasses at my feet, I remembered suddenly Elevsis and could almost hear again that curious humming in my inner ear, feel that vibration in my limbs. 'My answer is yes', I said to myself – without words. I roamed into a farther field. The scattered marble fragments were fewer here. Near the field's corner, among the grasses, I saw a gleaming stone and moved toward it. It was a fragment of a fallen statue – a woman's torso, without head or arms, and leaning slightly. I sat down on another fallen bit of marble and gazed at it. The stone breasts shone among the tossing grasses. 'Yes I am, I am this sexual self', I said. And stood up, trembling, and went over and knelt and put my hands against the shining ancient breasts. And said: 'I am this self that I am. I affirm it.' I sang to myself: 'Yes I am. And I will not be robbed of my sex. And I will not be shamed.' The stone breasts were cool under my hands, with the coolness of water found at a spring, life-giving. I felt the spirit of the stone enter my hands with this coolness and enter my soul. I sang (without any sound): 'Yes. It is the truth about me and so I will live it.'

It felt to me, I can remember, like a very bold action to be taking. Even though no one watched – except for the browsing animals. As I rose from where I had been sitting and took those few steps and knelt. It felt as though I were taking my very life in my hands when I pressed them against those cool breasts. I remember the crickets singing around me. I remember trembling. The trembling was like a life current that was shaking me. I knelt there a long time.

My book, as you can see, moves on from this moment for several chapters. Yet I could say that it is toward this moment that it has moved from the first page. And that in one sense the story that I am writing ends here. But it would be a lie to end it here. My story moves toward this moment and away from it, moves away from it and back to it again.

I wandered off toward the road, turning often to look back at that image in the grass. As I look back now. Someone was calling to the horses – with a melodious almost teasing whistle. They lifted their heads, then lowered them and ate a little more grass, then – as the whistling persisted – decided to trot off. After I'd walked a little way down the road a man on a motorcycle with sidecar drove along and I hailed him and asked for a ride into Ligorio, for it was turning dark now. I had to squat on the edge of the sidecar, which was full of cans. And at the little hotel where I'd left my knapsack I found that all the rooms had been taken. The man at the desk and I had not understood each other earlier. But as always one English-speaking Greek soon appeared – a gnarled man who told me that he and his wife had a spare room and put up paying guests. They would feed me, too. So I followed him home.

The main room of the house was living room and workroom too. In the corner was a loom, which one of his daughters worked – a large barefooted woman with sad eyes. Her cot was near the loom. And her spare dress hung from a peg. In another corner was a workbench and tools. We ate in there (I was given the one chair, the family sat on stools), but the meal was cooked on an open fire in a small adjoining room – where dried pomegranates hung from the ceiling: little fish broiled in oil, a few herbs added. And yogurt made from goat's milk, very crusty and good. And retsina. There was a cot in this room, too, for the younger daughter. Neither the daughters nor the worn-looking mother knew any English, though they spoke shyly with their eyes. It was the father who made conversation. A good deal of it was with one of their goats who kept slipping into the house – and at one moment snatched the older daughter's dress from its peg and ran off with it, the women in pursuit. 'I'll kill him tomorrow', he swore. He'd been planning to anyway.

'Want to go stable and pee?' he asked, before showing me my room. Several farm animals were in the stable. The naughty goat eyed me with a look infinitely mournful as I squatted in the straw. It knows its fate, I thought. The guest room was a large room with two beds and a number of honoured mementoes very carefully placed. He pointed out a lute he used to play, hung under a portrait of himself and his wife. And a little oil painting of a warship. His son was on the ship, he said. There were doilies on the tables, hooked rugs on the floor. He turned to me and puckered his lips: 'A kiss?' I shook my head. He looked surprised and sad but didn't try to insist. We said good night. A few minutes later he was at the

222

door again: 'Varvara?' Would I like goat's milk in the morning? I would like it very much, I told him, without opening the door. There was silence, and then I could hear him slowly walking off.

In the morning I decided to start off walking toward Mycaenae, and again to hail the bus when it happened to come along. He walked along with me for a while, for he had work to do in one of his several fields. He had wheat fields, he told me, a hundred olive trees, and grapes. Before he turned off the road he gave me, for my trip, a large hunk of bread and two onions. I thanked him and put out my hand, which he quickly raised to his lips. And then, before I could stop him, he kissed the inside of my arm, too. As I moved off, he called after me, 'I'll dream of you, my daughter! If I were not so old, I'd not let you go.'

I'd walked a mile or so – passing workers in the fields – when I saw three women and two small children resting in a field under a tree. They waved and beckoned: 'Ella!' – Come! So I joined them under the tree. They offered me wine (tossing out what was left in the cup – with a splendid gesture – before refilling it and passing it to me), they offered me bread and olives and a dish of scrambled eggs in oil. They knew no English, but were so very eager to hear who I was and why I was on the road that with the help of my dictionary we did talk a bit. When either they or I became confused about just what was being said – which was often – we'd begin to laugh. We spent much of the time laughing like this – the children laughing too. There would be a festival in the fields outside a nearby chapel, the very next day, they told me. Why didn't I stay and take part in it? The youngest of the women – the merriest laugher, very skinny, her head wrapped in a sweat-stained white cloth – told me I could stay the night at her house. I thought for a moment of saying yes. But first I should go to see the ruins at Mycaenae, I told them – for I had just so much time – but I'd return in the morning for the festival. They rose to go back to work now.

The day before, on the bus to Ligorio, I'd sat next a young schoolteacher who spoke some English and she had invited me to stop off and visit the two-room schoolhouse where she taught. I'd promised to visit her today. After a few miles walk I reached the town she'd named and when I spoke the word for 'school' a boy who for some mysterious reason was not attending school that day gestured for me to follow him and guided me to the right building – on a back street, near a rapid little river. On the banks of the river a group of women were on their knees slap-slapping their laundry against the wet rocks. I could still hear this sound every now and then from inside the school building. The teacher – Katerina – was surprised but very pleased to see me. She introduced me to the children and then continued for a while to teach the class. The children were doing sums – writing them on the blackboard and then chanting the answers. Their mouths in wonderful grimaces. Their chanting rather like the chanting I'd heard in the churches.

Katerina soon left the room to bring the other teacher in to meet me – a curly-headed man with yellow shoes who I learned later was her fiancé. She referred to him as 'Sir'. 'Sir says . . .' they took me into his room, too, to meet his class. I still remember the problem he had written on the blackboard. Katerina translated it for me. (Sir spoke no English.) 'A man has 142 children. A wolf eats 30. How many are left?'

At lunch time the children ran off to their homes and Katerina asked me and Sir to have lunch at her place – which was a room one reached by outside steps in a house next the village church. In the room were a large iron double bed with one blanket, a sea chest (stamped US), a small marble-top table and two chairs, a few clothes hung on a hook on the wall and a small suitcase. I asked for the bathroom and she led me downstairs again and, with visible embarrassment, to the stable attached to the house. She peered at me as if to ask: 'Does this upset you?' And when I smiled at her to let her know that it didn't upset me in the least, she smiled back, surprised and relieved. Then she waited for me at the head of the stairs with a pitcher of water, a towel, and a new cake of Hermes soap. And we all three washed our hands. Back in the room she put the soap away carefully. She'd put a clean striped cloth on the little table and now served us batter cakes, cooked in the kitchen she shared with others; cheese and olives and retsina. As there were only two chairs, she sat on the bed.

She too was full of questions about my travels. When she looked at me I could see that she was trying to imagine her own self wandering like this through a wider world than Ligorio. She carefully translated everything that I said for her fiancé. At one point he made the suggestion that I'd become used to by now – that *I* marry him and take him back with me to the USA. And she carefully translated this, too, though colouring a bit as she did so.

I told her I was headed for Mycaenae and she said that the next bus left at four. But couldn't I stay over and take the bus the next day? I would be back this way, I told her – for I'd be going to the festival I'd heard about. I tried out my Greek and explained now 'agapo choros' – meaning to say 'I love dancing'. But perhaps I pronounced the words strangely. A happy blush spread over her face. 'Thank you,' she said, 'I love you *more*.'

And now it was time for school again. As we passed the river I saw her glance at its darting waters and for just a moment her eyes held a look of such longing to be able to dart across new distances too that I stared at her. But in the next moment that look was veiled. Sir asked her some question and she turned to him with sweet gravity.

She had the children sing for me. And just before I left, she asked one little girl to go out and pick me some flowers. The girl returned with a few hollyhock heads – just the heads. She asked another girl to go and bring back roses – and that girl returned with a few nipped-off roses' heads. Then Katerina asked one of the older boys to guide me to the right place to hail the bus. In parting, she held my hands for a long minute. Katerina, I have often thought of you.

Mycaenae wasn't many miles from Ligorio. But I had to change buses and there was a long wait for the second bus. By the time I'd been dropped off at a crossroads near Mycaenae, the sun was low in the sky. I expected the ruins to be close to the hotel Katerina told me to ask for – La Belle Hélène. Two little boys I met on the road led me quickly there. But at the desk I learned that the ruins were still a mile or so away, up in the hills behind this little town. I left my knapsack at the desk, hurried out again and started off along the rutted road up into those hills – heard a small sound and turned and saw that the same boys were following me. I gestured to them and they came running up. The only bus that could get me back in time for the festival the next day left early in the morning, so my one chance to explore the ruins was now. But night was closing in. The man at the desk in fact had advised me that I'd not be able to see anything by the time I reached the site. I figured if I walked fast enough I might prove him wrong; but I was happy to have my guides.

The road wound up and round steeply to the left. My notes recall 'strange grey forbidding wondrous hills' surrounding us soon. We passed a shepherd and his flock on a slope above us and the shepherd's dog came rushing down at us, snarling. One of the boys gave it a kick, at which the shepherd came rushing down, waving a large stick. Was this to chastise the dog or to chastise the boy? We didn't wait to learn but dashed forward, up the road. And into the dark. For the sun had by now dropped behind the hills.

When we slowed our steps again, I noticed the lights from fires shepherds had built twinkling in the distance from various hills. The older boy took my hand and led me off the road to the left – into the hillside itself it seemed for a strange moment. 'Tholos,' he said – 'Agamemnon'. It was the first of the great 'beehive' tombs. I peered up and could dimly see the great stone lintel of its gateway high above our heads. Once inside I could see nothing. But the boy led me to the curved far wall and placed my hands against its stones. Then they both did a fierce dance, stamping their heels hard against the ground, and the echoes of their steps, rebounding from the walls, made the shape and size of the place known to me. I joined in the dance myself.

When we had climbed the road to the top of the hill, we came to the Gate of Lions – set in ramparts built of huge stones, the walls tunnelled in toward the gate, its great lintel again high above our heads. Above this lintel two stone lionesses – lacking heads – reared up on their hindlegs, with forefeet set upon a kind of altar. A sliver of moon was in the sky and I could just make out their sinewy presences. Squinting up at them, I remembered for a moment the dream in which I wrestled with an animal quite like one of these. The older boy again took me by the hand and we passed through the gate. And now he led me up a kind of ramp to the left – the younger boy giggling a little. Then pointed down into mysterious hollows. Led me – slow-motion so that I shouldn't stumble – down and up various steps. And sometimes over low walls. And to a lookout spot, where we could stare down at the faintly discernible plain of Argos and across to distant lights at the verge of the darkened sea. It could have been from here that Clytemnestra had watched for Agamemnon's ship to return from the war against Troy. And it was somewhere within these walls that she had killed him. And it was somewhere within these walls that she herself had been killed.

The boy led me down and around through the almost-dark, and then down down many steep steps into a pitch-black room where he placed my hand on an earthenware pipe – and spoke the word for water. This was a secret cistern, I would read later, disguised as a tomb – so those under siege in this citadel could always find water.

Then he led me up again and around and under some scaffolding into another great tomb, but this one no longer intact but open to the stars. And he spoke the name of Clytemnestra. The husband-killer. In the distance I could hear shepherds' pipes now. Teasing sounds – trembling on the air as thoughts can tremble in the mind without one's knowing that one is thinking them. I didn't at all at that time know what all my thoughts about Clytemnestra were. The plays that I had read named her killing of Agamemnon a crime. But his killing of one of their daughters – as a sacrifice to bring fair winds so that he needn't wait to sail off to war – this was justified. And the killing of Clytemnestra by her son, to avenge his father – this was justified too. By the 'gods'. The mother's anger alone remained unjustified – even her two surviving daughters wanting her dead. It would be almost twenty years before I would dare to admit to myself that I felt threatened by this judgement of who had a right to anger and who had not. (It was not until I read Kate Millett's words about the ancient story in *Sexual Politics* that I admitted it – with a bursting out from within me then of all my rebel feelings.) At the time I knew only that to think of Clytemnestra was painful, and I was glad that I was exploring this site under cover of night.

Cover of night. Years later now, I muse about my own mother's anger against her husband, my father. About the fact that it was under cover of night that she spoke to me of its cause. And the fact, too, that she never did actually name her anger 'anger'.

I remember her first confiding in me. I am sixteen. I am in love with Zoe. I have been lying in bed unable to sleep – so brimming with this love, which wants to spill over, wants to speak. I decide to tell my mother my feelings. For the only in any way comparable feelings I have ever experienced have been feelings for *her*. I tiptoe into her room. 'Are you awake still?' I ask her. She is awake by now. I whisper to her, 'I am in love, I am in love!' She listens, tender and unjudging. I am shivering. She makes room for me next to her in bed. I smell the sweet slightly milky smell of her. Which calms me – as it used to calm me when I was a child. Her long lank hair lies next to me on the pillow. And the dark lies next to us.

And she begins to tell me of a time when *she* was utterly in love. Not with my father. She had never been in love with my father –

227

only fond of him. Her mother had persuaded her to enter this marriage, assuring her that love would follow marriage. But it was love for another man that had followed. Some years later, after three of her children had been born. Then she had asked my father for a divorce. But he had refused. Arguing that marriage vows should not be broken. Sure of his correctness in this. When she had insisted, he had presented her with the most painful of choices: stay in the marriage and never see the other man again, or join the other man and lose her children. He would ask his sister to help him raise us, he told her. My mother had chosen not to lose her children.

I think back and can remember in her telling of the story no anger directly expressed. She expressed only her sense of loss: she could smell still the stale cigarette smoke in the telephone booth from which she called her lover – to tell him she could never see him again. I remember my own anger – and dismay – that my father, honourable in so very many ways, had felt it right to hold her captive, felt it right to claim sole authority to say what would become of *us*. But I could make out no anger in my mother's voice – strangely light – almost singsong – as if she were speaking of all this from a distance, safe distance. From cover.

Cover of night. It is some years later. My mother and I are making a long night-time drive together, after a family visit. Sharing the driving. Our eyes fixed on the highway before us, a narrow tunnel through the dark. We have been talking about a young couple we know whose marriage has just broken apart, though everyone had assumed the two were happy. I ask my mother, 'When you were first married, before you'd fallen in love, really in love with that other man – did you ever *think* that you were in love with Dad?' She is silent. Shrugs. And then in a dull voice she begins to tell me: 'Every night at bedtime I would simply go upstairs with him. I would perform my wifely duty. Every night . . .' And again I can make out no anger. She speaks almost as a medium would speak in a trance. I listen in pain and wonder. Eyes fixed on the highway.

And then I ask her: 'When Dad refused to let you leave him – when he told you he could take your children from you – weren't you terribly angry? Didn't you want some kind of revenge?'

'Revenge?' she asks, startled.

I say quickly, 'I wouldn't blame you at all if you had wanted it.

Perhaps to turn our affections from him if you could?' (I think she *has* wanted this.)

She says woodenly, 'He thought he was right.'

'Oh, I know,' I say, 'I know.'

As we hug good night, that night, at the end of the drive, I feel very close to her, and touched that she has been willing to speak to me as intimately as she has. But in the morning, to my dismay, she stammers out, 'That drive last night – I feel as though it were a bad dream I had dreamed. Trapped in the car, driving through a bad dream.'

I am sorry, mother.

I named your anger. A woman's anger is not supposed to be named. A woman's anger is supposed to be cause for shame.

Another memory rises in me. I am sixteen or seventeen. One day Zoe tells me that she's insisted to my mother that she (my mother) mustn't ever feel that she has to sleep with my father when she doesn't want to. Tongue-tied at her words – and all that they bring to mind – I inwardly fiercely assent. Fiercely assent, and yet and yet . . . One evening not long after, passing the open doorway of my mother's room, I see my father sitting there on the edge of her bed, waiting for her. In the raggedy old bathrobe that he has worn for years. There is a look about him so forlorn that it pierces me to the very core of my being. And – this is what I recall most especially – pierces me with a sense of shame, of guilty complicity. As though I were complicit in a form of murder. Regicide. As though I were standing regarding his naked body brought down – body of Agamemnon slain in his bath. I can still see him sitting there, both awesome and forlorn. And fear, love, anger, grief, a confused shame collide in me. Feelings hard even now to untangle. They were harder still to untangle those many years ago. Yes, I was glad to be moving through the ruins under cover of dark.

As the boys and I came at last full circle and were standing again at the Gate of Lions, I heard in the darkness the peeping of some small bird. It was an unlikely sound after nightfall. I had learned the Greek word for bird and I spoke it in surprise. The older boy nodded, and then ran toward the wall that flanked the gate, and I saw him clambering up it, finding footholds somehow in the cracks between the great stones. And then he came clambering down again, more slowly now and awkwardly. And he was holding out his cupped hands toward me in the half-light. I held out my own, and he put into them a tiny featherless bird – all skin and beak and still peeping timidly. I peered at it in awe, then quickly put it back into his hands. And he climbed the wall again and – carefully – returned it to its nest.

The night had grown cold. The older boy pointed at the younger now, who was shivering. I offered my scarf but he refused, in pride. And the older one gestured that we must head home. So we started back, walking as fast as we could over the rough ground. When we reached the slope where the shepherd's dog had come rushing down at us, he came rushing again, again snarling – the shepherd after him. And we ran and ran and ran downhill, holding hands, but the boys stooping now and then to pick up stones to throw. We'd slow down, but then seem to hear the sound of snarling again and would run again. When we were at a safe distance, the older boy suddenly took the younger on his back, to carry him pick-a-back. The little one was laughing now, with a tremulous laughter that I mistook at first for weeping. He was heavy for his friend and I suggested – with gestures – that we link hands and carry him that way. So we did for a little while. But then the boy slipped off our hands and ran along on his own.

We were still quite a distance from the hotel when the two stopped and held out their hands. They were asking to be paid now, for we had come to a sidepath that was a short cut home for them. It took me several moments to understand, for I'd assumed that they lived a little beyond the hotel – where I'd first met them. Their voices became anxious, I understood at last what they were asking, and – feeling badly not to have guessed more quickly, and wishing again that there were a better way to thank them – I paid them, and waved goodbye to them; then stumbled the rest of the way home alone.

The man who ran the hotel was astonished that I would leave in the morning without ever seeing the ruins by daylight. He had a proprietory feeling about the site, had left a scholarly book about it by my bedside. But I did take the early bus back to Ligorio. There I learned from an old man that the festival was at Haggus Johannus – two miles away; so I set out again walking. A truck full of soldiers came along. An old woman I had greeted – she was leading a goat along the road – gestured that I should hail the truck; and I did. One of the men gallantly gave me his seat in the cab. The soldiers, too, were headed for the festival; but first they had an errand to run at the seaport beyond. So I went along to see the port – and was invited to enjoy a dish of squid with them, at a little restaurant where the flies were thick but the smell of orange trees that lay on the breeze made one almost forget the flies. After this meal we roared back to the festival – carrying now a couple of extra people, who stood on the runningboard, clinging to the door.

There were two skipping circles of dancers in the field – a field that lay before a small whitewashed church. Others were sitting about on the ground, watching – sitting on blankets, on saddles. An improvised band played. I remember a violinist; I remember a woman shaking a tambourine. I went into the church for a moment, with the soldiers – a simple chapel whose ceiling hadn't quite been finished. When we came out, the soldiers joined the dance for a few rounds then jumped into their truck and were off again, shouting, laughing. I looked for the women who had asked me to come, but didn't see them. Had they been here for a while and had to leave? I looked about for Katerina, but didn't see her either. An old man who spoke English introduced himself and took me to meet his family: his wife, a tired-looking woman with very few teeth; his sister, who nodded and nodded at me; his niece, who stared into my eyes. I sat on their blanket with them in the shade of a grapevine and they gave me a drink of lemonade. A tiny girl approached. I didn't recognise her at first; then saw that she was the girl who had offered me delphiniums and poppies on the road to Epidauros. She smiled at me shyly and I smiled at her shyly. 'She says she gave you flowers on the road to Epidauros', the old man said. I nodded yes, yes. She looked at me for a moment with an odd twinkling in her eyes; then darted toward one of the circles of dancers. Two dancers unclasped hands to clasp hers and skip her away. I could see her glancing again in my direction as she circled by. Others gathered round me now. Two women in the huddle spoke to the old man. He told me, 'They say they saw you get on the bus for Mycaenae, and here you are again.' Then one of the women reached out her hand – beckoning that I should come with *her*. And she took me to meet *her* family.

The man at whose house I had stayed appeared, smiling broadly. And would I stay with them again, he asked. But the woman next to me shook her head, and took hold of my arm as though to say: 'No, she will stay with us.' And someone else was whispering: 'Stay with *us*. And *we* wouldn't ask you for money.' A vying began about where I would spend the night. 'Come for a little walk', someone would say – either in words or with gestures. And lead me away from the others. And then someone else would take me by the arm – as though cutting in at a dance – and lead me in another direction. One little old woman took my coat from me and my knapsack. To place them somewhere for safekeeping, I'd thought; but I noticed soon that she was keeping them tucked under her arm. To mark her claim? It was this old woman, I think, who first suggested, with gestures, that I join the dance.

She just assumed that I knew the steps. Happily, I did know them. For Lisa and Russell had taught them to me. Many times during my visits with them we had formed a fragment of a circle and danced around the room – or out in front of their house. So now I stepped into the dance. Seeing my intention, a dark-browed young woman who'd been standing next the old woman took me by the hand and led me in. Two dancers unclasped hands to include us. And we were in the round. Taking running steps forward, then the lovely swinging backward step, and forward again with a dip and a skip and more running steps. I saw the fat daughter who'd had her dress stolen by the naughty goat dancing in her mended dress, very gracefully, eyes alight. And her father was dancing now too. Old and young were in the circle. Not a full circle, as you know. A head to it and a tail. The dancer at the head of it sometimes improvising flourishes – leaps or kicks or twirlings. We circled, circled – to the lovely wailing music, in which bird calls and the rasping of crickets were woven.

I can remember still the lift of heart I felt treading that circle – with strangers who seemed, as we danced, familiars. And I can remember still how I wished that you were part of this round. And how I felt strangely that you were, somehow – that dancing here I grasped your hand. We circled, circled.

The young woman who had taken me into the dance now placed me at its head, and I found myself leading it. For a while it was a lovely feeling to be trusted in this way. Then I began to feel selfconscious. My confidence failed me and I signalled to her please to take my place.

I tired finally and dropped out. She dropped out with me and she and her sister and mother asked me with gestures to come sit with them and eat a bite. They gave me wine and cheese. Then I drew closer to the dance again, to watch. And the old man who had been the first to speak to me invited me into the circle again; so I entered it once more. And again felt my heart lighten; and again dreamed that you, too, circled in this dance.

After a while the two sisters approached the circle and beckoned to me, so I left it again. The mother was gathering up their belongings. It was time to leave, they gestured. And they were taking me home with them. Somehow the battle over me had been settled – though the old man who spoke English made a few final objections. I said some quick goodbyes. I looked for my coat and satchel. The old woman who had taken charge of them still had them under her arm and was already on the road. She was the young women's aunt, I would learn. The family had three mules and the four of us took turns riding and walking the several miles home – while those returning home by bus or bicycle, on horseback or walking at a fast pace, passed us, waving. Our fat mules were in no hurry. The aunt had climbed on to a bus and called out to me with a strong shout. Along with us came the family's small dog and also a goat and a lamb. I'd noticed the dog before this; she'd been begging cheese of me; but in the crowded scene I'd not noticed the goat and lamb who'd been browsing nearby. They now led our slow file – skipping on ahead, then circling back, not to lose us. The last mile that we went, the lamb began to gambol – sniffing the air of home? – taking bouncy leaps, with hunched back, like the leaps I'd seen playful kittens take; delighting in these motions, delighting in its bouncing self. I told myself not to forget this dance of its own that it was inventing, this dance of delight in being who it was.

A breeze had come up and I saw one of the sisters hugging herself, to keep warm. I took my pullover sweater from my knapsack and passed it to her. She smiled her thanks. And after she'd put it on, I saw her hands stroking the wool lightly – as though to compare it with the homespun she knew. The mules began to move a little faster now, and soon house and stable were in sight. The father was on the porch and looked at me in surprise.

It was a house with small whitewashed rooms and the simplest of furnishings – which I found very beautiful. Again supper was cooked over an open fireplace – tiny fried fish. I'd discovered that the sisters, though not the parents, knew a bit of Italian, and we attempted some conversation in that language; but for the most part we just looked at each other shyly, each trying to guess a little what the other's life was like.

There was a shouting at the door. It was the aunt – Helene. She marched up to me and exclaimed something. One of the sisters translated: 'She says that God came down and told her to go looking for you.' The old woman pulled up a low chair in front of the fire and began to talk to me. Then – realising that I understood almost nothing of what she was saying – turned to sign language. She signed that she would like to go travelling with me. She decided then to give me a lesson in Greek, began pointing at various objects in the room, naming them, waiting for me to repeat the words. This lesson went on and on. The others became restive. Trying to lighten things, I turned to them and said in Italian, 'Lezione' – lesson. One of the daughters nodded firmly: 'Si, silenzio' – yes, silence. 'Stamata' – stop now, she told her aunt. I corrected her quickly: I hadn't said 'silenzio', I'd said 'lezione'. But she didn't translate my correction. She wanted me to have asked for silence. The aunt began to apologise to me. I kept shaking my head at her: 'No – I thank you.' I didn't know what to do now. I didn't want to ignore the younger woman's wishes, but I didn't want Helene to think that I'd asked her to shut up. She looked rather bewildered, but after peering into my eyes decided that all was well between us. She decided, too, to go home. Stood up, took my hands in hers, then kissed me suddenly – and left. 'Troppo vino' – too much festival wine, said one of the sisters. We sat on a little longer before going to bed.

There were two beds in the house, I now learned. One in which the father and mother slept (I glimpsed it through an open door); one in the two sisters' room. This night these two spread a rug and a blanket on the floor and indicated that I was to take their bed. I objected in vain. They lay down swiftly – after each had stood for a moment in front of the icon in the corner.

They were up with the first light, were dressed by the time I fully opened my eyes. In working clothes today. Had I felt the fleas, one of them asked, grinning – with gestures imitating the flitting movements of the insects across her body. I grinned back: Yes, I had felt them – throughout the night. They brought me a basin of water in which to wash. And when *I* had dressed, they led me to a chair out on the front porch, and brought me a glass of goat's milk and a hunk of bread. I gathered they must have bolted something down already, themselves – while I was washing. They told me then that they had much work to do in the fields – 'molto lavore' – the whole family – 'capisce?' – did I understand? I nodded yes. They told me that a neighbour who spoke English would take me to catch my bus. He'd be here in just a minute. I nodded. While we waited for him, I admired the two blue irises blooming in their yard. One of them quickly broke off the head of one iris and gave it to me. We were all frowning now, anxious. They were upset, I think, at having to say goodbye abruptly. I was upset at feeling unable to say adequate thanks. And I think that on both sides we'd learned less about one another than we would have liked. We shook hands awkwardly. I began to babble disjointed words from several languages – English, Greek, Italian. And then the neighbour led me off – holding the beautiful ruffled flower in my hand, carefully.

The neighbour, it turned out, was taking the bus himself. He was going a far as Tyrins, but returning the same day. I decided to send a note back with him, and to try to write a more coherent thanks than I had been able to speak. And then I decided to ask him to take back with him too the sweater one of the sisters had seemed to like. But I still felt it to be an awkward thank you. I wrote in my notebook that night: 'How to give? How to give?' The fact that I would soon be seeing you again added its stress to those words. I wrote: 'How to dance? How to give?' On the long bus ride back to Athens – where I would pack to sail for Italy again – I tried to hold to the feelings I'd had circling in the festival dance. And I tried to hold to the feelings I'd had kneeling among the grasses with my hands at the fallen statue's ancient shining breasts.

16

On the ship, too, sailing to meet you, I tried to grasp my pride. I would not let the love I felt for you abash me. It was a power I'd been given, not a blight. Hadn't I learned this? Hadn't I felt it bring me back to life? I was wearing the gypsy bracelet now. I kept turning it on my wrist – to remind me of what I knew.

The ship was very crowded. I slept with my knees pulled up, wrapped in my quilt, for there wasn't deck room enough in which to stretch out. When we moved through the Corinth Canal I picked my way to the rail. High high up on the sheer cliff through which we passed stood the wee figure of a child – who uttered a wee faraway cry, no louder than an insect's cry, to bless us on our way. Then in the half-light I saw a smallish black animal racing up the cliff's side – though how it managed a foothold I couldn't imagine. I turned in astonishment toward the young man standing next me. He nodded, grinning, and named the animal. But the name he gave was strange to me.

Throughout the night the ship stopped at various islands; and at each stop, with a quiet-as-they-could-keep-it commotion, passengers clambered ashore. By dawn I could stretch my limbs out and really sleep. In that sleep I dreamed that you came forward to meet me and I kissed you on the mouth – and you rebuked me sternly. I woke later, cold and wet. My hot-water bottle had sprung a leak. Happily, it was a sunny morning. I stretched out, face up, and was soon dry again.

I was sitting on the bench that ran round the deck, writing in my notebook, when a young ship's officer passed by. He took my pencil out of my hand, to my bewilderment, and walked quickly off. I was hunting in my knapsack for another when he returned, smiling, and handed the pencil back to me, beautifully sharpened. And walked off again. Now did first-class travel ever offer courtesies like this?

The next night was stormy. The other passengers moved inside, into the stifling room with double-decker wooden sleeping shelves. But I decided as I had before to remain on deck, and sleep on the bench. I had clung to this bench through a storm after first saying goodbye to you. Now I clung to it on my way back to you. And again my spirit greeted the ship's shuddering and the hissing of the waves through which we persisted on our way.

The long train trip from Brindisi brought me to Rome in the evening. You weren't due in town until the next day; so I wandered through the streets renewing my acquaintance with them. A round-faced young American who'd sat next to me on the train tagged along for a while. We raced each other along the shore of the Tiber. (He won the race.) Then I told him I was headed for bed – but walked instead to the Piazza Navona and stared for a while at the lion in the central fountain there. And told myself again: I will not be shamed.

I had left a message for you at the Academy, and kept calling at intervals throughout the following day to ask whether you'd left any message for me. But for some reason you were never told of my calls, and it was another morning before you called my hotel, wondering where I was. I'd begun to doubt that you were very eager for this encounter. When we did meet, though – we met by the Spanish Steps – I could tell that you were happy to see me. Especially happy, even. Your eyes lit up as I drew near; your smile lingered. We had coffee nearby and exchanged a few tales; then set off on one of the many errands you had to run before you'd be free to take our trip. These errands took several days. There were errands and there were also farewells to be said. We'd meet Kurt somewhere for a drink or a meal; or someone else from the Academy. We spent very little time alone – except trotting down the streets together. And sometimes of course you wanted to see one of these people without me. I took one long walk with Aaron. I also spent some time in the café across from my hotel with a new acquaintance – a talkative German Jew from South Africa who had fascinating tales to tell. I still remember one of his tales – about a production of *The Tempest* he had staged at the university where he taught, using students from various countries, and allowing each actor to speak the lines in his or her own native tongue. Everybody in the audience knew the play anyway, he said, so no one was really confused; and this way each actor could feel at ease. You laughed with delight when I reported this to you. Sounded like life here at the Academy, you said. Everybody just babbling away to himself in his own tongue.

For a while, these days, I remained more calm than I had expected to be able to. But then I made a move that in one moment tumbled me out of equilibrium. My shipboard dream might have warned me; but I forgot that warning.

It was an evening that we'd set aside for packing your canvases. You'd spread them out on the floor of one of the large rooms at the Academy, because I'd asked could I have a good look at them before we rolled them up. And so had one of your fellow painters there, whose opinion you valued. Stan. He strode around the room, his large head thrust forward, surveying them. And he was very impressed. As well he might have been. It was an extraordinary body of work you had produced. Most extraordinary were the paintings of the children. You'd caught them so truly in their ragged grace. As he spoke his words of praise, I could see the colour rising in your cheeks. You nodded your head slightly – half asserting (I thought): 'I know it'; half asking: 'Do you really mean it?' But you knew he meant it; knew – I guessed – that he'd rather *not* have been impressed by a mere woman, but had to praise you in spite of himself. You poured us all drinks then. He toasted you – and left. It was almost midnight.

As he left the room, you let your pleasure really show at last. Tossed your head up with a lovely undisguised motion of pride. And turned to me. Your eyes were strangely flashing. I had been standing studying one of the paintings I most loved – three children in your studio caught in moody postures I'd seen them fall into between posings. I looked at you and you looked at me. I hadn't yet found my own words to speak. I stammered out some phrase now – 'Yes, you really are extraordinary, Lottie.' And your eyes grew wider and shinier still. And you looked so beautiful at that moment, so entirely like your freest self, that without thinking I stepped toward you and kisssed you, with fervour, on your mouth.

You drew back from me. Almost in panic. All the light left your face. You said sternly, 'Don't.'

And I was filled with shame. And with a sense of helplessness. I remembered my dream then. I felt suddenly as if I had staggered and fallen into the dream.

I told you quickly that I was sorry. And I told you that it was just the paintings – the kiss was for the paintings. But I couldn't recover my composure now. Though we set to work and were so busy packing, I'm not sure that you noticed. It was late by the time we finished, and you suggested then that I sleep in a room near yours that nobody was using. I accepted gratefully. And fell into the bed, and into a heavy sleep. And woke – late morning – still abashed.

You had been up long before me. I found you in the room in which we'd packed your paintings, talking with a woman you'd said I should meet – a gifted flautist, but better known as the wife of a much-published poet who was visiting the Academy. I tried to enter the conversation, but I couldn't shake off a feeling of awkwardness now – like the awkwardness I'd experienced when you and Elena were together, and Elena watching me. The feeling that I was a child among adults. Your friend had brought a bottle of ouzo and – though I'd had no breakfast – I foolishly accepted a drink. It made it harder still for me to pretend to be at ease – to pretend that I felt like one of you. I wrote in my notebook that evening: 'Felt a bit insane for a while. Face knotted. Horrid.' I found an excuse to leave – volunteered to run one of your errands that didn't require your presence. And I took lunch by myself. And slowly sobered, and slowly recovered some kind of poise.

I find among my notes a page that is undated. I'm not sure whether it describes a dream that I had then or whether it describes my waking vision of the peculiar state of helplessness into which I'd tumbled. Kneeling among the shining grasses in the field at Epidauros, I had known that my feelings for you were deeply natural. But now I had tumbled back into a fear that what moved me was not my own nature but some awesome force quite other than myself.

I wrote:

'I had stamped on it. Then in the sun it revived. One morning I stepped out the door and there it reared, smiling at me. I pretended not to see it, not to have to stamp upon it again. I took another way through the grounds. When I wrote to you, of course, I made no mention of it. Might you be coming? I continued to ask. Yes, I took another path through the garden. But everywhere I looked, it was smiling behind the leaves. Or I could hear the silky sliding of it down the path after me, a little way off, but at my heels. Music to my ears! Would *you* see it? Ah but (my heart raced) might not its smile charm you?

'You never came. Its smile was a little baleful after this news. It followed me broken-backed. But still it smiled. And then the morning when I was to leave, to join you (out of the corner of my eye I saw these things; I never glanced at it directly) the morning I was to leave, I went out into the garden by a path I had never taken before, a roundabout path, and looked neither right nor left and walked very fast – and into a little wooded place, and sat down on a stump. And then didn't even breathe. I looked at nothing. I didn't let myself listen. I just sat there. How long a time passed I don't know. But I know that I sat there, burning. And now I must go, I thought. And as I thought this – I felt it slide in at my coat and coil itself round my left breast, sweet and cold. I had never known such sweetness. Nor such terror. And I rose quickly, as if to pretend that I didn't know.'

Yes, I slowly recovered my poise that day. But it was a fragile poise, it was all pretence. I pretended – to myself and to you – that I hadn't alarmed you. And I pretended that I hadn't been shamed. When I first returned, I'd had the happy feeling that you drew some needed extra strength from my presence. Now I'd lost that feeling. But I pretended that I hadn't. And you tried to pretend, too, along with me.

We left on our trip. We drove first to Cerveteri – to see the Etruscan tomb paintings. Then – after a picnic in sight of the sea – on to Tarquinia, to see more Etruscan frescoes, and the extraordinary tomb scultures: atop each stone casket, lounging at full length, the sculptured scantily draped figures of the deceased; head reared up usually, as though they brooded now upon the lives they had led. Brooded serenely.

We had begun to be almost happy together now. We nodded at one another.

'What a people!' you marvelled.

You made some quick sketches and we drove on.

Towards day's end we reached Tuscania – to stare at two ancient churches, and most especially at the one atop a hill. A simple structure, as my memory shapes it for me, but down the otherwise stark facade several immense stone animals roamed. We shook our heads in wonder. And high in the church belfry a flock of crows began to clamour, as though to express the astonishment we had no words for.

'Are you glad now that you came?' you asked me. I was glad.

We spent the night in Viterbo. In separate rooms. I tried to persuade you that if we shared a double room, as we had in Sicily, it would be cheaper as well as more companionable – and you needn't fear that I would try to be amorous. But you were firm. My assurances were made sincerely. But of course I still did hope against hope that – somehow – you yourself would suddenly discover that you felt amorous. Throughout this trip, come bedtime, we were always to exchange tense glances as we said good night.

Monday we spent staring at paintings in Sienna and in the many-towered town of San Gimignano. Usually I much preferred to do such looking on my own. I could better use my eyes when someone else was not standing next me telling me what *she* was seeing. But I delighted, those days, to be with you. You spoke rarely. Though you did sometimes point, or draw in your breath – as when we walked into the town hall in Sienna and high on the wall, in fresco, Martini's haughty captain-at-arms on a battle-draped and hooded horse crossed by night a wide castle-studded landscape – clearly his domain. The night around him, an intense blue – this very night was his, the painter made one feel; the air itself was his. You exclaimed again later in the day at the fresco of a drunken naked Noah – a proud one, here, discovered, by his sons, in an unguarded moment. You touched my arm: 'Look!' – pointed your finger; half shocked at the sight, it seemed to me, and half gloating.

At the beautiful Duccios in the Duomo – New Testament scenes – you gazed without speaking. Your eyes, very simply, at school. You deserved a portrait yourself, I mused, stealing a look at you. It would be a portrait of one who is all eyes. Who almost leaves her body as she looks. You could stand before a painting which intrigued you almost endlessly. Following, sometimes, every brush stroke. And no, this didn't make me impatient. It often moved me to look again, myself – and notice much that I had not yet noticed.

A day and a half we spent in Florence. I revisited with you the Michelangelos, the Fra Angelicos, the Donatellos and Massaccios.

We didn't spend every minute of the time together. Each of us did a little wandering on her own. But the time we spent together was good time.

Then late Wednesday we drove on to Arezzo – and at sundown visited the church of San Francesco there, and the Piero della Francesca frescoes. We were standing behind the altar, studying the great painting of the battle to recover the Cross for Jerusalem, when you grabbed my arm suddenly and pointed back into the church. I'd heard a pattering of feet, but disregarded the sound. You hadn't disregarded it. A small choirboy was dipping a broom in the holy water font, and then he was whooshing it down the aisles, to tidy up. Evening Mass would begin soon.

You rolled your eyes at me and whispered, 'Do you believe what you are seeing?'

The priest entered and took his seat near us at the organ, and began moving his fingers noiselessly over the keys. The choirboy put down his broom and joined him on the bench. And then a block of little boys arrived – the smallest with his foot in a huge plaster cast; the priest moved over and some of these, too, joined him on the long bench, while others stood close. They began to rehearse the evening's music – in piercing, almost yelling voices, but true in pitch.

'Now we'd better get out of here', you said.

We drove toward Assisi. But we weren't sure that we'd taken the right road, and when we pulled in at a gas station to fill up, we asked directions. Three young men who had just pulled in themselves overheard us asking, and volunteered to be escorts. We didn't want escorts; we just wanted to be told the way. But they were laughingly insistent. We were too tired to know how to send them away – sat there dumbly shaking our heads. And when we were on the road again, they came up alongside from behind, waving and shouting; fell back, then came up alongside again – and again.

'What *is* the matter with them!' you kept asking me.

I couldn't help feeling that your anger was directed in part at me. As though you were saying, 'See – you want me to share your life with you, and look at how vulnerable we are, two women alone together! What is the matter with *you*?'

We drove on, looking straight ahead, and they finally went their way. It was late night by the time we'd reached Assisi and found a hotel and said our usual strained good nights.

A good part of the next day we spent looking at the Giottos, the Cimabues. And then we headed back in the direction of Rome. For the next day you had to deliver your car to the friends who were buying it; and we had to board the evening train for Naples, where your ship waited.

During that day's-end drive, I remember, I fell into a kind of daze. The scenes I stared at now seemed to be glimpses not of the actual world but of some world of fantasy into which we had wandered. We stopped in Perugia for tea. Its lovely square and church and splashing fountain seemed make-believe. We passed through Orvieto after nightfall. And the church there, too, high on a hill, and lit up for some feast, seemed a phantasm. In one ancient town through which we passed, a sculpted figure leaned towards us from atop a wall, and I remember turning towards you as though to confirm that I had really seen it. You nodded: I had seen it. You, too, seemed in a dazed state. Your face looked very drawn. It had been an odd trip. We'd not once spoken together of Leonard. You clearly hadn't wanted to talk about him. And I hadn't wanted to pressure you. Part of me was very curious to know what you expected your life with him to be like. And part of me wanted simply to pretend for a while that you were not about to enter that life, that our trip together would never end. I must have looked at you with a particularly miserable look as we said good night in Viterbo.

'Don't, Bobbie', you said.

We reached Rome the next day by late morning. And you hurried off to run some errands, and I hurried off to run some of my own; and then we met again to complete a few last errands together. You had fallen in love with a short black-and-white checked coat you'd seen in a shop window, but had decided it would be an extravagance to get it. I asked you to let me buy it for you and you let me. You put it on at once and wore it from that moment on. And I was pleased – because you looked happy in it, and because it felt a little as though you had let me put my arms around you in this way.

At my albergo earlier I'd found a note from Lisa and Russell. They'd spoken of taking a trip to Italy perhaps, and now here they were. So I left a note for them to join us for early supper at a little outdoor restaurant near the Acadamy. A few other friends of yours joined us, too. The meal was one of those at which each person keeps trying to turn the conversation in some different direction, and everyone looks bewildered. Then half the company saw us to the train. Your landlord from Anticoli turned up too. We headed there in two cars and Lisa and Russell seemed at first to have disappeared on the way. It turned out that Russell had decided to rush to their hotel and bring Lisa's drawings to show you. Right there among all the jostling people on the train platform he improvised an exhibition – holding up first one and then another picture, taken from a portfolio Lisa obediently held. She did look a little embarrassed – but continued to pass the pictures to him at his bidding. He raised his voice above the general hubbub and explained each one: 'These are Mykonos houses and flowers', 'This is our garden at home', 'Here – this one is one I did.' Your various friends meanwhile were trying to say their particular farewells. And each was glaring at Russell as though he were a madman. Russell didn't care. 'I don't believe in waiting for the "right" moment', he told us. The drawings were in fact quite lovely – as you managed to tell Lisa in the midst of the confusion.

And then the conductor was yelling for everybody to get on board. Your friends quickly embraced you. Your landlord kissed your hand. And we climbed on.

And stared at one another. For we'd soon be saying goodbye now too.

We weren't alone in the compartment. A stout middle-aged man with a florid face shared it with us. The few words he spoke to us were in Italian, and we weren't sure whether or not he understood us when we spoke English together. But whether he would understand or not, it was hard to disregard his presence.

Early in the long rackety trip through the night we fell into a curious quarrel. I had decided that after I'd said goodbye to you in Naples, I would travel through Spain for several weeks – then pay the visit to Pete in London he'd asked me to make. I'd written *him* suggesting that he join me in Spain, but he'd responded: 'Look, lady, I know these Latins are colourful, gay, irresponsible and quaint, but it's saline celtic blood that courses through your anglo-gaelic heart. You mustn't deny it if you are not to deny yourself. By which I mean to hell with this come and see me in Spain kick – YOU come see ME in England.' And I'd agreed to join him there toward the end of June. I'd planned to travel to Spain by train, third class. But a few days before, you'd remarked that your ship made one stop in a Spanish port. Why didn't I start out by ship – along with you? This seemed a lovely plan; so in Rome I'd inquired about tickets. You were going second class, and a second-class ticket would cost me a sum several times over the cost of the train ticket I had priced. I didn't quite dare commit that extravagance. But if I bought a third-class ticket I could well afford it. I spoke of this now. We couldn't have meals together, but we could easily enough meet again and again on deck.

You flared up – indignant. If I couldn't afford to travel *with* you, we should skip the whole idea. I was indignant, in turn – indignant that you were indignant. For if I weren't careful of my money, I'd have to cut my travels short. And – though I didn't speak of this – I'd already committed one extravagance, in giving you that coat. You were staring straight ahead of you now, eyes very black – with the look you'd had in the car when the three youths were harassing us; a look again that seemed to complain: And you have wanted me to share your life!

I was bewildered, as well as angry. I leaned my head against the shaking wall of the train and dozed for a while. When I woke – I think the snoring of the man across from us woke me – you were sitting there looking not angry but dejected. I told you now that as we grew closer and closer to saying a final goodbye, I seemed to be feeling number and number. Perhaps it made more sense anyway not to draw the goodbye out. You nodded. You, too, looked numb.

We said very little the rest of the trip – dozing on and off, side by side. It was almost 3 a.m. by the time we were saying good night in the hallway of a Naples hotel. You gave me, as I remember, a little kiss on the cheek.

You'd been told that the ship left mid-morning, so we'd arranged to be called at eight and we met groggily for breakfast – but then learned that the sailing wouldn't be until late afternoon, so we went gratefully back to our rooms and slept until lunch. At lunch time we found an outdoor café on the waterfront. Down the quay was the big liner, waiting for its passengers. It sat there: the end of our time together. I kept turning to look at it, in spite of myself.

We ordered clams, oysters, ricci – a farewell feast.

Some ragged children were jumping in and out of the water at the dock nearest us. And a few of them had clambered into a little boat moored there and were swaying back and forth, laughing hard, pretending that the boat was in motion. An old man in a bright blue rowboat began to call to us, gesturing. Didn't we want to hire him to take us for a jaunt? We signalled 'No', but he kept on calling, gesturing; then finally he gave up, with a shrug, but continued to call out – just to himself, to the air. There were a lot of sailboats in the bay. German tourists on most of them, you remarked; and made a face. And down the quay the big liner sat.

'In a certain way I do love you – and always will', I heard you saying – your voice so light that I could just hear the words. And very tender. But very final. You were saying goodbye. Your voice trembled a little. 'Anticoli was very real', you were saying. But even as you spoke these words you were shaking your head gravely. Real but out of reach. Not to be repeated. The ship you would board soon sat there just down the quay.

I couldn't find any words of my own to speak.

And then you found a stronger voice and you began to question me. Did I think I might write a book about this year of travel? I did think so. I'd been keeping a journal, hadn't I? I had.

Your voice changed again, became newly intense, as you began to tell me about a story of travel *you* had tried to write some months before. But you never had found the right way to tell it. It was a story about an impulsive trip you'd taken while you were visiting Crete. You had settled in at a small hotel in Herakleion, you said, and you were beginning to get some good work done. You'd gone off on a brief sidetrip and another traveller you'd met that day invited you to drive with him to see a certain out of the way and fascinating hill town. You'd been tempted, but felt you shouldn't really go – you should get back to Herakleion and to the quiet work you were doing there. So you'd told him no; and you'd taken the bus, as planned, back to Herakleion. But all the way back you'd been tantalized by thoughts of that town he'd described; and you'd decided suddenly to return to the place where he was staying and tell him that you *would* go with him after all. There would be no bus running for hours; so you'd decided impulsively to hire a taxi – though the fare would be high. You'd persuaded a young Englishwoman who was staying at your hotel to join you and share the cost. But on the way you'd fallen into a state of acute anxiety. 'Are you sick?' she had asked you – very concerned. And it had been *like* being sick, you told me. You'd been sick with the feeling that you were acting out of some unreasonable compulsion. Yes, the story – you said – if you could write it – would be a story about a certain kind of feverish compulsion that one follows, and it ends in disaster.

Had this ended in disaster, I asked.

You looked surprised at the question. Oh – nothing had happened. And actually you were glad you'd taken the trip, you told me. You'd never forget the sight of that town.

The disaster, I gathered, had been your own consternation of spirit. I suggested: Maybe you couldn't write the story because you weren't yet entirely sure how you did feel about having gone.

You thought about that for a moment.

'I know I felt sick the whole time', you said.

You'd done something like this once before, you added. While you were a WAAC, working for a photographic unit out in the Pacific during World War II, a couple of flyers had suggested that they smuggle you aboard a plane making a quick round trip flight to Saipan. It was a very beautiful island, they'd told you. Wouldn't you like to see it? And you'd gone with them. And got away with it, too – without being punished. And you'd never forget that island, either. But – you had suffered for it; felt sick that whole trip, too.

Now this is strange: it didn't occur to me at the time to ask myself why you were moved to tell me this story. And I'm quite sure that it didn't occur to you, either. But as I write of it now, it seems clear that you were saying to me, and saying to yourself: If I were to try to make my life with you, I would always feel as I felt on this trip – don't you see – sick in spirit, out of bounds.

We sat for a while, then, not talking about anything. But saying goodbye with our silence. And now and then we'd glance down the quay to where the liner sat.

The children who had been playing in the small boat near us clambered up out of it and ran off. You said that you'd better start seeing about your luggage. Some of it you had with you at the hotel; some had been sent on ahead by a travel agency. So we walked to your hotel to collect the bags from your room, and then walked to the agent's, a few doors away. The agent drove you solemnly down to the dock, to fill out innumerable papers. I sat on one of your suitcases, watching others begin their long farewells.

There were explosions of laughter all about us; there were explosions of tears. You finished your paperwork and suggested that we have a last drink together. So we walked slowly back to the café. And we had a last drink. You drank to me. I drank to you. And then we walked back to the ship. Its whistle was blowing now – a hideous and piercing sound. And the gangplank was down.

'Let's let some others get on first', you said. You pretended to smile. I pretended to smile. Your hands touched my hands for a moment. They were quite cold, I noticed. And so were mine. You pressed a kiss against my cheek – hard. Your mouth was cold, too, I noticed. You said, 'I have your letters. I'll keep those with me.' I couldn't think of anything to say. We said goodbye with our eyes.

You went up the gangplank.

When the gangplank had been lifted, some of the others who had come to say goodbyes began to throw streamers of confetti toward the decks – as if to hold the ship there by those papery tethers, hold the loved ones there still within our sight. Some of the streamers reached the deck and passengers clutched at them. Some fell short. One woman, standing beside me, threw her frail spiral short again and again, but kept hold of her end of it and would wind it each time around her finger, then toss it out again. Tears were streaming down her face.

The ship *wasn't* moving. Time seemed to be tangled in all that paper, and to have stalled. There you were, standing gravely at the railing, and perhaps you would always be standing there, I felt – still blessedly within my sight. And then the ship's whistle gave another, a final ugly blast. And the ship began to move. You raised your arm. I raised my arm. All the confetti streamers fell into the water.

On the train I wrote you:

'And so – you are gone.

As Pete writes, it *is* from the north that I come. I am not a gypsy from Crete. And so as your ship pulls out, I stand there like a stick or a stone and simply stare across at you. Nevertheless – it *is* weeping that I see you off, and it *is* gesticulating, and it *is* calling messages to you through the air – *at the same time* dancing for you, and my heart in it, and my hat sailed into the air as high as it can sail – quite as in that gypsy farewell. And it is right that as a ship pulls away it should become more and more difficult to see whether or not anyone is weeping, but you may still see a hat up there in the air for you. May you be going home truly, Lottie.'

17

It was in Spain that I wrote a first sentence for this book – though it wasn't until I returned to the States that I wrote more than that sentence. I can remember standing at nightfall in a dusty street in the town of Avila – a town that is encircled by a high many-turreted medieval wall. The sun had dropped beyond the wall and now dark drew its circle round us too. The words spoke themselves in my mind: 'This is a book of travel – of travail. Spell that either way.' I remember asserting in that moment: Yes, I have a story that wants to be told. And though I was still desolate – having lost you – a small flare of joy burst in me with that assertion, and went on burning.

I ask myself now: Why did the word 'travail' seem to me to contain in itself – as in a kernel – the fullness of the story that I had to tell? What labour of the spirit have I been trying to describe? I think I can see now that it has been the labour of accepting my sexual self; the labour of guarding it against scorn. My own scorn, of course, as well as that of others. Guarding it against scorn, and also – paradoxically – against jealous attempts to steal it from me. For rereading the pages of this book that I have written so far, I can see that often when I've felt myself to be in touch with the very deepest fires in me – as when I stood watching the dancing gypsy woman in the grove near Phaestos – whatever man has been standing near has wanted at once to try to steal that fire from me – to make it somehow *his*. 'Miss Barbara, kiss me!' Miss Barbara, give *me* your fire. I need it! (Has he not his own?) It was in Avila that I met an especially subtle would-be thief. But I am ahead of my story. Avila was the last town that I visited in Spain.

I had been travelling through that country for more than two weeks. By third-class train, as I'd planned. Glad to be making the trip this way. I was numb after saying goodbye to you, but it was hard to sit knee to knee with others in these crowded compartments and not wake again to some sense of ongoing life.

As my train was crossing the south of France, on the first lap of this journey, a large Frenchwoman had entered the compartment – set a wicker basket at her feet, set on the empty seat next her a little black satchel. As we bumped out of the station, the satchel began to squirm, the wicker basket uttered a grunt. I wrote in my notes: 'Ah, Lottie, don't ask me to travel any other way. Truly, how would you go: an antimacassar behind your head, or by Noah's Ark – out of which life began all over again?'

Out of which life began. But what new life would I be able to begin now? Was there life fire in me still? I doubted it. I doubted it. It had died down in me with your leaving. And what kind of new life was beginning now for *you*? I couldn't not wonder about this continuously. Though I told myself to stop. I told myself that I had better simply travel for a while – stare at what was in front of me.

We entered Spain through a long and filthy-aired tunnel. No warning was given to the passengers, so the train windows were open. We all began to choke – quickly buried our faces in our hands. 'A fitting entry, perhaps', I wrote in my journal. At customs, before a change of trains, the officials wore antique black hats like helmets – which gave them the awesome authority of figures out of some scary dream. I had only my lightweight typewriter, two shirts, a change of socks and underclothes, comb and toothbrush, a warm scarf, packed into my one small knapsack. (I'd left everything else with a travel agency in Rome.) They studied these simple items with the darkest of scowls before giving me the necessary nod to proceed. But the ragged Spaniards with whom I soon was travelling I found to be as friendly as Greeks. I brought food along with me always, but it was seldom that I was allowed to eat it. If I'd take an orange out of my pack, 'Here – this is a better orange', I'd be told. Or 'Here – you should eat *this*' – and a large slice of potato omelette would be handed me on a knife. Few of them spoke any English and my Spanish was scanty – I was learning it as I went. But with the few words we could share, they patiently questioned me, and gave useful information – such as the cheapest place to stay in the next city.

My first stop, Barcelona. City full of rich shops smelling of leather goods, glinting with beautifully worked silver. A few elegantly dressed citizens strolled in and out of these shops and along the grand avenues – the ramblas and rondas and grand vias. But most of those wandering the streets – and passing the shops without entering – were shabbily dressed. Many were crippled – had stumps of arms, or stumps of legs, got of course in the war by which Franco had seized power. Many were pedlars of trifles: combs or caramels or tin birds that whistled. Many more were beggars. I would visit one town – Aranjuez – where a sign on the city's wall warned: 'No begging or blasphemy'. This was like telling half the population to drop dead, I mused. For clearly there were many who could only fill their bellies *by* begging. And how were they to feed their spirits without cursing the powers-that-be?

I remember seeing a shabby boy sitting on a sidewalk in front of one of the fine shops, with a piece of hard bread on the ground next him, just sitting there in utter listlessness. A woman stopped to question him. Another woman walking past muttered quietly but with fury: 'Miseria miseria miseria!' A police officer who was passing stopped and tried to lift the boy up, but he began to cry, in fright. So he put him down again. The woman took him up in her arms and he began tearfully to respond to her questions and she walked off with him – followed at a little distance by the policeman.

I remember (in Madrid) passing a splendid fountain of a sculpted goddess seated in a chariot drawn by lions and then seeing a ragged woman sitting on a bench nearby, her head bowed into her lap. A child on a worn black pillow at her feet, playing with her skirt. The child not even trying to rouse her – used, I supposed, to her defeated state.

I began to wish that I had not chosen Spain to visit now, when my own life spirits were low. Face after face into which I looked seemed set in the rigour of unhappiness. A line from one of Chekhov's plays kept running through my head: 'I am in mourning for my life.' And I was in mourning for mine. I began to scan the faces, looking for some sign of zest. Some sign of my own hope of zest.

On the afternoon of my second day in Barcelona I entered a cobbler's shop. One of my shoes needed mending. The young cobbler and I began clumsily to talk, with the help of my dictionary. Two friends of his dropped in – Manolo and Pepe. They were workers in an automobile factory. Did I like this city, they asked. 'Bella, no?' But sad, I said. They quickly agreed. Either there was no work or you were overworked. I thought to ask: Was it possible to see flamenco dancing here? (*There* might be the life I sought.) They said oh yes, and Pepe offered to take me to see it that evening; Manolo offered to be our chaperone. So after dinner the two picked me up at my room and we began to wander night-time Barcelona. We never saw any flamenco. It turned out that the places which featured it were too expensive for us. Once we stepped just inside the door, heard the shrill distinctive breaking voice of a flamenco singer, caught a glimpse of the dance, and backed out again. But we did find dancing. It was the narrow streets of the old part of the city that we were wandering – beautiful now in the night, lights rebounding strangely from the close-crowded walls, which shone a mysterious grey. By day these streets had seemed to me only miserable, but now they were alight, alive. We turned a corner and the chatter of castanets was in the air, like a pulse – though I couldn't see where the sound was coming from. We turned down another street and music was spilling its length – from a large hurdy-gurdy. An old man was cranking it, and two raggedy thin girls were dancing together to its jazz, in the middle of the street. Steps which they invented themselves. Arms round one another. Nearby a very skinny man was roasting a chicken on a spit, while others stood close, laughing. My spirits lifted. A life persisted here, in spite of all. And my own life persists, too, I told myself. Believed this. Doubted this.

The train to Madrid made many local stops – took a day and a night. At the outskirts of Barcelona I glimpsed families living in shacks of little more than slats and paper; and in mere lean-tos built against the city's walls. I remember still a sight I caught of a patient woman standing outside one of those lean-tos, bent over to stir something in a little pot over a makeshift bonfire. She stirred it with such care – as though the dish she had concocted were a work of art. And art it must indeed have taken. Look what she makes of little, I chided and encouraged myself. Past the city's limits there were ragged people living in caves dug into cliffs.

Then we were in the countryside. Rich muddy rivers. Farms with terraces of careful stonework. Frequently villages. When we'd stop in a village, everybody would lean out of the windows to visit.

There were three men in my compartment who stayed on the train till Madrid. Two were friends. They shared one of those water jugs with a long spout, and enjoyed squirting water from a distance into one another's mouths. One of them also enjoyed reading aloud over my shoulder. I was studying my Spanish grammar. He'd read the English translations – drawing out the sounds, loudly, grotesquely; then shrug his shoulders at me. The third man – with a lean quite yellow face (the whites of his eyes were yellow, too, I think he had jaundice) – borrowed my dictionary and read it to himself, quietly. This man shared with me a delicious potato tortilla – though I showed him that I had my own food. He shook his head: It wouldn't be as good as his tortilla. The other two shared with me their bottle of wine. And when I took out my pocket knife to peel an orange and the man who'd been reading over my shoulder noticed that the blade was loose, he took it from me without a word, stood up, held it against the luggage shelf, and – to 'fix' it – hit at it with the now empty wine bottle. The bottle, not surprisingly, shattered, and some of the pieces dropped down the neck of his friend. But the friend merely stood up too and shook the glass down into his overalls. It seemed not to bother him at all when he sat down again. (This puzzles me still.)

Towards evening the train got very crowded. People were sitting on the floor in the aisles. Most of them began to sing, to forget their discomfort. I wrapped my woollen scarf round my head – against the chill of the night and against the glare of the overhead light, which was never turned off – and leaned against the window frame and, to the clamour of their singing, and to thoughts of you, thoughts of you (Lottie, Lottie, where am I travelling now? Why are you marrying? Why are we not together?), dozed off. When I woke in the early morning, the head of the jaundiced man was on my knees, bobbing about like a great marble. (Lottie, what is this head on my lap?) I hesitated to wake him, but the man in overalls – waking now too – pushed the man upright, uttering a series of oaths.

In Madrid there were fine shops again; and banks, banks – I had never seen so many imposing bank buildings. And limping past the fine buildings were as many crippled people and beggars as in Barcelona.

I spent much of my time at the Prado. Stayed on three days so that I could return and return there, going from room to room, painting to painting. I wrote in my journal: 'What a peculiar feeling it is – peculiar shock – when one encounters a real style. Even in a painter one doesn't particularly care for. Say, Tintoretto.' It was at the Goyas that I chose to stare the most. What life motion was in them. And especially in the later, very painful scenes – of war, oppression. I wrote: 'On way home from Prado felt elated for some reason. In spite of misery here. And my own misery. Reason of seeing such paintings, no doubt. It struck me about Goya: it was in what the catalogue names the "painful, disturbed" period of his life that he found his true style somehow.' Could I then not find my own true life style by facing what misery *I* knew?

One painting I returned and returned to was a painting by Hieronymus Bosch, of three moments in the story of Adam and Eve, the last – at which I stared and stared – the moment in which they leave the Garden of Eden. Making not the dismayed exit I had seen in so many paintings, but an almost jaunty exit. I wrote: 'Yes – he sees it: we have to escape the Garden; owe thanks to the serpent who winds itself round that tree and smiles its ancient smile. This Adam, a small skinny figure, holds out his hand for the apple with heart lifting, eye lighting. And he steps forth, hand raised, and a smile upon his lips. A jaunty flick of a smile. Yes, that is how we must step out. Feeling, yes, yes very naked. But able to smile that flick of a smile. Then one puts one's foot down as though it were the day of Creation all over again. Can I keep my balance? Can I walk – by myself?'

Of course it is with you that I had dreamed of stepping out – beyond the reach of the Father's eye, on to new ground, our own. Could I do it without you? That is what was facing me now.

I visited Aranjuez. I visited Toledo on its green hill, which I had seen first in El Greco's moody painting. I took a train for Seville. A day-long trip. South. (Lottie – come south with me again.) Stared out the window at the land carefully tended. At the changing reds of the Spanish earth. And sometimes now the earth was an amazing violet colour. (Lottie – come south.) I made friends with a soft-spoken older woman and her solemn son who worked for the telephone company. They taught me the names of flowers by the side of the tracks; and suggested that we meet the next day. It would be Saturday, and they'd be free to show me their beloved city. So the next day I strolled with them down narrow streets where purple vines hung overhead. Into parks and patios and courtyards. 'Hermosa, eh?' Beautiful, eh? the mother kept asking. Ornamented tiles underfoot and tiles in walls and sills. In the courtyards, palm trees and orange trees. One park through which we wandered was full of roses. She wanted to pick just one rose. Her son said no. It was strictly forbidden. Just one – to hold it to her hand and smell it, she pleaded. He told her no. She made a little face, but didn't dare to disobey him; smiled at me a sad little grimace of a smile. Yes, we have to forbid ourselves our loveliest desires, I wanted to cry to her.

I made another giro of the city with a young Italian doctor who approached me later at a sidewalk café and asked could he talk with me. He was 27 years old and had decided to take off three years and travel. 'But I find it annoying to go around alone', he confessed. Dan Balbao. I decided that he didn't have a sexual conquest in mind, did simply dislike being alone. Indeed when he learned that I was a few years older than he, he began to treat me rather like an aged though companionable aunt – to regard me even with a slight distaste, I thought. He was headed the next day for Algeciras. To attend a fiesta there. Would there be flamenco dancing, I asked. He thought there would be; so I decided to head for Algeciras myself. I had begun to hunger to see this dancing. Hoping to feel in it again that pulse of Spain which had persisted through all calamities. Hoping, too, that watching it might help me to believe surely in my own continuing pride. I was finding this more and more difficult. I'd think of you with Leonard. Feel the life go out of me. Try not to think of this. Try not to think of you at all. Feel dead indeed, then. No, the answer was not to forget you.

Next to me in the bus, Balbo chanted in eager tones: 'If God is a curious green cat, we shall see what we shall see.' It was his travel song. We weren't to see flamenco dancing in Algeciras, however. A scrubby seaboard town. Throngs in the streets – in party paper hats. Vendors selling more paper hats, or selling things like rubber eggs you squeeze and rubber chickens jump out, squawking, with their tongues stuck out. There were, to be sure, in the throng, a number of tiny girls dressed in the costumes of flamenco and – faces solemn – snapping castanets; but they snapped them mechanically. They had been doing this for hours and were very tired. They were heavily made-up, looked not like children but like small tired middle-aged women. There was to be a bullfight and the crowd had come to see this. Balbo took me to the bullfight of course. I kept remembering wistfully the Cretan frescoes in which those ancient people leapt over the horns of the bull rather than prove themselves by doing the bewildered beast to death.

Balbo was headed for Tangiers next, across the straits. He had a friend who had a villa just outside the city, and he suggested that I come along and spend a couple of days there. (He'd be staying on.) I almost didn't accept this invitation – for a long moment felt that I *shouldn't* travel to that farther shore. The figure of my father seemed to rear up from the waters, forbidding it as beyond limits. I shook myself, startled. I had been about to forbid this crossing to *myself.* I said yes.

I can recall still the smell of the North African wind – hot, fragrant, blowing from inland. I lay awake in bed the first night for a long time, filling my lungs with it. And remembering *your* sweet scent. Our bodies entangled. When desire surprised you – blew upon you, too, for that too short while. I also recall the dismay I felt when we roamed the streets of Tangiers, at the sight of the Arab women wrapped in their chadors – 'as in graveclothes', I wrote in my journal. The wind here seemed to invite one to act out one's deepest self. But the chador warned: if you are a woman, you had better kill off that self. In spite of myself I felt my flesh receive the warning.

I left for Spain again. In Granada there were gypsies, I'd heard. Maybe I could see *them* dance flamenco. Dance our *right* to be our deep selves.

I arrived in Granada past nightfall and when the padrone of the hotel I found, after some walking, told me that yes, there were gypsy dancers at an address he could give me, I decided to visit them that very evening. He wrote on a card with the address the price I should pay, and advised me to take in my wallet no more than that sum. Or, he told me with a grin, I would end by paying whatever sum was in the wallet.

The gypsies lived at the edge of the city, in caves – or rather, in whitewashed dwellings built somehow in the mouths of these caves. I entered a dimly lit room in which a few small tables had been set up for tourists. The only other tourists at the moment were two German couples. A group of gypsy women and girls were sitting in chairs ranged round the room against the walls. Three men provided music, and a slender boy served drinks. At the end of the room was a curtained archway. Just behind the half-drawn curtain a young girl sat, with a sleeping baby on her lap.

The boy served me some wine. The guitarists began to pluck out a tune. The women began to clap – a startling sound, loud as the sound of pistol shots. My ears were buzzing. I glanced at the girl and baby in the doorway. The baby, to my astonishment, was sleeping soundly still. I smiled at the girl, who smiled back at me, and bent and placed a tender kiss on the baby's cheek. One of the women rose, scowling. Tossed her head. She had thick hair the colour of straw. Stamped her feet. Swirled her long faded yellow skirt which had a design of large flowers on it. Snapped her castanets. Four others rose and began to stamp their feet. And then they all began to circle the room, clacking their castanets very loudly, swirling their long ruffled skirts. (The skirts – as they passed – kept slapping in the face of a young fat-cheeked girl who was still sitting against the wall, her hand out to protect herself.) They danced in sloppy abandon. They were giving the tourists what we had come for. Yes, here we are – ole! – gypsies, doing our wild gypsy dance for you. Ole!

The fat-cheeked girl rose and did a solo – a very fancy solo – bending way back at one point so that she practically lay back along the ground, her face in an almost trance. But not the trance of the dancer who has become one with the dance. The trance of sublime indifference. The first woman danced a solo. She shook her blonde hair loose. An artificial flower which had been stuck in it flopped to the floor. She shook her hair down over her face, her hands gesticulating wildly before her face. Abandoned to complete indifference.

I was very disappointed. And yet I couldn't not respect what these women were doing – were refusing to do – and marvel at the humour of it.

'Tres jolie, no?' the blonde woman – passing me – asked with a grin, as she ended her dance. Could she see what I was thinking?

When the time came to pay, I *was* asked for an outrageous sum. But I made a face and showed them the contents of my wallet, and they cheerfully enough took just what was in it. The woman with the straw-blonde hair gave me an affectionate pat on the arm. The girl with the baby on her lap – still sleeping soundly – smiled her sweet smile at me again.

The next morning I set off to admire the Alhambra, on its long wooded hill at the city's edge. After I had wandered through those airy rooms, with all their delicate traceries and arabesques – and then through the walled gardens, with their murmur of doves and murmur of fountains and running streams, and scent of boxwood – I shook myself out of the drowsy almost drugged state these palace grounds invited, and decided to return to the site of the gypsies, to see that place by daylight. As I approached the caves, three children ran toward me and hailed me. They had seen me the night before, they told me. I couldn't remember seeing them. They must have been peering from behind that curtain in the darkened archway. Two little girls and a boy. Bright bright black eyes, dishevelled hair.

Had I liked the dancing? They studied my face as I answered – staring at me with the wonderful direct stare of children. Where was I from? And I travelled alone? That was brave. Well, if I liked dancing – would I like to see *them* dance?

Oh yes, oh yes.

They laughed to see me so eager. The smaller of the two girls took me by the hand. They led me into one of the cave houses, where nobody was at home – a sparsely furnished whitewashed room.

Ole! The little boy danced first. Throwing up his arms, hands gracefully curled. Stamping, proud. And tossing his head. His skinny torso stiffly held now, his buttocks jutting out – proud. As the little girls shouted out a song for him and clapped, clapped.

They flashed looks at me. Did I like? I liked. His heart was in it.

The taller of the little girls danced next. Her fingers fluttered imaginary castanets. She stamped, she stamped. She tossed her wild hair. Yes, I liked. Here were the very same motions I had watched last night, but last night they had been the motions and nothing more. Now the dancers *entered* the dance.

And then the smaller of the girls began to move; straightened up, with an audible drawing in of her breath, stamped – and I drew in my own breath, and held it. The other children had been beautiful to watch – they danced with such spirit. And yet I had remained very conscious of the fact that they *were* children. But she – from the moment that she took that breath, raised her arms, began to flutter her hands, glancing over one shoulder, then over the other, her eyes taking everything everything in – she was neither young any longer nor old. She was – the life-pride which flamenco is. And her own pride, of course, revealed to her by the dance. And the pride of all that she was touching – the ground her feet stamped, as if in greeting; the encircling air which her tossing head and her weaving arms and snapping fingers greeted. She swayed her body in greeting to east to west to south to north. And finally – as the girl the night before had done – swayed so far back that her body almost lay along the ground. The girl the night before had made this seem a well-executed feat. But she – made it seem the very motion of life. And the ground seemed to rise as if to meet her, in welcome.

As soon as she had stopped dancing, she became a little girl again.

I took them to eat some of the small ices one could buy from street vendors. I parted from them with reluctance. Now I knew again that Spain was alive, in its pride. And I knew again that my own pride was alive.

I took a train to Avila – north and west of Madrid; rode all night and all day, this train more crowded than the train I had taken from Barcelona to Madrid. I spent the night sprawled, with others, on the floor of the entranceway to the coach, my knapsack under my head. I remember opening my eyes in the middle of the night to watch a man with a wooden leg carefully pick his way among the sleepers to get into the lavatory. Then – step by patiently precise step – make the return trip. He managed it with such calm and grace that I was suddenly happy to be lying there.

Avila. I can remember, yes, standing out in the street near the small hotel I'd found, at sundown, the evening of my arrival, and telling myself that I would write this book. I would address it to you, I told myself. It would be the story of a long walk through the dark. And the story of trying to learn to dance that walk. It would be a celebration of my love for you. The story of this love's

260

difficulties. But the story, too, of learning to know it to be a gift. The book would move towards the moment in Elevsis when I knelt among the grasses and pressed my hands against the shining breasts of the tumbled statue.

I went to bed early that first night, for I was very tired; and I slept half the next day away. Then I went out and began to explore the town. Town in which St Theresa was born and had her visions. She heard God speaking to her through the sound of flowing streams, I had read. I went out through one of the nine gates in the wall to look at the surrounding plain – striped with the shadows which the many towers cast. A stream ran its curling way nearby, and I stared at the wall's reflection which it carried – now golden, now rosy, the stones changing colour in the water under the day's changing light. And I listened for the stream's voice, thinking of St Theresa. But it was not this sound but another sound that took me by surprise. A sound in the air above me. I looked up. There were storks nesting in the crenellated tops of many of the wall's towers. And they were doing their own dancing up there – shuffling about on the twigs of their nests, stretching necks and wings, clacking the castanets of their great beaks. And sometimes of course they sailed out over the plain, trailing their long legs. I watched them with awe and delight. Lottie, Lottie –

I went back through one of the gates and began to wander inside the walls – musing, as I walked, about my book. There were many others at this hour strolling through the town, and a good many taking the same direction that I was taking. But I began to be aware of one particular stroller who was keeping pace with me, a little to the side. He wasn't looking at me directly – or wasn't when I glanced at *him* – but I began to know that he would take any turn that I took, and that he was waiting for some moment he'd choose to speak to me. A neatly dressed middle-aged man with a tense not-quite-handsome face. I strolled now into the piazza where the fortress-like cathedral stood, guarded by its stone lions – the beasts crouched up on pedestals, and all of them linked together by a chain hung from each of their muzzles. I found a step to sit on, for I wanted to make some notes in my journal. And now he came up to me.

He hoped I would forgive him, he began. But he could tell that I was an American, and he would like the chance to talk English again. He had lived in the States for a while. Could he walk with me a little?

I told him of course, and we began to stroll through the town together. Down the cobbled street that ran alongside the cathedral – the Street of Life and Death (set in the cathedral's wall were medallions of a young woman's face and a staring skull). Into the wider streets. Past shops. The convent in which St Theresa first lived. Into the plaza with her statue. Past the post office, where the letter slot is a lion's mouth open in a yawn. He was pointing things out to me, telling me a little about the history of the town. I wanted to look hard with my own eyes, so I was abstracted as I listened, and I could tell that this bothered him. He wanted me to give him more attention. And he wanted to walk closer to me than I wanted. So I hung the satchel I was carrying between us. This annoyed him, too. We sat for a while on a low wall, because there was something I wanted particularly to stare at – the glowing bricks of some old building. He drew close. I inched away. He drew close again. I moved again – and put my satchel on the wall between us.

Why didn't I just get up and say goodbye at this point? If he had been cruder in his attentions, I would have felt more free to. But he was subtle, managed to seem quite well-mannered all the while. Even haughtily so. I felt the need to be courteous to him.

When we strolled into the piazza where there were several outdoor restaurants, he asked me to have a sherry with him and I accepted. And then he walked me to my hotel.

He would like to meet me after dinner, he told me. And now I did say no.

'Why not?' he asked.

I said, 'It wouldn't be right.'

'Why not?'

'It just wouldn't', I said.

Then he reached quietly for my hand and set it upon his wrist. 'Feel my pulse', he said. Very quietly.

'Look,' I decided that I had better say – 'I am engaged.'

'Oh?' He looked at me hard. 'And why are you travelling about by yourself?'

I invented a quick lie. My fiancé was in school in London. And very busy with his studies. So I was making this trip that I had always wanted to make. But I would soon be joining him.

I met his eyes.

He made a little bow and left.

But the next morning when I stepped outside my hotel, he was standing there waiting for me.

'I've been in a fever all night', he accused me.

His words made me angry. I told him, 'I'm sorry, but that's not my fault.'

The day before I had said that I would be in Avila for only a day or two. Now he began to urge me to stay on. 'You're cruel if you won't. You must.'

I must – because he wanted it! I didn't answer. Just gave him an angry look – and began walking. He kept pace beside me, urging, 'Say that you'll stay!'

So I stopped. 'I don't want to stay', I told him. 'And I have to be alone now.' I'd told him during our walk the day before that I was a writer. 'I have to think about something that I'm writing', I said.

He argued with me. Very quietly. His voice always low, well-bred. I should have said a brief goodbye and walked away. But there was a look in his face that made me feel guilty, in spite of my guiltlessness. He did look as though he hadn't slept all night. I told him I'd meet him later for another sherry if he liked.

As we walked together toward the café in late afternoon he again tried to walk so close to me that our bodies would touch. Again, to balk him, I switched my satchel from one shoulder to the other. And again he was annoyed. He chose a table in the café that was at the greatest distance possible from others. I gestured for him to sit first – for I wanted to make sure that he didn't *sit* too close to me.

He stared at me. 'The woman sits first.'

'I have a reason', I told him – and remained standing.

He remained standing, too. But then he glanced around, saw that the people at the nearest table were looking at us; and, angrily, he sat. And I took a chair that was a comfortable distance away from him.

To change the subject quickly, I began to question him about himself. He was glad enough to be the subject of conversation. He took from his wallet a photograph of himself as a much younger man. Smiling, elegant. 'This is how I *once* looked.' He said this with a kind of anger, too – anger at the years which had taken that face from him. He was a scholar, and sometimes a teacher. This is what had taken him to the States. During his stay there, he had married an American woman. Why she was still over there and he was here in Spain he never fully explained, and I didn't press him for an explanation. She worked for some magazine, he said. Then he drew out of his pocket a recent letter from her and passed it to me. It was a letter in which she begged him to write to her more often. Was he proud of the letter? He wasn't, at any rate, ashamed to show it to me. I passed it back. And now I didn't feel like asking him more questions about his life.

The waiter brought our sherry. It was a particularly good, very old sherry – dark and spicy. (My notes read 'Dark secret sherry'.) Sipping it, I suddenly longed for you with all my heart and soul.

And now *he* began to put questions to *me*. I was brief and elusive in my answers. But he ignored my curtness. Just kept putting his questions.

And then he said quietly, 'You look so damned sad.'

I ignored the remark. Tasted my sherry.

He repeated the words. 'You look so sad.'

And suddenly I didn't know how to elude his words any longer. I said angrily, 'OK – I *am*. I am sad. So?'

'Why are you sad,' he asked, 'if you are on your way to see your fiancé?'

And he just kept looking at me, with his black, rather narrow eyes.

The sherry was circling in my blood.

'OK', I said. 'I'm not engaged. I don't have a fiancé. I'm in love, but the person I love doesn't love me. All right?'

He grew more quiet still. And sat looking at me, fixedly. His narrow eyes brightening oddly. All this while I had been carefully avoiding his touch. Now, to my dismay, I felt his eyes touch me, in spite of myself – reach to the quick of me. And I didn't know how to avoid their touch. For suddenly my love for you, and my sorrow at your leaving, flooded me. And though I tried to veil my feelings, I couldn't.

Some part of me wanted to be read.

I had written in my journal, making notes for this book: 'One passes even in one's own country as a stranger, even among one's friends, unknown. This love walled within one, unrecognized.'

I had written: 'Can I speak? One wants to speak. It is as if one had not spoken for years. One day one feels: If I do not speak . . . the world will break.'

Of course the words I had just spoken to him were only half a truth.

He wasn't reading my words, though. He was reading my face.

Now he was saying, 'To sit and watch you touched by that love is as sweet for me, almost, as to touch you myself.'

I glared at him.

He ignored my anger. He asked, 'Are you acting? Just to please me? Do you do that to your eyes to inflame a man?'

I told him, 'I do not!'

He said, 'Your face! Your face! You are on fire!'

And now my spirit rebelled more and more against him. And yet I couldn't veil myself. I sat there in dismay, bewildered. All my feelings for you brimming in me. I welcomed these feelings – I knew them to be a gift, and a power. Even if unrequited. Even if unrequited. Yes, I was on fire. I wanted to be able to be. I wanted to burn freely. I didn't want to have to encircle myself with a wall like the wall round this ancient town. I didn't want to be veiled. I wanted to be read.

And he was reading me. But he was stealing me from myself.

Finally I stood up. In outrage – though bewildered still. I said, 'All right. Yes, it's so. And now I'll say goodbye to you.' I hurried back to my hotel, all my deepest feelings in disorder.

When I left the hotel that evening to walk to the station, he was there, waiting to walk with me. I saw that I couldn't prevent him, so I walked very fast – though he kept asking me please to slow down. It was clearly hard for him to walk as fast as I was walking. And he wasn't trying now to be sexual, I noted. He seemed to want to say more to me than he had said about Spain under Franco. He wanted to let himself rave a little, to spill out some of his anger. So I did finally slow down, out of respect for this wish.

'Hitler,' he said in a low voice – 'Hitler turned upon other countries; but Franco has turned against his own people. He is a beast', he said. 'I couldn't even tell you.' He was trembling.

'Feel my arm, feel my right arm.' And he took his hand and placed it on his upper right arm. It was very skinny and without muscle.

'What did they do to you?' I asked, horrified.

He just shook his head. He seemed to want some kind of motherly blessing from me now in parting.

I shook hands with him through the window of the train. 'Write to your wife', is all I could think of saying to him – as the train pulled out into the night.

I arrived in London very angry at myself. And in that state of anger, let myself forget for a while who it was I had learned that I was. I look back now and try to understand this. How was it possible to forget what I had thought every bone of my body had learned? But this would be a lying book if I were to pretend that I didn't forget – and omitted these next pages.

'High time you turned up here', Pete chided me. And I felt myself agreeing. Shouldn't I perhaps try to forget my feelings for you? I had named them to myself a gift. But when they had brimmed up in me, in Avila, they had made me feel only helpless – made me feel a prey to that man. Mightn't this always be so? The book which I had been writing in my head became garbled for me. Was I capable of the work of the spirit it was meant to narrate?

Pete had his own small walk-up apartment by now – had moved out of the rooms provided by the school. 'Why don't you stay the whole summer?' he suggested. And I let myself think to myself: Perhaps I should. Didn't I perhaps need a guardian?

I remember climbing the stairs to his rooms.

His light voice is saying, 'You'll make us a little supper.'

I answer, 'Sure'. Though something in me takes alarm.

Something in me takes alarm, and yet – as he sits beaming at me across that supper, raising his glass of wine to me, I find myself recalling Flo's curt words: 'People do marry.' Yes, they do. I remind myself: Every woman to whom I have offered my love has decided to marry. I find myself wondering again: Will it always be so? Wondering again: Is it possible then that marriage is the path *I* must take? And just possible that this smiling young man lifting his glass to me is the one I should marry? If I were married to him, would you, would Nell, feel then at last at ease with me? And is it just possible that I would feel at ease with myself?

I remember his thin naked body in my arms again. Companionable. I am prompting myself: Yes, he and I *could* learn to love.

I remember sitting together on the edge of the bed in the dimly lit room before lying down together. I see, in the vague light, his slim penis standing up, slightly arched, there in his lap, and he smiles at me a little sideways smile I don't know how to read. I think of an ancient Greek vase painting I've always loved, in which a naked reclining youth with a curving erection is playing upon a flute – his penis rising as if in delight at the music; or the music, perhaps, invented in delighted response to the swelling penis. This penis rising at the sound of music – or (I muse) it could be at the music of love – seems a beautiful branch to be growing from a man's body.

But moments later, as he lies above me, it becomes ugly to me, grotesque.

He is speaking to me – lightly, not harshly, but my whole self flinches, as if slapped by his words. 'I'm fucking you', he is telling me – in his light voice, that a moment ago had seemed to me a brother's voice. And with a jolt I recognize once and for all that he never will dare to be the brother-spirit that he really is. He never will know me and I never will know him. For this penis thinks itself Lord and Master, I realize. It has been taught to think itself Lord and Master. And I am not the one to unteach it this inanity, I realize too. And I know that the thought of marriage to Pete is madness. My spirit stands still – absolutely attentive at last. Knowing: This is not possible. Recalling at last my promise to myself, kneeling among the shining grasses near Elevsis: 'I am this self that I am. I affirm it. Yes, I am. And I will not be robbed.'

Did I speak of any of these feelings to Pete? No. We didn't know how to speak. I stayed with him another day or so – embarrassed to leave as abruptly as I'd like – and then I bought a ticket on a boat back to the States. Pete was not really surprised. It was time, I told myself, to sit in one place and try to write this book.

And now the image returned to me of the jaunty Adam painted by Bosch – about to depart the Garden. (Today I know that I was seeing in this jaunty figure the figure of a rebellious Eve.)

The Serpent (ancient Mother of us ALL) advises: 'Yes, keep trying to leave the so-called Garden. It has not been a garden for you; it has been a prison – a prison of the mind. Though you have been led to believe that you should be thankful to The Keeper.'

She tells me, 'Take and eat, keep eating, this apple of disobedience. It will cause you trouble, but it is the knowledge of who you really are.'

The angel at the gate raises her arm, to send me on my way.

My journal ends: 'And to that angel I cry: "NOW DRIVE ME FORTH!"'

... put out your hand before you.

Alice Walker
In Search of
Our Mothers' Gardens
Womanist Prose

'Womanist is to feminist as purple is to lavender'

This is a phrase from Alice Walker's own definition of the special quality of her 'womanist' prose. The depth of thought it implies is reflected throughout this major collection of the essays, reviews and articles she has written over the last fifteen years.

The pieces deal with art, with being black, with being female, and with the need for us to acknowledge our earliest loyalties. They include Alice Walker's rediscovery of black writers like Zora Neale Hurston, her retrospective view of the Civil Rights movement, a visit to the 'new Cuba', and her final coming to terms with a childhood accident which nearly blinded her. Above all they are full of the excitement of discovery, the sense of humour, and that ability to explore the most complex of issues in crystal clear prose which Alice Walker's many admirers know so well from her fiction.

£4.95

Joanna Russ
How to Suppress Women's Writing

How to suppress women's writing?
Begin by saying/writing/thinking:
She didn't write it.
But if it's clear she did the deed:
She wrote it, but she wrote only one of it (*Jane Eyre. Poor dear, that's all she ever . . .*)
She wrote it, but look what she wrote about (*the bedroom, the kitchen, her family. Other women!*)
She wrote it, but 'she' isn't really an artist, and 'it' isn't really art (*it's a thriller, a romance, a children's book. It's sci fi!*)
She wrote it, but she had help (*Robert Browning, Branwell Brontë. Her own 'masculine side'*).
She wrote it BUT . . . Congratulations! You have just belittled/distorted/neglected/suppressed women's writing. But don't worry. It's a tradition . . .

Joanna Russ has written an explosive, irreverent, angry and very funny book, which rediscovers women's literary heritage. She reveals how it has been belittled in the past, just how impressive the reality is, and how (and why) women's writing is now finding new forms.

'A book of the most profound and original clarity. The study of literature should never be the same again' Marge Piercy

£3.95

Janet Frame
To the Is-Land
An Autobiography

Winner of the James Wattie Book of the Year
Award, New Zealand, 1983

The first volume of the autobiography of one of the
finest novelists writing in English today, *To the
Is-Land* is a haunting account of Janet Frame's
childhood and adolescence in the New Zealand of
the 1920s and 30s. Its simple yet highly crafted
language brings alive in vividly remembered detail
her materially impoverished but emotionally intense
railway family home, her first encounters with love,
and death, her first explorations into the worlds of
words and poetry.

Janet Frame, awarded a CBE in 1983, is author of
ten novels. These include, published by The
Women's Press, *Scented Gardens for the Blind*
(1982), *Faces in the Water* (1980) and *Living in the
Maniototo* (1981), winner of the Fiction Prize, New
Zealand Book Awards, 1980.

£4.95

Janet Frame
An Angel At My Table

An Autobiography: Vol II

Winner of the New Zealand Literary Award for
Non-Fiction, 1984

An Angel At My Table is the story of New
Zealand's greatest living writer's struggle from
painfully shy adolescence, through banishment
to the back wards of a succession of mental
hospitals, to self-knowledge as writer. It is an
unforgettable book, the triumphant
achievement of an artist at the height of her
powers. This is the second volume of Janet
Frame's three-volume autobiography. The first,
To The Is-Land (The Women's Press, 1982), her
magical account of childhood, won the Sir James
Wattie Book of the Year Award, 1983.

Hardcover   £7.95

Barbara Wilson
Murder in the Collective

Two print collectives, one left-wing and one
radical lesbian, plan to merge. But hidden
tensions explode when one of the collective
members is found – murdered.

Penny is determined to uncover the truth,
however disturbing. No one is free of suspicion.
The Filipino resistance movement, the CIA, a
drunken feminist on a binge, a fugitive in the
attic, arms running, blackmail and a pair of
unusual contact lenses are all involved before
the mystery can be solved.

Barbara Wilson sustains a marvellously tortuous
plot at the same time as a cool wit through this
hugely enjoyable story. She is also the author, as
Barbara Ellen Wilson, of *Ambitious Women* (The
Women's Press, 1982).

£3.50